HOW TO RESEARCH YOUR SECOND WORLD WAR ANCESTORS

SIMON FOWLER

First published 2025

The History Press
97 St George's Place, Cheltenham,
Gloucestershire, GL50 3QB
www.thehistorypress.co.uk

British Library Cataloguing in Publication Data.
A catalogue record for this book is available from the British Library.

ISBN 978 1 80399 449 9

Typesetting and origination by The History Press.
Printed and bound in Great Britain by TJ Books, Padstow, Cornwall.

The History Press proudly supports

Trees for Life

www.treesforlife.org.uk

EU Authorised Representative: Easy Access System Europe
Mustamäe tee 50, 10621 Tallinn, Estonia
gpst.request@easproject.com

CONTENTS

'I lived upon this earth in such an age
when man was so debased, he sought to murder
for pleasure, not just to comply with orders,
his faith in falsehoods drove him to corruption,
his life was ruled by raving self-deceptions.'

Miklós Radnóti, *Fragment* (1944)[1]

PREFACE

For most people, the Second World War is ancient history, in a way that the Battle of Waterloo, or even the Great War, is. Yet, in many ways, however, the war is still fresh – it is almost as if it ended last year. If you mention 'the War' in conversation everybody knows which war you mean. Hundreds of books are published each year on all aspects of the Second World War, many of which enter the bestseller lists. There are endless television programmes, both factual and fictional, of varying degrees of accuracy. It is, of course, taught in school. And, perhaps more seriously as the problems faced by society today become ever more difficult, it is all too easy to fall back into a nostalgic world where Britain was still top dog, when we were led by a charismatic leader, and where the country was united in one common aim. Most importantly, the national story is that Britain came through near collapse in 1940 and endured a great deal until the final and emphatic victory was achieved five years later.

Unfortunately, to be brutal, the truth is somewhat different. In comparison to the Americans and the Russians, by the end of 1943 Britain was no longer top dog, either militarily or economically. There were widespread doubts at the highest levels about the prime minister's abilities. Among ordinary people, there was a serious debate about the shape of the post-war world, which saw Winston Churchill unceremoniously ejected from power after the General Election in July 1945.

This book aims to help you research your ancestors' part in the war. It was impossible to remain unaffected by the events at home and abroad and almost everybody played an active part in the Allied victory. Many families have stories amusing or horrific about the experiences retold by grandparents or aunts and uncles that have been passed down through the generations. Or you may remember nightmares as your father's or grandfather's subconscious struggled with his experiences on the battlefield.

The Second World War was a global war. Troops from many nations were stationed in Britain: Australian to Yugoslav. And the country welcomed (to a greater or lesser degree) tens of thousands of refugees from Europe, who were either fleeing Nazi persecution, wished to take the fight to the enemy, or found themselves unable to return home due to the occupation of Eastern Europe by the Soviets. Therefore, this book, where possible, has included material to help readers find out more about men and women from the United Nations (as they were known from 1942) who served in the UK as well as for the refugees and the survivors of the Holocaust.

It is assumed that you are new to family history, so there is material about how to get started and the key genealogical sources that can help. There are also bullet points suggesting how the records might help your research and pitfalls for you to avoid. Unfortunately, it may sometimes be difficult to find information. You may be lucky, but too often you won't necessarily uncover very much. On the other hand, the chase is part of the joy of family history and who knows what you will find en route.

My personal interest in the war is threefold. There are surprisingly few family stories, as neither my parents nor their relations were in the forces. My father, who was a radiographer in London, told me shortly before his death about X-raying the survivors of the direct hit by a V2 on the Woolworths in New Cross in November 1944, when 160 people were killed and another 135 seriously injured. My mother spent much of the war as a nurse in the East End, having arrived as an 18-year-old refugee from Germany six weeks before war broke out.

Against my better judgment – or so I thought – I was persuaded to write a history of Richmond, where I live, during the Second World War. It turned out to be a fascinating project. In many ways, the town was a microcosm of British society at the time – there were air raids (one in ten houses were damaged in the bombing), people worked in the Hawker's aircraft factory in Kingston or commuted to war work in London. Meanwhile, local children played happily in the ruins while their grandfathers were on patrol with the Home Guard. Precious days off were spent on the River Thames or in Kew Gardens. There were several hush-hush establishments and even an Italian prisoner of war camp. And, of course, many local men and women served in the forces, although until recently it has been difficult to find out much about them.

Over the past decade, I have been a professional researcher at The National Archives (TNA) at Kew and at other archives and libraries across London, checking the records for clients who wanted to know more about their family's history during the war and I have incorporated some of this research here. I still find it an exceptionally interesting topic and I hope you will agree – if for no other reason than that the experiences of ordinary people are, for the most part, different from those shown on TV or described in books.

Simon Fowler
February 2025

ROUTINE ORDERS

Each battalion, battery or battleship, as well as RAF squadron, published daily or weekly orders keeping everybody informed of what was happening and issuing instructions on all aspects of military housekeeping, from volunteering for special forces to the kit that had to be packed for a move.

These are the routine orders for the book:

THEN AND NOW

To ease understanding, the names of places are given as they were used during the Second World War. So the concentration camp at Oswiecim, for example, is referred to being at Auschwitz, and the city of Volgograd was then known as Stalingrad.

THE MONEY

Before decimalisation in February 1971, the British pound consisted of 20 shillings (abbreviated as *s*) with 12 pennies (*d*) in each shilling, meaning the pound consisted of 240 pennies.

To add to the confusion, there were also guineas, made up of 21 shillings. The guinea tended to be used for more aristocratic purchases. Things such as professional fees, land, horses, art, bespoke tailoring, furniture and general 'luxury' items were usually priced in guineas as opposed to shillings

HOW MUCH WAS IT WORTH?

According to the Bank of England, £1 in 1939 was roughly worth £50 today; that is the pound today has just 2 per cent of its value in 1939.[1] There was considerable inflation during the war, partly because there was a shortage of consumer goods, which increased prices, but also because of heavy taxation on almost every item sold. For example, a pint of bitter beer in a London pub in 1940 cost about 8*d* (which increased to 1*s* 1*d* by the end of the war, although most drinkers preferred mild – a weaker darker beer, which cost 4*d* (11*d* in 1945). Most pubs in the capital charge well over £6 for a pint of bitter today.[2]

Men and women in the services were not well paid, particularly when compared with Australians, Canadians and, especially, their American comrades, something that caused real resentment. It wasn't for nothing that there was considerable grumbling that the American GIs were 'overpaid, over-sexed and over here'.

The higher their rank, the more a soldier was paid. In addition, there were extra allowances for long service or having particular skills as a tradesman, such as signalling or being an engineer. The pay of a private varied between 2 shillings and 6*s* 3*d* per day; a lance corporal between 3*s* 3*d* and 6*s* 6*d*; corporal 4*s* to 7*s* 3*d*; and sergeant 6s to 8s 9*d*.[3] Officers were paid rather more: a second lieutenant in 1942 would receive 13*s* per day, and an allowance of 7*s* 6*d* if he was married, although from this there were mess bills to pay. In 1940 a pilot officer in the RAF (a fairly junior rank) was paid £237 per annum, or £4 10s per week. According to Tom Cotteswold, writing on the Key Aero forum: 'While the money was not enough to set up home on, as a pilot officer I ran a 2-litre car, went to the pub most nights, and to London clubs and shows as required!'[4]

When troops went overseas, they were generally paid in the local currency, although British Military Authority banknotes were introduced in 1942 mainly for North Africa, Italy, Greece and the Balkans. They were needed to ensure the economies of the countries that Britain occupied could still keep going. As a result, even the lowest-paid soldier could afford to drink in local bars and eat in local tavernas. Many brought home fond memories of cuisines that otherwise they would never have encountered, and were pleased to visit Indian and Greek restaurants once they arrived in Britain during the 1960s and 1970s.

WEIGHTS AND MEASURES

Although the metric system was not as alien to soldiers as it had been during the Great War, British, Commonwealth and American forces largely used imperial weights and measures, although there were some variations between British and American measures.

The key conversions are:

- 1 gallon = 4.5 litres
- 1 mile = 1.6 kilometres
- 1 pint = 568ml
- 1 ton = 907 kilograms
- 1 yard = 91 centimetres

THE ARCHIVES

The key archive where the vast majority of British records relating to the Second World War are held is The National Archives. It is usually referred to as TNA. More about the Archives and how to use it can be found in Chapter 2.

There are two major genealogical websites – Ancestry and Findmypast – both have a great deal of material about the war, but you have to pay to access the records. In the longer term, Ancestry is likely to be the most useful as it is where, over time, you will be able to access the service records, though at the time of writing Findmypast is better. However, there is a lot of overlap between the two sites.

WEBSITES

Instead of giving detailed webpage addresses, which would slow down the flow of the text and could easily be corrupted, you will normally find just the name of the website. Just type the name into your chosen search engine and then navigate your way to what you are looking for.

Websites come and go all the time. If one suggested in the text is no longer working, a copy should be available on the Internet Archive's Wayback Machine: www.archive.org.

BOOKS

There are tens of thousands of books about the Second World War, from the popular and general to the deeply technical. The books included here are not meant to be a comprehensive list; they are either key histories or, more often, those I have found useful in my own research.

Titles to look out for are:

- Anthony Beevor, *The Second World War* (Orion, 2014)
- Katie Clements, *Total War: A People's History of the Second World War* (Thames & Hudson/Imperial War Museum, 2021)
- Daniel Todman, *Britain's War: Into War, 1937–1941* (Penguin, 2017)
- Daniel Todman, *Britain's War: A New World, 1942–1947* (Penguin, 2021)

ERRORS AND OMISSIONS

The book is current at 1 January 2025, but records are regularly being released or digitised, so it is worth keeping an eye on the appropriate social media or through family history magazines for updates. Of particular interest will be the release of the service records for the British Army, Royal Navy and Royal Air Force over the next few years.

Should you wish to know where the quotes used in the book came from, look at the endnotes starting on p. 256. The endnotes may also include additional information used to expand upon points in the main text.

Errors and omissions are mine alone. If you spot a mistake or would like to suggest a resource I have left out, please get in touch.

I

INTRODUCTION

The Second World War was one of the most traumatic events in modern British history, probably in world history. It profoundly affected the lives of every man, woman and child in the United Kingdom. And not only in Britain of course. Tens of millions of people were involved in the war across the globe. For most it was a catastrophe. After the Fall of Singapore in February 1942, for example, the peaceful civilian population was treated almost as badly by the Japanese occupiers as the British and Allied service personnel who became their prisoners. Innocent Europeans from Biarritz to Bucharest, Newcastle to Naples, lost their lives, endured incredible hardships or were forced to flee towns and villages where their families had lived for generations.

We like to think of the Second World War as being just one worldwide conflict. In effect, however, there were three separate wars with relatively little linkage between them. The British were largely involved in the war in Western Europe between 3 September 1939 and 8 May 1945. Some historians see this as a continuation of the First World War, with a twenty-year truce between the two conflicts.

The Russians fought Germany on the Eastern Front, in a horrific war of destruction between 22 June 1941 and 9 May 1945. And, although Britain, America and the Soviet Union were formally allies, this did not mean very much in practice. The West was hardly involved on the Eastern Front, although it supplied large amounts of equipment and munitions. And, in reality, Stalin did what he liked, with little regard to what Churchill and Roosevelt thought about it.

The war in the Far East began in July 1937 with the Japanese attack on China and concluded dramatically with the dropping of atom bombs on Hiroshima and Nagasaki in August 1945. The Germans and the Japanese were allied, but there were very few ways in which either nation could help each other in practice. Britain was very much the junior partner to the US in the war with Japan.

The war devastated much of Europe and Asia and it took many years for the world to recover. In Britain there was rationing for almost a decade after VE-Day and shortages of material and labour hampered recovery. Much of Central and Eastern Europe had been destroyed to an extent that shocked British visitors. It is not for nothing that the year 1945 is called *Jahr Null* – Year Zero – in Germany. Six million Jews, Roma and Sinti people, LGBTQ+ people and political prisoners had been murdered by the Nazis. Millions of people became refugees, fleeing vengeful occupiers or devastated cities. Millions of others were traumatised by their experiences in the front line, on the home front, or from being imprisoned in camps. It is little wonder that the peoples of Europe decided that they did not want to go through another war. Churchill and other politicians across Europe discussed how to prevent another war destroying the continent for a third time.

NATO was formed in 1949 to defend Western Europe from Russian aggression. What became today's European Union started with the integration of steel and coal industries in the early 1950s, leading to a more formal union as a result of the Treaty of Rome in 1957.

By comparison with Germany and Russia, British casualties were light – about half of that of the First World War, although a fifth of these were innocent civilians. But there were no longer really any civilians; everybody from the age of 8 to 80 was expected to play their part in the war effort. In a few memorable words, Winston Churchill summed up the contribution the whole of British society would make towards victory in a BBC radio broadcast on 14 July 1940:

> This is no war of chieftains or of princes, of dynasties or national ambition; it is a war of peoples and of causes. There are vast numbers, not only in this Island but in every land, who will render faithful service in this war, but whose names will never be known, whose deeds will never be recorded. This is a War of the Unknown Warriors; but let all strive without failing in faith or in duty, and the dark curse of Hitler will be lifted from our age.[1]

Unlike most family history guides, this book is not about events and the records that describe them, some of which occurred hundreds of years ago. It concerns the recent past, that which historian Juliet Gardiner calls 'fingertip history'; that is, recalling an age so close that you can still just about touch it.[2]

Most readers will have memories of stories told by old relations of their wartime experiences, or perhaps, less happily are aware of the nightmares and the physical and mental traumas endured by fathers and grandfathers.

The Guernsey journalist Frank Falla, for example, spent nearly two years as a prisoner in Germany for writing and circulating an underground newspaper. Falla's health was permanently affected by his experiences. Writing in his memoirs *The Silent War*, he described how pneumonia left him with spots on the lungs and he became a 'chronic bronchial sufferer', as he put it. He also suffered from PTSD for two years, during which he experienced 'severe sweats at night and haunting hallucinations that I was back again in my prison cell at Naumburg'. Fortunately, he was able to return to his pre-war career and made a very happy marriage. But many of his later years were spent in ensuring his fellow islanders received compensation from the Germans and he later wrote his memoirs; an action that helped him to get the bitterness out of his system.[3]

It is natural to want to know about our parents' and grandparents' wartime careers. They probably told us snippets about their experiences, even if their memories might be rather disjointed. Many veterans felt unable to discuss the horrors they had experienced with their children and, perhaps, even with their wives. This book hopes to enable you to put flesh on their stories. But be warned. It is not unknown for veterans to embellish their tales!

During the war, almost everybody actively participated in the war effort, whether as soldiers on the Normandy beaches, working a lathe in an aircraft factory, or helping in a British Restaurant. Every morning the mother of one of my clients packed first-aid boxes that were given to soldiers, before returning home to cook lunch for her family. Their experiences, of course, vary greatly from unbelievable heroism to unbelievable tedium and everything in between. Some of our ancestors had 'a good war', but most muddled through as best they could.

The last veterans are disappearing rapidly. As this book was being written, the deaths of men and women who had taken part in the war were announced almost on a daily basis. Among them there were the deaths of HM Queen Elizabeth, aged 96, who had served in the Auxiliary Territorial Service, and the last survivor of the Dambuster Raids, Sergeant George 'Johnny' Johnson DFM, at the age of 101. Charles Lurcher, believed to be the last survivor of the evacuation from Dunkirk, and Pippa Latour Doyle, who was the last surviving female SOE agent, both died aged 102. Aged 23, Pippa had been parachuted into occupied Normandy to gather intelligence on Nazi positions in preparation for D-Day and remained there until Paris was liberated in August 1944.

To have any clear memory of the Second World War as a child you would have to be now nearly 90.

British records relating to the war are now largely available to researchers. They are reasonably complete, although much ephemeral material was destroyed in the 1960s. So far as is known, there have been no losses comparable to the destruction of the army records in September 1940, which saw the loss of a huge number of personnel and related documents of the First World War.[4] Only the Special Intelligence Service (MI6) and to a large degree the Security Service (MI5) have not released their records. In addition, some personal records are closed to public access for eighty-five years or longer. An increasing proportion of the key genealogical material is online with much more to follow over the next few years. All the key sources and their locations (both online and in archives) are described in the book.

It helps that many key sources, such as war diaries, newspapers and war grave records, will be familiar to anybody who has already researched their ancestors who fought in the Great War. The two wars were just two decades apart, after all. In addition, the major genealogical resources – particularly the birth, marriage and death registers and probate records – continued to be kept during the war.

For the first time, however, media other than newspapers, played a major part in both recording the events of the war and interpreting them for audiences at home. On occasion, they can still pack an emotional impact today as well as showing how our parents and grandparents experienced the war. And who knows if your ancestor was filmed in a crowd or appeared in a photograph. Again, there is a section describing the sources you might use here.

The book also suggests ways of researching the servicemen and women who were stationed in the United Kingdom from the Commonwealth, America or occupied Europe, or spent time here as prisoners of war.

Britain also took in tens of thousands of refugees before, during and after the war. The best known were the German and Austrian Jews who were forced to flee the Nazis. And as the Cold War began, Poles and other Eastern Europeans who could not return home for one reason or another settled here. Again, there are suggestions on how to find out more about them.

There is also a section about researching the Holocaust. Some of the survivors came to Britain and many British people, including my mother, lost family in the camps.

THE ORGANISATION OF THE WAR

It's useful to know something about how the war was directed, even if our ancestors were on the whole very small cogs in a very large machines. You cannot understand your father's or grandmother's wartime lives without understanding this.

The Second World War was a total war in which the economies and societies were fully engaged in battle with an enemy whose society and economy was similarly organised. Individuals were as engaged as society as a whole, whether as a soldier in the front line or his wife in the munitions' factory.

In Britain, everybody was expected to participate in National Service – that is the central direction of labour and individual citizens. For the first time, women were as fully involved in the war effort as their husbands, boyfriends and sons. Even outside work, men and, to an extent, women, were encouraged to volunteer for civil defence work or to dig allotments to supplement rationing. Women were expected to look after their families in addition to their war work.

Memoirs and anecdotal stories suggest that most people – in Britain at least – enjoyed their war service. Certainly, it seems to have been the highlight of my parents' lives and those of their friends. The comedian and writer Spike Milligan later wrote that, 'The experience of being in the army changed my whole life.'[5] Most service personnel were in their twenties and thirties – young enough to learn new skills, even basic ones like driving, and to take advantage of the opportunities they were given.

For some, it was life changing – in good and bad ways. Young women in particular seem to have relished the chances to do something new, whether it be working in a munitions factory or in the SOE.

Many men were traumatised by what they saw and never fully recovered from their experiences. Before the war, comedian and author Spike Milligan, for example, was an assistant storeman in Bond Street. He was called up to the Royal Artillery in 1940, where he honed his musical and comedic skills in a variety of music parties. However, he eventually experienced a mental breakdown after his experiences in North Africa and during the battle for Monte Cassino in Italy. After a period of recovery, he worked as a wine waiter at an officers' rest camp. Soon after leaving the army, he became a musician before his big break at the BBC. However, Spike's mental health always remained fragile. He described his wartime experiences in a series of autobiographies.[6]

CENTRAL DIRECTION

There were essentially two British prime ministers during the Second World War.[7] Neville Chamberlain was in charge for the first nine months before being replaced by Winston Churchill in May 1940. Chamberlain was rather a colourless man and not a natural war leader. At the time, he was blamed for lack of preparedness for war, that is 'appeasement'. But many historians now agree that the Munich Agreement, in September 1938, allowed a vital extra year for Britain to rearm.

Twenty years ago, Churchill was voted the greatest Briton in a BBC poll and, despite his many faults, it is hard to disagree. He brought to the fore an absolute determination to win the war, at a time when defeat seemed inevitable. He was a charismatic figure; somebody – with the cigar, the reassuring bulk and the boyish smile – who could reassure and inspire ordinary citizens in wartime.[8] His colleagues were less complimentary about him in private, and although they cheered him as being the great victor, the electorate brutally ejected him and the Conservative Party from power at the 1945 General Election. This was possibly the greatest political upset in British political history.

Joseph Stalin, Franklin D. Roosevelt and Winston Churchill at the Tehran Conference in July 1943. This was the first time that the war leaders had met face to face. (Wikimedia Commons/US Signals Corps)

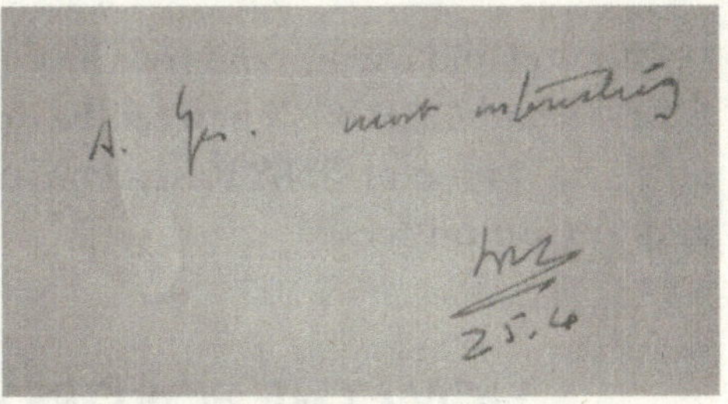

Winston Churchill's signature in a file on Operation Biting, the raid on the German radar station at Bruneval. (TNA PREM 3/73)

Churchill led a small War Cabinet made up of half a dozen or so senior ministers who had direct responsibility for the war effort. He believed that members should hold 'responsible offices and not be mere advisors at large with nothing to do but think and talk and take decisions by compromise or majority'. His deputy was Clement Attlee, the leader of the Labour Party, who largely looked after domestic affairs, allowing Churchill to concentrate on defence and strategic planning, and also indulge his fascination with special operations – the subjects in which he was most interested. With the exception of Anthony Eden, the Foreign Secretary, the other members of the War Cabinet are now only usually remembered by historians.

The military direction of the war was through the Chiefs of Staff Committee. It was formed of the military heads of the three services. The committee was formed in 1923 but came into its own during the Second World War when it planned many military operations and encouraged the services to work together. General Sir Hastings Ismay acted as its secretary as well as a direct conduit to the War Cabinet (which, in practice, meant Churchill).

THE RECORDS

Although of little or no genealogical value, the records of the central direction of the war are interesting if you wish to know more about particular decisions or military actions.

Formal Cabinet minutes (known as Conclusions) were taken by the Cabinet Secretary. Memoranda were circulated by ministers to Cabinet providing background or asking for decisions to be made by Cabinet. In addition, committees – both ministerial and official (that is, made up solely of civil servants) – were established as and when needed. The system is still in use today. All Cabinet conclusions and memoranda are available online on TNA's website in series CAB 65 and CAB 66. It is probably easier, however, to use the Cabinet Papers website.

Much useful material can also be found in the files of Prime Minister's Correspondence in series PREM 3 and PREM 4 and CAB 21 (these are not online). Also of considerable interest are the Churchill Papers held by the Churchill Archives Centre in Cambridge.

Minutes and Memoranda of the Chiefs of Staff Committee are in series CAB 79 and CAB 80. They can be downloaded from TNA's website.

There is a useful TNA Research Guide to Cabinet records: 'The Cabinet and its Committees'.

HOW THE FORCES WERE ORGANISED

It is very easy to get bogged down in the minutiae of when and where each unit was serving as part of which superior force. Unless you decide to do an in-depth history of a particular battalion or regiment, you really don't need to have this information at your fingertips. Ordinary soldiers were generally only interested in the unit in which they were serving and perhaps had a pride in being part of a particular army, such as the Eighth Army. An airman's loyalty was largely to his squadron or unit, or even, for many individuals in groundcrew, to the aircraft that they lovingly maintained, and seamen to their ship. In many cases, the real loyalty lay with the comrades they worked, lived and drank with.

In some ways, at least to the vast majority of privates, seamen and aircraftsmen, the organisation of the services was a bit like being at school. Students would know the form teacher and others who taught them – perhaps equivalent to the junior officers (lieutenants and second lieutenants) and the non-commissioned officers (sergeants), with corporals as the prefects, but they might know only by sight the head teacher and heads of subjects – that is, the senior officers.

Britain's armed forces were (and still are) divided into three services with distinct roles, although there was some overlap. During the war, the services generally worked well together under the direction of Chiefs of Staff and the supreme Allied commanders for each theatre of operation. In one of his first acts when he became prime minister in May 1940, Churchill established a Ministry of Defence to ensure that the services were under his direct control and to ensure that they collaborated with rather than against each other, which sometimes had been the case during the First World War.

The **British Army** provided the infantry, armour (that is tanks) and artillery (guns). In addition, there were corps providing common operational support across the service, notably the Royal Engineers and the Royal Army Corps, but also smaller units such as the Royal Electrical and Mechanical Engineers, the Pioneer Corps, the Army Catering Corps and the Royal Army Pay Corps. Most special force units, including the Special Air Service (SAS), were also part of the army.

It was also the largest of the three services. By the end of the Second World War in September 1945, over 3.5 million men and women had served in the British Army, which had suffered around 720,000 casualties (that is men and women killed, incapacitated in some way, or taken prisoner by the enemy) throughout the conflict.[9] Just under a million men served in the Royal Regiment of Artillery, by far the largest unit in the army.

The Army's organisation changed considerably during the Second World War in order to meet changing situations. New formations were created and disbanded as and when it became necessary. This section is only the briefest of overviews, for more detail refer to G. Forty, *British Army Handbook 1939–1945* (Sutton, 1998). The more comprehensive histories of campaigns and battles may also list army formations of whose work they describe.

More about formations can be found in the Orders of Battle, often referred to as Orbats. The Orders give the war establishment of each army, corps and division and when subordinate units join and leave them. They are listed in full in H.F. Joslen, *Orders of Battle of the Second World War* (2 vols, HMSO, 1960). Military archives and TNA have copies, and it is also sold by the Naval and Military Press. A selection is also available on the Orders of Battle website.

The British Army was divided into several numbered **Army Groups** under the control of the supreme commanders in the various theatres of operations, who in turn answered to the Combined Chiefs of Staff in Washington DC. The Army Groups comprised both British and American formations as appropriate. The 18th (and then the 15th) Army Group, under General Harold Alexander, was responsible for armies in North Africa and Italy. General Bernard Montgomery commanded the 21st Army Group in north-west Europe after D-Day. This was renamed the British Army of the Rhine, following the Surrender of Germany in May 1945. In Burma there was the 11th Army Group initially under General George Giffard, who was succeeded by Lieutenant General Oliver Leese and in the last weeks of the war General William Slim.[10]

Reporting to the Army Groups were a number of field **armies**. The most important of which were the Second Army which saw action in north-west Europe between D-Day and May 1945 (together with the Canadian First Army), the 8th Army which served in the Middle East and Italy, and the 14th Army which served in India and Burma. Your fathers or grandfathers should not have been part of the 4th or 6th armies, which were fictional bodies that were successfully created to deceive the Germans into believing that the D-Day landings were going to take place near Calais.[11]

These units were not fighting ones. Their role was to plan and prepare for battle to ensure that the objectives set by the politicians and the supreme Allied commanders were met.

A subdivision of the armies was the **Corps**, which was usually commanded by a lieutenant general. It normally consisted of two or more army divisions together with additional artillery, engineer, reconnaissance, signals and other units that could be used by the corps or attached to divisions for specific operations. It should not be confused with the Arms of Service (that is formations such as the Royal Artillery, Royal Armoured Corps and Royal Army Medical Corps). Thirteen corps were created during the war.[12]

Divisions were the highest echelons to actively engage in action. There were 11 armoured divisions, 42 infantry divisions, 2 airborne divisions and even, for a short while, a cavalry division.[13] An infantry division was normally made up of a headquarters commanded by a colonel, three infantry brigades and an artillery group. In addition, there could be a wide range of specialist units. In the 51st Highland Division, serving across north-west Europe after D-Day, there was an Ordnance Field Park (for ammunition), a provost company (for policing) and a postal unit.[14] Armoured divisions would have included additional facilities to maintain, store and refuel tanks and other armoured vehicles.

Beneath them lay **Brigades**, which were mainly infantry, but included some more specialist armoured and parachute groups too. Their structure was not dissimilar to the Divisions, which were made up of three battalions, a headquarters and troops such as REME workshops.

But the most important fighting unit was the infantry battalion, which at full strength consisted of about 1,000 men. Battalions were part of a regiment. Each regiment had a depot, which had a number of administrative duties, including keeping the regimental archives.

Regiments, with the exception of the Rifle Brigade and King's Royal Rifle Corps, were linked to particular counties or cities. The affiliation is usually clear from the regimental title, such as the King's Liverpool Regiment or the East Surreys. In peacetime, the regiment recruited from the communities in its area. During the Second World War, this link was comprehensively broken; recruits were sent to units where there were vacancies, and increasingly where their skills could be best used by the army.

In peacetime, the regiment was made up of two battalions of regular soldiers, one of which was normally based at home, while the other was overseas, generally in India. In addition, the Third and Fourth battalions were territorial units made up of part-time soldiers or reservists, that is, veterans who could be recalled in time of war. The numbers of battalions grew as the army itself grew.

The Worcestershire Regiment, for example, started the war with two regular battalions and added another six as the war progressed.[15]

An infantry battalion was made up of a Battalion Headquarters Company and four companies. It was usually commanded by a lieutenant colonel, with a major as second in command. Other important figures would be based at battalion HQ, such as an adjutant. An adjutant was responsible for battalion administration and the write up of war diaries; a quartermaster who would oversee stores and transport; and a medical officer, who was on detachment from the RAMC.

The regimental sergeant-major (RSM, the most senior non-commissioned officer) would also be based here, alongside several specialist positions such as quartermasters, cooks, signallers and an orderly room clerk, which were taken up by sergeants. Each company was commanded by a major or captain and was referred to by its letter, normally A to D. A company sergeant-major (CSM) and 'quarterbloke', who served as the company quartermaster sergeant (CQMS), were also required.

Companies were then divided into four platoons, under the command of lieutenants and second lieutenants, otherwise known as subalterns. Each platoon was then split into a further four sections. Generally, an individual section consisted of twelve men lead by an NCO, typically a corporal or sergeant.

The **Royal Air Force (RAF)** was divided into a small number of 'commands' at home, including Bomber, Coastal and Fighter commands, and air forces overseas. The commands in turn divided into groups generally on a geographical basis. For example, 5 Group, Bomber Command, was responsible for stations and squadrons in Lincolnshire, and during the Battle of Britain, 11 Group, Fighter Command, had responsibility for much of south-east England and East Anglia.

At the heart of the RAF units were (and remain) squadrons, which are the main form of flying unit. Individual squadrons were assigned to particular tasks – as bombers or fighters – and were equipped accordingly. Each squadron was commanded by a wing commander and normally comprised two or three flights. A flight would normally be equipped with eight aircraft with a squadron leader as officer in charge. Aircrew would fly the machines, but they would be maintained and provisioned by the groundcrew. A Spitfire fighter would be flown by just a pilot, but heavy bombers, such as a Lancaster, might have a crew of six or seven, each with a specialist role: pilot (who commanded the aircraft during a sortie or mission); the navigator; flight engineer; wireless operator; bomb aimer (who also operated the front gun turret); and upper, mid and rear gunners.[16]

In the UK, squadrons were based at permanent stations. The station might house several squadrons and be commanded by a group captain. They provided a variety of common services from air traffic control, maintenance of the runways, emergency services and accommodation for everybody. The numbers housed could be large. At its peak, RAF Elsham Wolds in north Lincolnshire accommodated 2,500 officers and men. Overseas stations might be rather less fancy, perhaps no more than a strip in the desert or jungle with facilities in tents.[17]

In addition, there were training units of every kind, of which the best known are the Empire Flying Training Schools in Canada, Rhodesia and the United States that provided basic training in conditions far better than those available at home.

At the heart of the **Royal Navy** was the ship. Even shore bases, sometimes referred to as 'stone frigates', are given ships' names. HMS *Ganges*, for example, was the boys' training school near Ipswich, and many a sailor sat on his heels waiting for a posting at HMS *Pembroke*, the barracks at Chatham Dockyard.[18]

The navy was organised into a number of commands and fleets, as well as the Royal Marines, Submarine Service and the Fleet Air Arm These are explained in more detail on the Naval History Net website.

During the war, the Royal Navy sent around a thousand ships and submarines to sea, from aircraft carriers and battleships, each with a crew of many hundreds, to motor torpedo boats manned by an enthusiastic young and undoubtedly bearded skipper, an engineer and a couple of deck hands.[19]

MANPOWER AND CONSCRIPTION

One constant determined British military policy during the Second World War – that of the lack of manpower. Men and women were needed in the forces, but they also were needed in the factories and the farms to supply munitions and food. Writing after the war, the official historian noted: 'The manpower budgets were the main force in determining every part of the war effort from the numbers of RAF heavy bombers raiding Germany to the size of the clothing ration.'[20]

To maximise the effective use of manpower, conscription – formally known as National Service – was introduced. Initially it was only for men aged 20 and 21 for 6 months military training. The scheme began in April 1939, 5 months before the formal declaration of war.

However, you could join up without waiting for your call-up papers. Some 300,000 did so. The advantage being that volunteers could choose which service to join and, perhaps as importantly, allowed men to escape otherwise tedious work in a factory or office for what they hoped was a more adventurous life.

In addition, half a million men had volunteered to join Air Raid Precautions, another sign that people had woken up to the threat of Nazi Germany. Previous attempts to find volunteers for ARP work had been very disappointing; before the Munich Crisis of September and October 1938 war had seemed very distant.

Full conscription was introduced in September 1939 for all men between the ages of 18 and 41. Continuing shortages of manpower meant that the conscription scheme was eventually extended. From April 1941, all able-bodied men and women between the ages of 18 and 60 were required to perform some form of National Service. This might mean full-time service in the Home Guard or Civil Defence (as the ARP became). For most, it meant joining the armed forces or a reserved occupation at home. Britain thus became the first nation to conscript everybody regardless of sex. In Germany, for example, women and girls were eventually conscripted in the last few months of the war, although in practice many women in their teens and twenties had been a member of a Nazi youth organisation or a women's auxiliary service.[21]

Initially, conscripts could choose which service they joined. Because of the romance attached to it, the Royal Air Force was inevitably the most popular choice and had the pick of candidates. The British Army being the least popular, a higher proportion of army recruits were said to be dull and backwards than in the other services.

Within the army, men were assigned to regiments based on the need to keep numbers up rather than to meet a man's particular skills or aptitudes. This was a shocking waste of manpower. The Army Council was told that, 'The British Army is wasting manpower in this war almost as badly as it did in the last war. A man is posted to a Corps almost entirely on the demand of the moment and without any effort at personal selection by proper tests.'[22]

From the middle of 1942, recruits initially joined the General Service Corps for their first six weeks of basic training and assessment at a Primary Training Centre so that their subsequent posting could take account of their skills and the army's needs. About 9 per cent were identified as tradesmen, with particular skills, 6 per cent as potential officers, and 14 per cent were referred for further psychological assessment.[23] Although it wasn't perfect, the scheme generally managed to put round pegs into round holes.

RESERVED OCCUPATIONS

Not all men and were conscripted into the armed forces, however. Many remained in civilian 'reserved occupations' which were considered to be vital to the war effort, such as miners, farmers and workers in aircraft factories. Initially, employers could request that the call up be deferred for a valued employee. But as the demand for men in the services continued jobs were increasingly filled by women as their menfolk were called up. Members of the Women's Land Army for example replaced labourers on the land. By 1943, most workers in aircraft factories were women, only the inspectors, foremen and the most skilled workers were men.[24]

BEVIN BOYS

Coal mining suffered a severe shortage of manpower, which was particularly important because Britain's factories and homes depended almost entirely on coal for fuel. In a bid to tackle this, Ernest Bevin, the Minister of Labour in December 1943, introduced conscription. One in ten young men who were due to be called up to the forces would instead be heading down into the mines. Men were selected by ballot. There was no appeal against this selection.

These conscript miners were known as 'Bevin Boys'. Some 21,800 young men became Bevin Boys, alongside another 16,000 who chose to go down the mines rather than join the services. Famous Bevin Boys included Stanley Baxter, Eric Bartholomew (Eric Morecambe), and Brian Rix.

Some men hated their time in the mines. Bert Mitchell remembered that:

> The conditions were diabolical, I dreaded it from the moment I went there I just couldn't get attached to it at all. I actually hated it. The conditions, crawling along two or three miles to the coal face to work ... plus the fact that the people weren't very kindly to us because they seemed to think that we were doing what their sons ought to be doing.[25]

Mr Dowden had a happier time:

> We were regarded as a different species to the miners. We spoke quite differently to them and this was a cause of much amusement and misunderstanding. As I had worked at the Post Office the blokes wanted to know if I spent all my time licking stamps![26]

FINDING OUT MORE

There are no service records for Bevin Boys, but some records are held at the National Archives. Simon Demissie summarised their holdings in a useful blog posting in May 2013. There is a valuable BBC TV documentary on the Bevin Boys first broadcast in 1983 on the BBC Archive website. The Bevin Boys Association has much of interest on their website: their archives are with the Imperial War Museum.

ARMY OFFICERS

By contrast with all previous wars, officers had to spend at least a year in the ranks before being recommended by their commanding officer and passing an interview and other tests at a selection board. Announcing this policy in 1939, the Secretary of State for War, Leslie Hore-Belisha, stressed that:

> In this Army the star [that is the 'pip' on the lieutenant's uniform] is within every private soldier's reach. No one, however humble or exalted his birth, need be afraid that his military virtues will remain unrecognised. More importantly, no one, who wishes to serve in the army need consider his state minimised by starting on the bottom rung.[27]

During the war, some 200,000 men and women received commissions, the vast majority of whom had come via the ranks.

Although the army was a much more democratic body than it had been in 1914, it still preferred men from the right public-school background. The writer Alan Wood spent a year as a gunner before someone discovered that he had been educated at Oxford: 'I was promptly given a recommendation for a commission and a handsome apology for being kept in the ranks so long.'[28]

Officers who came from the ranks often found it difficult to deal with the aristocratic and upper-class elites who still formed the majority of pre-war officers. Being an officer also involved some financial sacrifice, largely because junior officers' pay was less than that of an experienced NCO. There were also other expenses such as mess bills, which might be a quarter of a junior officer's salary. Henry Longhurst, serving in the Royal Artillery, pointed this out in an April 1941 article in the *Sunday Express* headed: 'No drinks or smokes on an officer's pay'.[29] Matters improved when pay and allowances increased to provide for the payment of mess expenses.

'Fighting Fit in the Factory', one of the many posters produced by the Ministry of Information to boost the war effort. Artist A.R. Thomson. (Wikimedia Commons/TNA INF 3/160)

Commanding officers were also often reluctant to allow good non-commissioned officers to apply for commissions. The result was that fewer men were being promoted from the ranks than had been expected or met the army's increasing needs.

The system was reformed in 1942 with the introduction of War Office Selection Boards, which thoroughly tested applicants for suitability regardless of rank or background. *Picture Post* declared that the new system was one of the most progressive initiatives of the war.[30] Not everybody was so sure. George Macdonald Fraser felt that, 'The general view throughout the army was that [the boards] weren't fit to select bus conductors, let alone officers.'[31] It was a view that Churchill privately shared, although he was persuaded not to take any action.

Even so, the proportion of officers who had been to public school fell from 84 per cent in 1939 to just 15 per cent at the end of the war.

WOMEN IN THE WORKFORCE[32]

Just before the start of the war the government established the Women's Auxiliary Territorial Service (ATS) to replace men who had been conscripted into the army. In addition, separate formations were established for the RAF, that is the Women's Auxiliary Air Force (WAAF) and the Women's Royal Naval Service (WRNS). Until the introduction of conscription for women in December 1941, membership of all three bodies was voluntary. In addition there was the small Women's Transport Service (WTS).

In 1940 the decision was made to significantly increase ATS numbers. Women between ages 17 and 43 were allowed to join the service. By September 1941, the ATS had 65,000 members. The range of duties also increased, and women now served as office, mess and telephone orderlies, drivers, postal workers and ammunition inspectors.

The country remained short of workers in vital industries. In March 1941 Ernest Bevin, the Minister of Labour, made a speech where he asked for

100,000 women to volunteer their services. The newspapers reported that he said: 'I have to tell the women that I cannot offer them a delightful life. They will have to suffer some inconveniences. But I want them to come forward in the spirit of determination to help us through.'[33] It had little impact. Perhaps his patronising tone had something to do with this.

By the end of 1941 legislation was introduced to compel women to undertake National Service. Unmarried women and all childless widows aged between 20 and 30 were called up and permitted a choice between joining the services, the Women's Land Army or working in a factory. By the end of 1943, it was estimated that some 7,750,000 were in paid employment that in some way connected with the war effort. Of these, nearly half a million were in the armed forces and a similar number were full or part-time members of the Civil Defence, Home Guard, Royal Observer Corps or the Women's Land Army.[34]

Eventually married women could also be directed into war-related civilian work, although expectant mothers and mothers with young children were exempt.

Joyce Storey went to work at Magna Products at Warmley, near Bristol, a big engineering firm with huge wartime contracts:

> My first impression of this great all male domain was not a good one, and the dust, grit and grime mingled with a strong smell of oil, along with all the lathes and machinery, awed and scared me.[35]

With the exception of a few women agents in Special Operations Executive, women were not allowed to fight in combat zones. However, as more men were called overseas to fight, their duties extended to becoming radar operators, military policewomen, members of anti-aircraft gun crews and many other operational support tasks.

No. 490 Heavy Anti-Aircraft Battery was the first Anti-Aircraft unit which included women as well as men on the establishment acting as range finders and plotters.

According to Sir Frederick Pile, 'They became one of the wonders of the world. Women marching, eating, drilling, working with men!' He said that the only real problem had been with the head of the Auxiliary Territorial Service (ATS), who complained 'bitterly that our specially contrived living conditions [at the site] were "disgraceful".'[36]

When Churchill visited this unit, which was based in Richmond Park, during the summer of 1941, he 'seemed most impressed: he repeated several times that it was a remarkable and satisfactory innovation.'

2

STARTING YOUR RESEARCH

Starting to research your family history can be a daunting experience. However, it's a bit like swimming. Once you are in the water it is fine.

To use another simile, family history can be compared to a jigsaw puzzle. There are lots of pieces that may (or indeed may not) fit together to build a picture of where you come from and your ancestors' lives. But you have to start somewhere, open the box and spread the pieces on the table – so to speak. And the only place you can do this is at home. This is particularly the case when you are researching men and women who served during the Second World War.

Start by thinking about what you know already. Naturally, the more information you have to start off with, the better it is – but if you know next to nothing, there's no need to panic. You are looking for certain clues in order to progress the research. In particular, you need to establish what they did in the war, as how you research an individual will depend on their wartime career.

Sign at the long-abandoned Down Street Underground Station. (Author)

- If they were in the services, do you know which one – British Army, Royal Navy or Royal Air Force? In which regiment, ship or unit did they serve? If you are interested in your mother, grandmother or aunts, were they members of the Auxiliary Territorial Service (ATS), WRNS or Women's Royal Air Force. Were they an officer (lieutenant, captain etc.) or other rank (private, aircraftsman, able seamen, corporal, sergeant etc.)? And finally, did they survive the war?
- If they were not in the services, what did they do? Were they in the Merchant Navy, or in a reserved occupation (that is worked in a factory or office in the UK)? Or were they in the Women's Land Army, Home Guard, Air Raid Precautions Warden (ARP) or Auxiliary Fire Service, or a special constable? Perhaps they were at school or a housewife keeping the household together during some pretty hard times.

You might already have some of this information. I already knew that both my parents worked in hospitals and my in-laws were doctors in the Royal Army Medical Corps (RAMC). Even if you don't know very much, without too much effort you may pick up some useful clues by thinking about what older members of your family told you about their wartime experiences and by going through any family papers you may have.

MEMORIES

The chances are that there are some family stories. It is likely that this sparked an interest in finding out more about their experiences of the war.

Your parents and grandparents may have talked about their time in the military or during the Blitz, or if they were children during the war about collecting shrapnel or running wild in the bomb ruins. Occasionally, they may have talked about people who were killed in the war. One of my sisters-in-law remembers how her mother never really got over the death of her brother during the Tunisian campaign of 1943. And I've been contacted frequently by clients who want to find out more about the deaths of uncles and great-uncles during the war.

Often the memories are rather disjointed and sometimes hard to place. Very few people have clear, well-ordered memories. It's not like a detective show on the telly where a witness still has vivid recall of a crime that happened decades ago. My father-in-law, who was an army doctor, spoke about forcing a train driver at gunpoint to take his train across the desert.

It seems like something out of the film *Lawrence of Arabia*. But when this was and where, I'll now never find out, as it didn't seem right at the time to press the old boy for more details.

And sometimes they didn't want to bring up bad memories or experiences that may have upset their families. My wife remembers that her father got really annoyed when she once innocently asked about his experiences of Belsen: he was a pathologist who must have been one of the first people into the concentration camp when it was liberated in April 1945.[1] Most managed to suppress their memories, but occasionally they might surface. A correspondent once told me about his uncle, who had been a Commando:

> He talked very little about his war but my cousin and uncle remember him opening up a couple of times and talking about raids from fishing boats in and around Greece. He specifically mentioned a raid on Crete. My nan said he told her about a raid when he had to take out the sentry. He used his knife and was horrified to have killed a very young soldier. Apparently, he had got very drunk before telling the story and was in bits. Never spoke of it again.

It's a good idea to share the wartime stories you remember with other family members. They may well recall other memories or have different interpretations of what you thought you knew. My brother and I have very different recollections of what our parents told us.

Indeed, your own memory may play tricks on you. I thought I had correctly remembered what my mother told me about her wartime experiences, but my brother put me right. And, irritatingly, she had talked much more to my cousin than to her own children, and particularly not to her historian son! As I researched her story, I found that I had misremembered dates and facts. Or perhaps she had. Again, we will never know.

You need to be aware that family stories aren't always accurate. They may have been embellished for public consumption, or very occasionally the individual has become enmeshed in his own story. Years ago, I was contacted by a client who was convinced that his father had been an official assassin. No such person existed, although the British government negotiated with an unnamed New Jersey hitman in 1944 to assassinate Hitler, before it was realised that the increasingly deranged dictator was more use to the Allies alive than dead.[2]

Oral history researchers have found that interviewees have a tendency to imagine that they were present at great events, either because they remember seeing newsreels or TV programmes about them or conflate several different events into one. It is also easy to make assumptions: just because Uncle Fred was in the army during the Second World War it does not mean he stormed the Normandy beaches; he could just as easily have been a stores clerk at Catterick. An awful lot of men remember the concentration camp at Bergen-Belsen and it is easy to believe that they helped liberate it on 15 April 1945, but the truth is that many British troops were taken to see the site in the days and weeks after liberation, or watched graphic newsreels in the cinema.[3] It turns out that the 'assassin' actually spent his war years as a film projectionist showing movies to the troops, no doubt feeling that he should have had the exciting wartime career that was portrayed in the films he watched night after night.

If you have elderly relations who remember the war, it is worth trying to record their memories before it is too late.

FAMILY PAPERS

Now is the time to start rummaging for family papers and memorabilia. What have you and your family got stored away? Go through the trunks in the attic, the files in the garage and the boxes under the stairs – and ask family members to do the same. You are after anything that might give a clue to their wartime service: official documents such as discharge documents; identity cards and leave chits; photographs; diaries; letters; medals; and newspaper cuttings.

You may occasionally find physical reminders of a man's service. A correspondent recently wrote that he had his Uncle Doug's medals including the Military Medal (MM) as well as his fighting knife, bayonet and angled torch that he carried on ops. Uncle Doug had been a Commando serving on missions in Yugoslavia and Albania.

You are after facts and you are after clues. In particular, you are looking for clues about your family during the Second World War. Just before starting this book, I found a long-forgotten box of papers in the garage, with my parents' identity cards, some photographs of my mother with friends and a few – frankly creepy – love letters to my father from an old girlfriend. You might be luckier finding letters home from relatives in the forces, which should give details of their service number and unit and roughly where they were stationed. All vital information!

Key clues include:

- Details of the units individuals served with in the forces and especially service numbers, as this will allow you to get their service records more easily.
- Details of civil defence units served with such as the Home Guard, Air Raid Precautions (ARP), or Auxiliary Fire Service (AFS). Alternatively there might be material about working in a factory or an office.
- Other official documents, such as identity cards and ration books, call-up papers, letters about being rehoused.
- Any letter or other document with an address that can be checked in the 1939 Register.

DIARIES

A friend recently showed me his father's diary kept when he was a prisoner of war in Germany, showing how boring life was behind the barbed wire and the constant uncertainty about whether he would ever return home safely. For some men, particularly those in captivity, keeping a detailed diary was important. Indeed, the Red Cross sent blank diaries to camps to allow those interned to record their daily thoughts.

The Imperial War Museum (IWM) has the very moving diary of John Edward Roden Parsons, who was a sapper (private) in the Royal Engineers. The IWM's catalogue describes it as being a 'Very detailed ms [manuscript] diary covering his experiences as a prisoner of war on Sumatra and subsequent liberation, February 1942 – November 1945, in four small notebooks, loose sheets of notepaper, and on the backs of letters received whilst a prisoner (circa 25 pp)'. In the introduction to the typescript that accompanies the original diary, Parsons wrote that he had kept the diary from the capitulation of Singapore until the last entry, which reads 'passed Aden today' on our way home:

> Had the diary been found by the guards, the consequences for me would have been somewhat unpleasant; this necessitated recording only those events to which the Japanese would not take too violent exception. I am now uncertain as to how and where I hid the diaries during our fairly frequent searches; though in fact the guards were more interested in weapons and radios, nevertheless I did manage to hold on to a much-shortened bayonet and an army issue compass till towards the end when I was obviously too weak to escape, I threw away the bayonet and sold the compass to guards.

> In retrospect I feel that I was altogether too concerned with the state of my health, not expectedly food or rather the lack of it, loomed larger the longer we were in captivity… to my shame they [the diaries] they often appear querulous and self-centred but that was how I was affected by some unpleasant times.[4]

In my experience, most diaries, however, contain nothing but scribbled notes and possibly the occasional mention of a place. One I came across recently seemed mainly to contain lists of gambling debts.

OFFICIAL PAPERS

There may also be a variety of official correspondence that sometimes turns up in people's papers. Most families seemed to have kept their identity cards. In late 1939, everybody over the age of 6 was issued with an identity card that had to be carried at all times. The cards gave the owner's name, address and previous addresses, together with a unique National Registration number that was written on the inside of the card. The local registration office stamped the card to make it valid. The cards were necessary in case families became separated in the event of bombing or if the children were evacuated to another part of the country. People also had to produce their identity cards along with their ration books when they were claiming their share of food or clothes. Cards were finally abolished in 1952.[5]

It is worth seeing whether you have a pay book and/or a certificate of service in your family papers, as these will provide basic details about an individual's service in the military. Pay books contain brief details about an individual including service number and units served with, plus notes about their pay. Certificates of service were issued to men and women who were honourably discharged, to be shown to potential employers if required. The army's certificate took the form of a booklet with a deep red cover. It looks similar to a pay book.

Regardless of service, the certificates and pay books will give brief details of the individual (including service number), the units the recipient served with, and when and where they served overseas. There should also be a reference from their commanding officer. This almost always attests to the individual's hard work and intelligence.

There might also be correspondence about enlisting in the forces or exemption from service. (See also Chapter 3 below.)

Certificate of Transfer to the Army Reserve.

Date of transfer........

Rank........

Cause of transfer........

Corps from which transferred........

Service with Colours on date of transfer :—

........years........days.

Description of soldier on transfer :—

Year of birth........ Height........ft........ins.

Complexion........ Eyes........ Hair........

Marks or Scars........

.... Signature and rank.

Place........

Date........ Officer i/c........Records.

Certificate of Discharge.

Date of discharge 12th April 1940

Rank W O II S.S.M.

Cause of discharge For the purpose of being appointed to a Commission Para 383 (xvii) K.R.35

Corps from which discharged.

Service on date of discharge :—

(a) With Colours 13 years 11 ... days.

(b) In the Reserve — years — days.

Total Service 13 years 11 ... days.

Description of soldier on discharge* :—

Year of birth 1911 Height ft ins.

Complexion Eyes Hair

Marks or Scars

.... Signature and rank.

Place Canterbury

Date........ Officer i/c........Records.

* Not required to be completed in the case of a man discharged from the Army Reserve.

An example of an Army pay book. (Author)

PHOTOGRAPHS

The chances are that you have a photograph or two of the soldiers you are researching in uniform. As well providing a direct link to the past, the insignia and badges can tell you something about his service. Military uniforms can reveal clues, but photographs of service personnel are notoriously difficult to interpret. Many men took a small camera with them to war. The reason for this may be that it was likely to be the most exciting time of their lives, and the camera would record this experience. Although technically cameras were not allowed, they were tolerated provided they weren't used to take photographs in the front line or anything that might help the enemy if the camera fell into the wrong hands. There may be a posed studio photograph of an individual proudly wearing his new uniform. More often, they are shots of a man in crumpled battledress grinning at the camera with a cigarette cupped in his hand or a group of soldiers standing relaxed by a tank or lorry. Civilians too took photographs of bombed-out houses, children and days out at the seaside or in the countryside.

Old photographs are wonderful but can they all be identified? After all, who is ever going to forget Jack and the gang. But, of course, we do. All too rarely, however, is there anything scribbled on the back with anybody's names. My mother's photograph album is full of photographs of her family and the nurses and medical staff she worked with, but there are no more than a few cryptic captions, usually a forename, and nothing else, which makes working out who these people were and what became of them almost impossible.

Experts at military museums should be able to help you work out what the photographs of men in uniform are telling you.

TOP TIPS FOR IDENTIFYING PHOTOGRAPHS

- Is there any writing on the back; or if the photograph is mounted are details of the photographer and their address given?
- If the individual is in uniform, can you identify the unit from cap or tunic badges?
- Are there any rank badges, such as sergeant's chevrons or a lieutenant's pips?
- Are there any trade badges, such as crossed flags for signallers?
- Does the background give a clue? If the soldier is posed in front of a Roman ruin, this might mean the photograph was taken in Italy or Greece. Sometimes it is obvious that the snapshot was taken in Paris, because of the Eiffel Tower, or near the Acropolis in Athens. Or there may be a two-letter RAF squadron code on the aircraft a man is standing nearby, so he must have had a connection with that unit.

THEIR FINEST HOUR

Their Finest Hour is a project from Oxford University that aims to collect and digitally archive everyday stories and objects from the war. The goal is to save and preserve this material before it is lost forever. As well as records and artefacts from acknowledged war heroes, the project wishes to reflect the experiences of everybody affected by or involved in the Second World War, regardless of where they came from and how they contributed to the war effort, whether in factories, in the forces, at school or at home.

Find out more at https://theirfinesthour.english.ox.ac.uk

MILITARY UNIFORMS

The uniforms worn by members of the British Army was radically different to that their fathers wore during the First World War. Most men and their officers wore battledress – a loose fitting and durable jacket and trousers designed for more mobile warfare, Introduced just before the outbreak of war in 1939, it was inspired by contemporary wool 'ski suits' which were less restrictive to the wearer, used less material, were warm even while wet and were more suited to vehicular movement than Service Dress. The jacket was normally worn over a woollen shirt. Officers wore a tie or had their shirt collars open, whereas the men under their command wore collarless shirts buttoned at the neck. Officers' battledress, particularly those who on the staff or in positions of command, was often tailored to give a smarter better fitting look. Even so there was some grumbling. One major in a Smart Guards regiment is supposed to have declared: 'I don't mind dying for my country but I'm not going to die dressed like a third-rate chauffeur.'[6]

Battledress changed slightly during the war, partly as the result of shortages of cloth but also to meet the needs of specialist troops. Tank crews, for example were issued with a 'tank suit' which, according to George Forty, was 'warm, waterproof and comfortable, although the rain always collected in the crotch when in the sitting position (for example, when driving a tank)!'[7]

Battledress – in RAF blue – was adopted by the Royal Air Force. Darker blue versions were worn by the Civil Defence units (ARP). It was even used by U-Boat crews who were issued with suits captured during the Fall of France, and were widely worn by German soldiers in the last few months of the war.

Troops in North Africa and particularly in Burma and the Far East wore a tropical uniform consisted of green cotton shirt and trousers, ankle boots worn with puttees or anklets, and bush hats. Shorts seem particularly common and were worn by all ranks, including seniors commanders.

Distinctly coloured berets became very popular. The most famous were the maroon ones worn by members of the Parachute Regiment, the khaki of the SAS and the black ones worn by members of the Royal Tank Regiment, which was famously modelled by General Bernard Montgomery.

Unforms were customised by various badges and flashes which signified the army, corps or division a man belonged to. The ranks of officers would be shown by a pattern of stars (known as pips) and crowns worn on shoulder straps. Sergeants and corporals would have chevrons on their sleeves – one for lance corporal, two for corporal and three for sergeant, with a crown over the chevrons for staff sergeants and warrant officers. In addition, there might be tradesmen's badges and those for other skills such as bomb disposal.

There does not appear to be a website devoted to interpreting uniform insignia in a simple way, although there are a few books that might be worth consulting (see further reading below). Wikipedia does have several useful articles on British military uniforms, with several illustrations.[8] For badges, the British Badge Forum might be a good place to start.

The uniform of a British officer showing his rank with the pips on his collar and his regiment. (Skipton Museum)

Further reading

Graham Bandy, *Identifying Cap Badges* (Pen & Sword, 2022)
Peter Duckers, *British Military Medals* (Pen & Sword, 2021)
Malcolm Hobart, *Badges and Uniforms of the RAF* (Pen & Sword, 2013)
Brian Jewell, *British Battle Dress* (Osprey, 1992)
Robert Pols, *Identifying Old Army Photographs* (Family History Partnership, 2011)
Neil Storey, *Military Photographs and How to Date them* (Countryside Books, 2010)

CONCLUSION

Occasionally, there are neither family memories nor family papers. A client was trying to research her great-grandfather, but did not know whether he was in the forces or not. The 1939 Register (see below) revealed that he was a radio engineer, a skill that would have been extremely useful in the services as well as to civilian employers. Potentially a useful clue, unfortunately he also had a common name. I had to admit defeat.

CARING FOR FAMILY PAPERS

Always look after family heirlooms by keeping them out of direct sunlight and store them in a cool place away from potentially leaking pipes. You should also avoid handling them as frequent touching may well damage them. If you are going to use original photographs or documents (such as marriage certificates) a lot in your research, make copies.

In the long term, think about what happens to your family papers when you have gone. Offer them to a service or regimental museum if they contain a lot of military material, or to your local museum or archive if your family served largely on the home front.

CONDUCTING AN ORAL HISTORY INTERVIEW

If you are lucky, you may have elderly relations who remember the war or perhaps grew up in the immediate post-war years. If so, they may well have memories about their parents and their friends' experiences.

People, especially the old, tire easily. Don't try to do too much at one time.

It is preferable to see the interviewee in person, rather than use Zoom or conduct a telephone conversation. If you have them, take old photographs to help refresh the memory. People like to look at pictures and can often supply names for unknown individuals in a family snapshot.

Be tactful, polite and understanding.

If you intend to use a recording device (there should be one on your phone):

- Always ask before switching it on, people often get very nervous when faced with a microphone. I've often found they will relax and tell you the really interesting gossip once it has been switched off.
- Make sure it is working before you start the interview.
- Have plenty of spare storage and batteries or make sure your phone is fully charged.

Work out what you want to talk about and think of some simple questions beforehand to get the conversation started. Don't interrupt. Let your interviewer speak. Your job is to just encourage, sympathise where necessary, and keep your interviewee on topic. Just remember those irritating TV interviews with politicians where the journalist constantly interrupts. If it helps, prepare a checklist of subjects you want to discuss, but be prepared to abandon the checklist if something more interesting emerges.

I also use a notebook to summarise what the interviewer is saying. This can be a lifesaver, because it can be time-consuming (and sometimes expensive) to transcribe the recording.

FOWLER'S LAWS OF MILITARY GENEALOGY

Over many years researching soldiers, sailors and airmen I have come up with several rules that may help you find your military ancestors:

- The closer your ancestor was to the fighting – or if he was killed in action – the more there is likely to be about him. If he was in the front line there should be operational records to provide more background, although he is unlikely to be identified by name.
- There is likely to be more about officers than for other ranks. They may be mentioned in war diaries or squadron record books, where other ranks are not.
- Service records, particularly those for the army, should be studied closely, as they often provide a lot of useful information about units served with, when the individual went overseas (if indeed they did), promotions and demotions. Disciplinary offences, the award of good conduct and long-service medals and any affected pay and pension may well also be recorded. In theory, every day of a man's service should be recorded in some way.
- If you want to fully to understand an ancestor's experiences of war it is best to start by reading campaign and regimental histories before using the operational records, as war diaries and the like are not always easy to interpret and on occasion can be misleading.
- The records are only as good as the clerks and adjutants who completed them. Names are misspelt, initials are used rather than full names and so on.
- There are many more records existing than are currently available online. Most of them will never be digitised. To get a full picture of your ancestor's military service you should visit TNA or the appropriate service and regimental museums.
- There are always exceptions! There may be nothing about a war hero, but by chance a mass of stuff may survive for an ordinary soldier or sailor.

You never know what you are going to find. That's the joy of this kind of research.

WHERE TO FIND THE RECORDS

WEBSITES

So much relating to the Second World War is now online. There seems to be something on almost every aspect. An increasing amount can be found with the commercial data providers, but a lot of free material is available. There are links to several hundred sites in the book, but I'm certain many more have been missed out.

If you find a link has broken or the website has disappeared altogether, then you should be able to find the missing information on the Internet Archive's Wayback Machine, www.archive.org. Since 1996, bots sent out by the Internet Archive have been crawling through the internet, taking snapshots of websites and preserving them. Like newspapers, the content published on the web was ephemeral – but unlike newspapers, no one was saving it.

Incidentally, the British Library collects websites created in Britain at www.webarchive.org.uk

GENEALOGICAL DATA PROVIDERS

There are two major commercial genealogical data providers, which make a huge range of genealogical datasets or collections of material available to subscribers: Ancestry (www.ancestry.co.uk) and Findmypast (www.findmypast.co.uk). Both offer a range of subscription packages; there is some overlap in what they offer. Incidentally, both offer occasional free access to their military record sets, particularly over the Remembrance Sunday weekend in November. Many libraries subscribe to Ancestry, although fewer provide access to Findmypast.

Both are fairly easy to use, but neither are terribly good at explaining what the records are and how they might help your research.

The biggest problem, however, with both these sites is in narrowing down your search to the individual, or individuals, you are researching. It is normally better to use specific collections of material rather than a general search of the whole collection. Ancestry has a Card Catalogue that provides a searchable listing of all record collections. Just type in the name of a topic, such as 'prisoners of war', and it come up with all the relevant record sets. Findmypast's equivalent is 'all record sets', which works in a similar way.

Here are the most important Second World War holdings for each company. Both also have a wide range of smaller collections that may occasionally be useful.

ANCESTRY

- 1939 Register
- 1911 Census
- Service records (due to be completed by 2029)
- War diaries (Army) (only Middle East at time of publication)
- Women's Land Army

Ancestry has put many of its military record sets into its Fold3 service for which there is an additional charge.

FINDMYPAST

- 1921 Census (which is also available on Ancestry)
- 1939 Register (a better set than Ancestry's)
- 1911 Census
- British Army casualty lists
- Nurses' records
- Prisoners of war lists

There is currently an additional charge to use the 1921 Census.

FREE WEBSITES

Here are a few key websites that provide background on the war and how it was fought:

- British Military History: www.britishmilitaryhistory.co.uk
- British Newspaper Archive: www.britishnewspaperarchive.co.uk
- Imperial War Museum: www.iwm.org.uk/history
- Wikipedia: https://en.wikipedia.org
- WW2 Database: https://ww2db.com
- WW2talk forum: http://ww2talk.com

Many more are listed elsewhere in the book.

MUSEUMS

If you have to choose just one British museum for its Second World War material it has to be the Imperial War Museum, or rather museums, as it has branches in London, Manchester, Duxford as well as the Cabinet War Rooms and HMS *Belfast* in London. Its holdings are mind-blowing and the exhibitions expertly curated.

Imperial War Museum
Lambeth Road
SE1 6HZ
www.iwm.org.uk

Inside the main gallery at the Imperial War Museum in London with a Spitfire and a German A4 (V2) rocket. (Author)

SOCIAL MEDIA

Social media is not something I am an expert on, so this section is much shorter than it probably deserves to be.

However, the various forms of social media are an important way of sharing information and finding out the latest news.[9] If you are a user then you are probably well aware of this. If not, well perhaps it is time to find out.

The most useful services are:

Facebook

There are numerous groups devoted to all aspects of the Second World War. Some are public for anybody to visit, but others are closed so you have to apply to join, normally a mere formality. If for example, you are interested in the events of the Second World War in Burma, you can join and post on the WW2 Burma Research Group. The Medal of KAR (King's African Rifles) Facebook group is a historical research page, open to everybody, dedicated to all those who served in the Northern Rhodesia Regiment, King's African Rifles, Royal West African Frontier Force and Rhodesian African Rifles. At the time of writing, it consists largely of photographs of Zambia's impressive Remembrance Day commemorations in Lusaka.

Twitter/X

Here you can follow historians, contribute to debates or ask questions. Similar services are Mastodon and Threads, but despite the turmoil surrounding its ownership, X remains the place to be (at least at the time of writing). Instagram seems to be mainly for photographs and TikTok for young people.

BOOKS AND LIBRARIES

Many, many forests have been cut down to provide paper for all the books published about the Second World War. But how do you find the right book for the subject you are interested in? Details of almost all the books published in Great Britain and Ireland can be found on the British Library Catalogue.

To search library catalogues worldwide, use WorldCat. Not only does it tell you what books there are but where you can find them. A search for books about the concentration camp at Bergen-Belsen comes up with over 4,500 different titles, published in a dozen different countries and kept by libraries worldwide. Helpfully, it will tell you where the nearest copy to you is located.

Your local public library will have an online catalogue, accessible via the council website, for books it holds. In addition, through the inter-library loan scheme it should be able to borrow any book, although it may take months for it to arrive.

Most university libraries provide access to members of the public. They may have collections and resources generally unavailable elsewhere.

BUYING BOOKS

Local bookshops should be able to order any book in print. But if you prefer to buy books online, Bookshop.org is an excellent alternative to you know who.

Of course, the book you want may be long out of print. This is where Abebooks comes in. It sells books on behalf of second-hand bookdealers. It's easy to use and the prices are generally very reasonable. Books are also sold on eBay.

OLD BOOKS

An increasing number of books have been digitised and are available online, normally free of charge. They tend to be for titles that are out of copyright. This generally means that they were published more than eighty-five years ago and often come from the shelves of American libraries. The main online libraries are the Internet Archive and the Hathi Trust. It's easy to do a keyword search across the whole site or within specific books.

An alternative is Google Books, which includes many modern titles, but here they normally reveal just an extract rather than the whole book. Amazon also provides teaser extracts for many books.

There are several publishers that specialise in publishing books about the Second World War, including The History Press. The largest such company, however, is Pen & Sword which seems to publish an inexhaustible flood of such books. The Naval & Military Press republishes a number of original histories and reports but is better known for selling military history books, often at greatly reduced prices.

In addition, the Imperial War Museum has republished a baker's dozen of 'Wartime Classic' novels. John Foley's *Mailed Fist* and Peter Elstob's *Warriors for a Working Day*, for example, are fictionalised accounts of life in tank regiments in north-west Europe.

PHOTOGRAPHS

By 1939, photography was no longer expensive or rare. As a result, many families possessed a camera used to take shots of weddings and days out. So it was not unusual for men and women to take their cameras with them into the forces or to go out to photograph bomb damage or VE-Day teas. Provided cameras weren't used where they might be of help to the enemy – for example in the front line – the authorities were generally relaxed about their use.

In addition, the Ministry of Information and the services had teams of official photographers who seemingly recorded almost every aspect of the war at home and overseas. The quality of their work is much better, but they lack the spontaneity and freshness of a soldier taking pictures of comrades larking about on their tank.

Local archives and local studies libraries may have collections of photographs from the war. In Richmond, I have found, for example, albums of photographs of ARP wardens and their posts and also some snaps of shelters being built on the Green.

The largest collection of official photographs is held by the **Imperial War Museum,** an increasing proportion of which is online – click on the 'Objects and Histories' menu. It is a real treasure store of images, many of which can be downloaded for your own use. There are many photographs of individuals (mainly officers who had been awarded gallantry medals), ships and aircraft, air-raid shelters and volunteers handing out cups of tea.

Service and regimental museums, as well as local archives and museums, will also have collections donated by individuals or companies or acquired from official sources.

Use these records for

- Visualising what our families looked like during the war.
- Noting uniforms and other details, such as the location where the picture was taken; they may give clues about an individual's wartime career.
- Understanding wartime scenes that your ancestors might have been familiar with.

Children sharing their collections of shrapnel. (Museum of Richmond)

Pitfalls

- All too often it is impossible to identify individuals, as names were not written on the back of the photo or noted down elsewhere.
- The quality of photographs taken by untrained photographers may be very poor, due to camera shake and poor exposure.
- What subjects were photographed was random. They depended on what interested the photographer or, to an extent, what they were permitted to take.

FILMS, NEWSREELS AND THE WIRELESS

Unlike the First World War, where primitive technology and the reluctance of the army high command to allow the cameras anywhere near the front means that there is relatively little film, the position had completely changed by 1939. Now the authorities realised that the war, both overseas and on the home front, had to be covered comprehensively as honestly as possible and, just as important in a way, to engage and motivate audiences. Our view of the war is coloured even today by this coverage: the stiff upper lip in countless movies, dramatic shots from newsreels, and a few surviving sound clips from radio broadcasts.

Millions of people visited the cinema each week, where it was warm and you could forget the dreariness of everyday life for a few hours. Each programme consisted of one or two feature films, a short film, often a cartoon or something made by the Ministry of Information, and a newsreel including a variety of pieces on the war as well as lighter stories.

By 1939, most households had a radio set. The BBC broadcast a wide range of programmes on the Home Service (equivalent to BBC Radio 4 today) and the Forces Programme (think Radio 2). Initially, programming was worthy but dull, but it became much livelier as the war progressed. The most popular shows were the *Brains Trust*, where experts discussed questions posed by the audience, and the comedy *ITMA* (It's That Man Again), with its range of characters and catchphrases that soon entered the language.[10]

Many listeners also tuned into the German propaganda station *Germany Calling*, at least until the BBC began to improve its programmes. Its star was William Joyce, better known as Lord Haw-Haw because of his upper-class accent. His broadcasts became famous for detailed announcements about particular places that only the locals would have known about.

SOURCES

The IWM has an incomparable film collection. At its heart is the uncut record footage filmed by combat cameramen. Much has been digitised and is available on the museum's website through the 'Objects and History' menu.

There are also a number of regional film archives, which also have films of the period, generally, but not always, about life on the home front. For more information visit the British Film Archive website.

YouTube is a brilliant resource, with much to explore. In particular, there are many newsreels uploaded by British Pathé and British Movietone, as well as the official ones made by the Ministry of Information. Some are still extremely powerful; for example, the films about the Liberation of the Bergen-Belsen concentration camp, while those featuring Richard Massingham remain very amusing. There are also many short documentaries of varying quality and accuracy made by modern historians and educators. Those by Mark Felton are constantly good, although rather marred by a monotone narration. Rather charming are the stop-go animations in Lego of key incidents in the war.

For technical reasons, few radio broadcasts from the war years survive. However, the BBC's Genome website provides access to every issue of the *Radio Times* published between 1923 and 2009. There's a link to the BBC Rewind that allows access to old television programmes, but there are none for the wartime period because the TV Service closed down on the outbreak of war and didn't resume until 1947.[11]

Use these records for

- Getting a feel for the war your ancestor experienced.
- Learning about aspects of the war that are of interest.

Pitfalls

- It is very unlikely that you will see anybody you recognise in these films.
- Wartime material was shot and edited to get across a particular, usually positive, message. In particular, the commentary given in the most patronising tones may well grate!
- Rushes and offcuts may be difficult to interpret.

ARCHIVES

At some stage, you may wish to visit an archive to do research using material that isn't online. This may seem a daunting step, but it isn't really. There's usually a lot of advice available for new researchers on the archive's website. In addition, the staff will be very pleased to help you.

Here are some tips to get you on your way:

- Before you visit, check the archive's website:
  - To make sure that it has what you are looking for.
  - To ensure whether it will be open when you plan to visit, as archive hours are increasingly being reduced as the result of cuts to services.
  - Find out what you need to bring with you, such as proof of identity and address to obtain a reader's ticket.
- Allow plenty of time to get to the archive and to find your way around.
- Bring pencils, a notebook and/or a laptop. Pens and loose collections of notes are not allowed in search rooms, so leave them at home or with your coat and bag.
- Don't forget a camera (or use your phone) to take pictures of documents. Many archives charge a small fee for a permit.
- Of course, obey reading room rules that ask researchers to only use pencils and handle documents carefully.[12]

THE NATIONAL ARCHIVES

The National Archives (TNA) at Kew in south-west London is the official archive of the United Kingdom and England and Wales. It largely holds the records of central government (aka Whitehall) and the armed forces. There are separate national archives in Scotland, Northern Ireland and the Republic of Ireland, although these institutions hold few military records relating to the Second World War. TNA is by and away the largest – and most important – archive in the British Isles and can compete with any worldwide for the completeness of its holdings and ease of access.

As a result, it has a superb collection of material for the Second World War. For most purposes, TNA is the only archive you will need in your research. Helpfully, TNA has digitised some key records, which are described in the relevant chapters below. And its importance will be enhanced over the next few years with the transfer of army, navy and air force service records from the Ministry of Defence.

The National Archives at Kew. (Author)

However, there are several difficulties:

- Relatively little is yet online, and it can be difficult to find (that's why you bought this book).
- Many files have been destroyed, particularly on trivial matters, so if you want to know the name of the troopship in which Great-Aunt Maureen sailed on to the Middle East, or the fate of the tank Uncle Jack drove or the type of army watch he wore, then you will be unlucky. Such records were discarded decades ago because of their ephemeral nature, although occasionally this material turns up at other museums and archives. The RAF Museum has, for example, a lot of material relating to individual aircraft.
- In addition, files can be very badly described in the catalogue, because many of the records relating to the war were transferred to the Public Record Office (TNA's predecessor) in the late 1960s in a great hurry. As a result, file descriptions are very often very general. Fortunately, TNA is beginning to tackle this problem, in particular it has recently indexed by name the escape and evasion reports submitted by service personnel after their return home. In the process, some fascinating stories have been revealed for the first time.

Getting started

TNA's website – www.nationalarchives.gov.uk – has two essential tools to help researchers:

- Research Guides
- Online Catalogue

In addition, there is the Live Chat service, which is open between Tuesday and Saturday, between 9 a.m. and 5 p.m., where friendly and knowledgeable staff can provide answers to your questions about all TNA's services and collections.

If you want to look at original material, such as unit war diaries, you will need to visit Kew in person, or employ somebody to copy the records for you.

Research Guides explain the records in very simple terms. They describe what records are at TNA, what is available elsewhere, and what is online. Often there are links to the appropriate page on other websites. There are more than 150 guides, with many relating to the Second World War. They can be found on the 'Help with your Research' pages on TNA's website.

Research guides are a very useful way of finding out more about particular sets of records. (TNA)

The **Online Catalogue** (sometimes called Discovery) contains details of more than 32 million descriptions of records held by TNA and more than 2,500 archives across the country. In addition, over 9 million records are available for download. It's extremely good and very flexible, but it can be off-putting to the casual user as it looks quite confusing. There's a link to Discovery on the home page. Click on 'Search the catalogue' and you are taken to Discovery's welcome page, which looks very similar to Google. You can type your search query here, perhaps the name of an ancestor or a former RAF station near you. There are two ways of narrowing the search, that is by date (say, 1939 to 1945) and whether the material is at TNA or at another archive. You can also do an Advanced Search, which allows you to filter your search in a number of different ways.

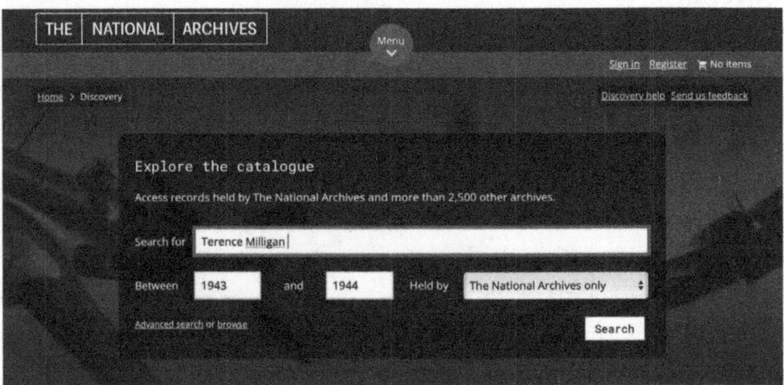

The search box to TNA's Discovery Catalogue. (TNA)

Discovery is a very sophisticated search engine, but does take time to get used to. Remember that:

- File descriptions have rarely been modernised, so if you are researching the D-Day landings you also need to look for files relating to operations Overlord and Neptune. And, more controversially, the English language has changed, something that is not always reflected in the catalogue. However, this is not usually a problem with material from the Second World War.
- Discovery contains details of hundreds of thousands of men and women who served in the war. But just because there is no obvious mention of your ancestor it does not mean that there is nothing about them; perhaps they may appear in a list of prisoners of war or survivors of ships sunk by the enemy, which still have to be indexed or digitised.

READING THE CODE

Each TNA record has a unique reference, which you will need if you order an original document while at Kew, or download an online document, and which you should cite as evidence on your family tree or if you are writing a book or article.

Like all archives, TNA collections are arranged by the depositor. In the case of TNA, this is the government department that created the records. Each department is assigned a two- to four-letter or departmental code: WO for War Office, ADM – Admiralty, AIR – Air Ministry, DEFE – Ministry of Defence, and so on.

Departmental records are broken down into series. A series is a main grouping of records with a common origin and function or subject matter. Each one is assigned a unique number within the departmental code, such AIR 28 – Air Ministry and Ministry of Defence: Operations Record Books, Royal Air Force Stations, or WO 171 War Office: Allied Expeditionary Force, North West Europe (British Element): War Diaries, Second World War.

Within each series, each unit of production (generally a file or bound volume), is usually referred to as being a piece reference, so the station record book for RAF Biggin Hill between 1932 and December 1945 was assigned the reference AIR 28/64. Occasionally, a large file is broken down into two or more items.

Contact details

The National Archives
Kew, Richmond
TW9 4DU
Tel: 020–8876 3444
www.nationalarchives.gov.uk

MUSEUMS AND ARCHIVES

As well as TNA, there is a network of military museums, archives and libraries that may have something about your ancestors. They are rarely your first place to start your research as almost all the key resources are with TNA, but if you really get into the subject then they can be very useful. If they have anything of particular importance to family historians then this will be mentioned in the main text. Almost all museums and archives have online catalogues of varying ease of use and completeness. An increasing number also are putting scanned material on their websites. This is the approach taken by the **National Museum of the Royal Navy**, which does not really have a traditional online catalogue.

MUSEUMS

As well as displaying their collections, military museums also maintain archives, both of the museum's own history and also collections deposited or otherwise acquired by the museum. Generally, these are collections of diaries, memoirs and other private papers, photographs and other ephemera. Most museums have online catalogues and lists of collections are also available on TNA's online catalogue.

The most important military museum by far is the **Imperial War Museum** (IWM), which has collected material relating to wars and conflicts since 1914. An increasing proportion of material, particularly photographs and films, is available through the website (for more about photographs and films see above). Among the archives are collections of diaries, letters and oral history interviews with service personnel and civilians.

There are also national museums for each of the services that collect not dissimilar material. In London there is the **National Army Museum** and the **RAF Museum**. Portsmouth Dockyard houses the **National Museum of the Royal Navy**. London also has the **National Maritime Museum** in Greenwich, which has a number of naval exhibits and a very good research library. A special mention must be made of **Bletchley Park**, the wartime home of Britain's codebreakers, which is now a museum with an excellent exhibition devoted to the exploits.

- Imperial War Museum: www.iwm.org.uk
- National Army Museum: www.nam.ac.uk
- RAF Museum: www.rafmuseum.org.uk

- National Museum of the RN: www.nmm.org.uk
- National Maritime Museum: www.rbg.co.uk
- Bletchley Park: https://bletchleypark.org.uk

On a local level, there is a network of regimental museums, some of which maintain their own archives while others have deposited theirs with county archives. The museums are well worth visiting, particularly if you have ancestors who served in a particular unit. They are all listed by the Army Museums Ogilby Trust.

There are some forty aviation museums with many different emphases on what they collect and display. Many also have archives; where this is the case there is normally information on their websites. A partial list is given by Military Airshow. In addition, there are a number of museums on former RAF stations, such RAF Hornchurch and RAF Biggin Hill. There are rather fewer naval museums. Most are part of the National Museum of the Royal Navy, but important collections are held by the **Liverpool Maritime Museum** and the **Scottish Maritime Museum** in Glasgow.

Most local museums include displays about the experience of war in their district. There are several national museums devoted to wartime life, such as Eden Camp in North Yorkshire. Of more immediate use is the **Second World War Experience Centre**, which has a large collection of material, private papers and oral history, a small proportion of which is online.

Some of the best museums are actually run by enthusiasts, volunteers for the most part. What they lack in slick presentation and technological gizmos is more than made up by the collections themselves and the enthusiasm and knowledge of the volunteers on duty. I really recommend Oban's **War and Peace Museum**, where there is a genuinely informative display on how the war affected the town and the relationship with the various British and Allied units stationed around the area. Most of the items have been donated by local people or by veterans and their families who had happy memories of being stationed at this Scottish seaside resort.

LOCAL AND SPECIALIST ARCHIVES

There is also a network of archives, most of which will have material about the Second World War. The largest of these is the **British Library**, which has the national newspaper collection, records of the Indian Army, and almost every book published in the United Kingdom. The largest Scottish archive is the **National Records of Scotland**: Scotland's national archives.

In Ulster, the major archive is the **Public Record Office of Northern Ireland**, universally called PRONI. There are also specialist national libraries for Scotland and Wales. The **National Library of Scotland** has a superb collection of UK-wide digital resources, including military lists and Ordnance Survey maps. Another important Scottish source is the **National War Museum** at Edinburgh Castle.

Every county in England and Wales and Scottish regions has its own archive. Most cities and London boroughs also have local studies libraries. In addition, there is a wide range of company and other archives – from British Airways via Barclays Bank to Marks and Spencer and Bristol University. Almost all have online catalogues and most welcome researchers, although opening hours may be restricted. The Archives Hub has descriptions of many archival collections and it is easy to carry out a search across them all, for example to find resources about convoys. For archives in London, AIM25 provides a similar service.

- British Library: www.bl.uk
- National Library of Scotland: www.nls.uk
- NLS Digital Resources: www.nls.uk/digital-resources/
- National Library of Wales: www.library.wales
- National Records of Scotland: www.nrscotland.gov.uk/research
- National War Museum: www.nms.ac.uk/national-war-museum
- Public Record Office of NI: www.nidirect.gov.uk/campaigns/public-record-office-northern-ireland-proni

Archives can sometimes be hard to track down. Almost all are listed by TNA as part of the Discovery Catalogue (which also includes details of many overseas). You can search by town or by archive name. The catalogue should be able to tell you at which archive a particular collection of material can be consulted. Contact details for archives specifically mentioned in the text will be found in the appropriate place below.

GETTING STARTED – THE RECORD SOURCES

As well as talking to the family and searching the loft for any papers and photos there's some basic genealogical research that you can do that might provide some useful clues and background information. Here are some key sources:

BIRTH, MARRIAGE AND DEATH CERTIFICATES

National registration began in England and Wales on 1 July 1837 (Scotland – 1855, Ireland – 1864). The system has remained largely unchanged since then.

At the time of writing, certificates in England and Wales cost £11 each, although an increasing number are available as PDFs at a cheaper rate. Although the information contained naturally varies depending on the event, they all have occupation columns for new fathers, grooms and the deceased, which should reveal whether they were soldiers or veterans. When ordering a service record, you may need to provide a death certificate to prove that the person you are researching has been dead for more than twenty-five years. Attaching a scan of the document to your application (if you are doing this online) will suffice as proof.

English and Welsh certificates can be ordered online via the General Register Office website or by phone at on 0300 123 1837. Scottish certificates are all online through Scotland's People. Indexes to Irish births, marriages and deaths for the period (both Northern Ireland and the Republic of Ireland) are available through the FamilySearch genealogical website, but you have to order the certificates from the General Register Office for Ireland or, in Northern Ireland, the General Register Office for Northern Ireland.

There are also indexes which will broadly indicate when and where an event took place, that is often enough to confirm roughly when a birth, marriage or death occurred. Indexes for England and Wales are compiled quarterly (the March quarter contains registrations between 1 January and 31 March and so on). They can be found on each of the commercial data providers' websites and at FreeBMD. The most detailed birth and death indexes, but not marriages, are actually on the General Register Office website, although you will have to register to get access.

REGIMENTAL REGISTERS AND RELATED RECORDS

Also of interest might be regimental registers, which record births, baptisms, marriages, deaths and burials of service personnel and their families at home and abroad. Indexes to this are on both Ancestry and Findmypast.

TNA has a small number of regimental registers of births, baptisms, marriages and burials in series WO 156. For the navy there are similar registers in ADM 338, and in AIR 82 for the RAF. Findmypast also has details of births, marriages and deaths at sea, including for both Merchant and Royal Navy for the period of the war. They will tell you the date of the event and the ship it took place on.

There's a useful TNA research guide found on TNA's website that explains the registers 'Birth, Marriage, Death in the Armed Forces'.

Use these records for

- Confirming dates of births, marriages and death.
- Providing details of parents.

Pitfalls

- Very occasionally, births and deaths were not registered, perhaps because they occurred outside the UK or Ireland.
- A reasonable number of marriages were 'common law marriages', which were not celebrated in church or in a registry and therefore cannot be found in marriage records. The partners thus 'lived in sin', as the phrase went.

WILLS

It was natural for soldiers to make wills before going into action. Indeed, the army pay book, which was issued to all soldiers, included a simple will form. Generally, any possessions were left to the individual's spouse or parents. The navy and RAF had similar arrangements.

If an individual made a formal will it would have been proved by the Principal Probate Registry (in England and Wales). Details were published in the National Probate Calendars, which list all wills proved, with the name of the deceased, his occupation and home address, date of death, the value of the will and who the executor was. Entries may be six months or later after the date of death. Captain Frank Rowland, Royal Artillery, was killed on 10 May 1943 in Tunisia. In his will, which was proved on 11 October 1943, he left £285 10s to Honoria Mary Saunders, presumably his sister, and seemingly nothing to his parents. Calendars are online at Ancestry and, for free, on the Principal Probate Registry's website. You can search for both ordinary wills and those specifically made by service personnel. You can also buy copies of wills for £1.50 each – which is a rare genealogical bargain. Indexes of soldiers' wills can also be found on the gov.uk website.

The National Records of Scotland, in Edinburgh, holds Scottish wills. It is a very different system to that found south of the border; to find out more see the NRS's research guide 'Wills and Testaments'. There are also

4,700 wills for Scots soldiers who died during the Second World War that can be found on Scotland's People website. Indexes to Northern Irish wills for the period of the war can be searched on the PRONI website.

THE CENSUS

Census records are an important source for family history, revealing unique information about ancestors. They have been taken every ten years since 1801, although the actual returns listing individual people only survive from 1841. The most recent one to be publicly available is that for 1921, which means that anybody over the age of 18 or 19 at the outbreak of war who was born in England, Wales and Scotland should appear in it.

In 1921, a full entry on a standard household schedule will contain:

- Full address of the property
- Names of persons in each household
- Relationship to head of household
- Age
- Sex
- Marital status
- For those under 15 the census recorded if both parents were alive, father dead, mother dead or both dead (1921 census only)
- Place of birth and nationality for those born outside the UK
- Occupation and employment including place of work or whether in education
- Number of children or stepchildren under the age of 16

They are fully indexed and it is pretty easy to find an ancestor in these records.

Servicemen, and their families, serving overseas in all three services were recorded. Native bearers, servants or civilian employees are not included, nor are British officers and other ranks serving in the Indian Army. Of particular interest are the returns for wives and children of service personnel, although it can be difficult to match them up with their menfolk.

SOURCES

The 1921 census for England and Wales, the Isle of Man and the Channel Islands is currently available through Findmypast and Ancestry. The 1921 census for Scotland is available on Scotland's People website.

The 1911 census may also be useful. It is very similar in layout and content to that of 1921. This is available on both Ancestry and Findmypast, with the Scottish census also on Scotland's People. The 1911 Irish census for the whole island is available free of charge on the National Archives of Ireland website.

Use these records for

- Providing background information about the people you are researching, and their families, which may be next to impossible to obtain from other sources.

Pitfalls

- A small people are missing from the 1921 and earlier censuses for one reason or another, usually because they were away on census night and were recorded as being resident in a hotel or visiting friends and family.

Because of the political situation, no census was taken in Ireland in 1921. The 1926 census for Southern Ireland will be available in April 2026.[13] It is not known when the 1926 census returns for Northern Ireland will be released.

THE 1939 REGISTER

The key resource for researching individuals who lived during the Second World War is the National Register, usually called the 1939 Register. It is doubly important for family historians as it is the only national survey between the 1921 and 1951 censuses. The 1931 census was destroyed by fire in December 1942, while no census was taken in 1941 because of the war.

Although there are many similarities to a census, the 1939 Register is not one. In part, this is because some items of key data were not recorded, notably place of birth, but also because it was meant to be a 'living register', being updated, when necessary, by the town hall. In particular, when women married, their married names were normally added.

The register was taken on Friday, 29 September 1939. The information was used to produce identity cards and, once rationing was introduced in January 1940, to issue ration books.

The register only contains civilians. It did not include men who had joined up. However, the records do include members of the armed services on leave and civilians on military bases.

Forms were handed out to householders, then collected and checked by enumerators on the following Sunday and Monday. During the collection process, the enumerators issued completed identity cards for each resident. Thus, anyone who did not register would not receive an identity card. And without an identity card it was not possible to obtain a ration card.

The following details are included:

- National registration number
- Address
- Surname
- Forenames
- Date of birth
- Sex
- Marital status (Including whether an individual was divorced.)
- Occupation (The 1939 Register required people to explain exactly what they did. They were asked to be as specific as possible, giving details of the trade, manufacture or branch of a profession. Housewives are normally described as being engaged in 'Unpaid domestic duties'.)

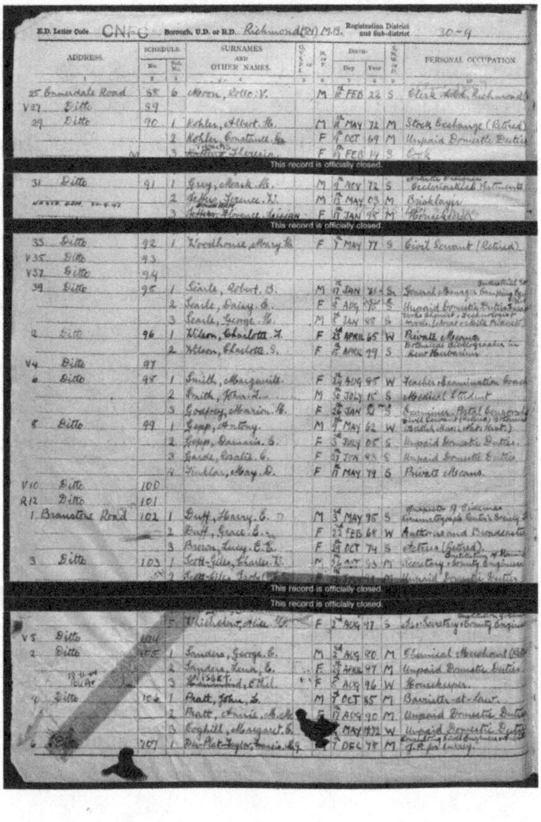

E.D. Letter Code CNFG Borough, U.D. or R.D. Richmond (S) M.B. Registration District and Sub-district 30-4

Address	Schedule No.	Sub No.	Surnames and other names	O.V.S.P.I.	M or F	Birth Day	Birth Year	S. M. W. or D.	Personal Occupation
1	2	3	4	5	6	7	8	9	10
25 Ennerdale Road	88	6	Moron, Rollo V.		M	16 FEB	22	S	Clerk [illegible] Richmond
V27 Ditto	89								
29 Ditto	90	1	Kohler, Albert H.		M	11 MAY	72	M	Stock Exchange (Retired)
		2	Kohler, Constance [illegible]		F	9 OCT	69	M	Unpaid Domestic Duties
		3	[illegible]		F	14 FEB	14	S	Cook
[redacted] This record is officially closed.									
31 Ditto	91	1	Guy, Mark M.		M	9 NOV	72	S	[illegible] Ecclesiastical [illegible]
[illegible]		2	Jeffers, Terence W.		M	13 MAY	03	M	Bricklayer
		3	Jeffers, Florence Lillian		F	17 JAN	98	M	[illegible]
[redacted] This record is officially closed.									
33 Ditto	92	1	Woodhouse, Mary K.		F	7 MAY	77	S	Civil Servant (Retired).
V35 Ditto	93								
V37 Ditto	94								
39 Ditto	95	1	Searle, Robert B.		M	17 JAN	71	M	General Manager [illegible]
		2	Searle, Daisy E.		F	8 AUG	[illegible]	M	Unpaid Domestic Duties [illegible]
		3	Searle, George H.		M	8 JAN	98	S	[illegible]
2 Ditto	96	1	Wilson, Charlotte J.		F	23 APRIL	65	W	Private Means
		2	Wilson, Charlotte S.		F	17 APRIL	99	S	Botanical Bibliographer in Kew Herbarium
V4 Ditto	97								
6 Ditto	98	1	Smith, Marguerite		F	24 AUG	85	W	Teacher Examination Board
		2	Smith, John L.		M	14 JULY	15	S	Medical Student
		3	Godfrey, Marion H.		F	26 JAN	[illegible]	S	Examiner, Postal Censorship
8 Ditto	99	1	Gapp, Antony		M	7 MAY	62	W	Civil Servant (Retired) [illegible]
		2	Gapp, Damaris E.		F	3 JULY	05	S	Unpaid Domestic Duties.
		3	Garde, Rosalie E.		F	27 JAN	93	S	Unpaid Domestic Duties.
		4	Tinkler, May D.		F	17 MAY	79	S	Private Means.
V10 Ditto	100								
R12 Ditto	101								
1 Branstone Road	102	1	Duff, Harry E.		M	3 MAY	95	S	[illegible] Cinematograph Renters Society
		2	Duff, Grace E.		F	22 FEB	64	W	Authoress and Broadcaster
		3	Brown, Lucy E.E.		F	29 OCT	74	S	Actress (Retired).
3 Ditto	103	1	Scott-Giles, Charles W.		M	[illegible]	93	M	Secretary County Engineers [illegible]
		2	Scott-Giles, [illegible]						Unpaid Domestic Duties
[redacted] This record is officially closed. This record is officially closed.									
		5	[illegible], Alice W.		F	2 AUG	97	S	Asst. Secretary County Engineers
V5 Ditto	104								
2 Ditto	105	1	Sanders, George E.		M	2 AUG	90	M	Chemical Merchant [illegible]
		2	Sanders, Lena E.		F	27 APRIL	97	M	Unpaid Domestic Duties
[illegible]		3	NISBET [illegible], Ethel		F	5 AUG	96	W	Housekeeper.
4 Ditto	106	1	Pratt, John L.		M	7 OCT	85	M	Barrister-at-Law.
		2	Pratt, Annie [illegible]		F	17 AUG	90	M	Unpaid Domestic Duties
		3	Coghill, Margaret E.		[illegible]	[illegible] MAY	[illegible]	W	Unpaid Domestic Duties
6 Ditto	107	1	Du-Plat-Taylor, Francis M.G.		[illegible]	7 DEC	78	M	Consulting Civil Engineer [illegible] J.P. for Surrey.

An entry from the 1939 Register for Ennerdale Road in Kew. Entries redacted are for persons thought to be still alive. (TNA/Findmypast)

The right-hand page has not been scanned as it contains various codes used for National Registration and National Health Service purposes. However, there are often marginal inscriptions added subsequently by clerks at the town hall, about an individual's war work, such as whether they were an ARP warden or a member of the Auxiliary Fire Service. Occasionally, there may be other annotations, perhaps giving a date of death.

Entries are redacted if the individual is believed to be still alive. To protect individual identities a 100-year rule was introduced. Provided the date of death can be proved, you can request the entry to be opened.

The 1939 Register for England and Wales is available on both Findmypast and Ancestry. If you have a choice, Findmypast is better as it offers a variety of ways of searching. You can search, for example, by address (perhaps to see who was living in your house), or by occupation (all the bus drivers in your town), which can be useful for local historians as well. It is also easier to get redacted entries opened.

The Registers for Scotland and Northern Ireland are still closed to public access, but you can request entries for particular deceased individuals. For Scottish entries, more information can be found on the National Records of Scotland website.

In Northern Ireland you need to submit a Freedom of Information Act request to PRONI. They will also only supply details of people who are deceased. You may be asked for evidence of their death.[14]

No records for the Isle of Man or the Channel Islands appear to survive.

Use these records for

- Finding out about your ancestors and their families right at the beginning of the war.
- Researching their civilian occupation. This may give a clue as to the war work they became involved with.
- Discovering entries that may indicate any voluntary service undertaken.

Pitfalls

- Entries for children may have been redacted.
- Service personnel will not appear if they had already enlisted.
- Inevitably, some data will be found to be inaccurate. It has been suggested that people falsified their dates of birth to avoid conscription, although I have not found any such cases.

- For some reason, people may be missing: perhaps they might have been overseas or otherwise away at the end of September. Or their name is given incorrectly; perhaps they gave their first name, which otherwise was never used.

Further reading

- National Registers of Scotland: www.nrscotland.gov.uk/research/guides/national-register
- The National Archives: www.nationalarchives.gov.uk/help-with-your-research/research-guides/1939-register

TNA also has a helpful webinar about using the 1939 Register on its YouTube channel.

NEWSPAPERS

Newspapers remain the least used of major genealogical resources, although this is changing as papers are digitised and placed online. If you have an ancestor who was killed in action, won a gallantry medal, or even helped with the Women's Royal Voluntary Service, it is worth seeing whether there is a story in the papers.

According to Professor Tim Luckhurst, Britain and Ireland have a wide range of different types of newspaper. By the Second World War, the Fleet Street daily papers were increasingly dominant because they were available in every newsagent every morning and could afford to employ the best writers. Eighty per cent of British families bought one of the mass circulation dailies: the *Daily Mail; Daily Mirror; Daily Express; News Chronicle* or *Daily Sketch*. Two-thirds of middle-class families also bought a quality title such as *The Times* or *Daily Telegraph*. Newspapers were immensely popular, although they were not widely trusted. The most important was *The Times*, but the bestselling titles were the *Daily Express* and the soldiers' favourite, the racier *Daily Mirror*. Most counties or regions had one or more daily newspapers as well, the best known of which was the *Manchester Guardian* (now the *Guardian*). In Leeds there was, for example, the *Yorkshire Post*, in Liverpool the *Liverpool Daily Post* and in Hull the *Hull Daily Mail*. Such papers concentrated on stories about the region. In addition, there were national newspapers in Scotland and Ireland.

Most towns also had one or more weekly or bi-weekly newspapers. In Richmond upon Thames, for example, the two main papers were the *Richmond and Twickenham Times* (which also published a mid-week edition called the *Thames Valley Times*) and the *Richmond Herald*. It was also not unknown for the *Middlesex Chronicle* and the *Surrey Comet* to include stories about the area.

Because of wartime shortages, even the national newspapers were rarely more than eight or twelve pages in length. As a result, articles are much shorter than they were before the war and there is little about debates in the council chamber or local sport that had once been the mainstay of papers. The advertisements are a joy; there are an awful lot of adverts for stomach powders and indigestion medicines, which suggest that the wartime diet did not agree with everyone. There are prominent listings for local cinemas and theatres.

Local newspapers, in particular, provide a wealth of information relating to individual soldiers, sailors and airmen.

There are frequently short obituaries for men who died on active service, often with details of their family and some other details about them. However, the exact date and circumstances of their death are rarely given, although they are easy enough to find on the Commonwealth War Graves Commission (CWGC) website. A typical entry comes from the *Midlothian Advertiser* for 9 February 1945:

> Cpl Robert Barrie, Durham Light Infantry killed in action in Holland was a native of Bo'ness, and a popular juvenile footballer. He had been in the army for about three years and went overseas at the time of the Normandy landings. He was about to go home on leave when killed. Mrs Barrie and an infant of ten months are left. Their home is at Douglas Terrace, Carriden.

In fact, his forename was Richard. Richard was killed on 17 January 1945 and he is buried in the Nederweert War Cemetery in the Netherlands.[15]

There may also be stories about the award of gallantry medals. On 22 January 1944, the *Falkirk Herald* described the award of the Distinguished Flying Cross (DFC) to Pilot Officer R.B. Berwick of Slammanan, near Falkirk, who had, the paper reported, been on thirty-eight sorties. The citation for the award said that on one operation 'he had been wounded in both legs by a cannon shell which smashed the inter-communications and radio, he refused to have his wounds attended to until the damage had been made good, and so contributed greatly to the success of the mission.'[16]

The real joy of newspapers for the period are the stories about life on the home front. Many stories could easily have been written about peacetime events, like political meetings, cattle shows and court reports, but most describe how the town and the paper's readers were affected by the war. Editors had to contend with censorship, which affected coverage of air raids and descriptions of the damage done by enemy bombers. Even so, there will be stories on all aspects of the war from Spitfire Appeals to complaints about behaviour in public air-raid shelters, and the arrival of American troops.

Food and rationing were always popular topics. The first British restaurant opened in May 1941 in the village of Ham, which was close to the giant Hawker aircraft factory in Kingston. 'The menu was sufficiently appetising, and plentiful to satisfy any ordinary needs,' reported the *Surrey Comet*, adding that the WVS volunteers 'have no time or funds to supply the frills and fancies of cooking, nor do customers expect them'. The paper concluded that, 'With a penny cup of tea to wash it down, this made as good a meal as the ordinary German would sell his Swastika to get every day.'[17]

SOURCES

The best source by far is the British Newspaper Archive (BNA). The project is digitising thousands of British and Irish newspapers, including Fleet Street titles like the *Daily Mirror* and the *Daily Sketch*, many regional daily papers, together with weekly local 'rags' and a few magazines. Over the next few years, the website aims to scan all the newspapers and magazines held by the British Library, for which it has permission from the copyright owners.

You have to subscribe to get the full benefit from it, but if you do a basic search, it will often provide the gist of a story. Subscribers to the Findmypast Pro or Premium subscription also have access to the BNA. However, it is by no means complete and more newspapers are being added every week, so it is worth checking every few months until your local paper is uploaded.

The site is easy to use. Aside from getting side-tracked reading the advertisements and other news stories, the only real difficulty is that you might have to plough through the same story that had been picked up by dozens of different papers, although this is rarely a problem during the Second World War.

Back issues from a number of Fleet Street papers are also available online in a variety of places. In particular, it is worth looking out for The Times Digital Archive. Many libraries subscribe to the archive and if you have a library ticket you may be able to access this database from home.

County archives and local studies libraries should also have sets of local newspapers on microfilm, although they are not always easy to use.

The armed forces published a variety of newspapers and magazines – either for distribution to everyone in a particular theatre of operations or service, or for a particular unit. The best-known service newspapers were *Union Jack* and, for the army, *The Soldier*, which was first published in 1944 and is still going strong. As well as news of the war and the home front there are likely to be articles (often involving laboured humour or in-jokes) on life in the unit, cartoons and photographs.

Unit newspapers or magazines can be very hard to track down, but both the British Library and the Imperial War Museum have extensive collections. Occasionally, copies can be found in unit war diaries or RAF operation record books. A comprehensive list can be found in Michael Anglo, *Service Newspapers of the Second World War* (London: Jupiter, 1977). Regimental or service museums may also have copies.

Use the records for

- They are a brilliant source for the home front locally during wartime.
- They often include stories about individual servicemen and women, particularly if they won a gallantry medal or died in action.

Pitfalls

- Newspapers, even local ones, were heavily censored to prevent the enemy picking up any intelligence of use to them. This meant they were not allowed to feature important stories, or more often included them weeks after they took place. It was not unknown, however, for newspapers to include a story about an event or individual constructed in such a way that it would be clear to keen readers, but not to the Germans (or to the censors in London).
- Just because there was a war on, it didn't mean that newspapers neglected the long tradition of making mistakes, such as misspelling names and getting dates and addresses wrong, or promising to follow up stories but not doing so.

MINOR SOURCES

ELECTORAL ROLLS

By 1945, all men and women over the age of 21 had the right to vote and their full name and address were included in the electoral roll. During the war, councils published rolls of 'Absent Voters', which include details of electors who were in the services. Often their service number is given, usually with the regiment or unit they served with. Electoral returning officers took their responsibilities seriously, although inevitably there are omissions and errors. It is often said that the service vote swung the 1945 general election in the Labour Party's favour.

They are an underrated source. Many registers for the war period are available on Ancestry, although they are surprisingly difficult to use. Local studies libraries and county record offices may have copies on the open shelves and these may be easier to use if you live within easy distance.

Use the records for

- To confirm an individual's service number.
- To identify the unit and, often, the company or other sub-unit he was attached to at the time the register was compiled.

BIOGRAPHICAL DICTIONARIES

Just possibly you may have an ancestor who was either well known (or became famous) or came from a 'good' family. There are numerous directories and dictionaries that can provide additional information. The best known are *Who's Who*, *Who was Who* (which consists of old entries from *Who's Who*) and the *Oxford Dictionary of National Biography* (ODNB). The actor Dirk Bogarde's army service is described in his entry in the *Dictionary*:

> He joined the army intelligence photographic unit as an interpreter of aerial reconnaissance pictures. He took part in the battle for Normandy and the liberation of the Bergen-Belsen concentration camp … and also served in India and Singapore, making copious sketches, some of which are held in the British and Imperial War museums. However, his war ended on a tragic

> note when the jeep he was driving through Calcutta on VJ-Day skidded in the monsoon rain and killed two deserters in a prisoner escort. He was exonerated, but never drove again.[18]

If you are a library member you should be able to access these resources online; your council website will tell you how. In addition, there are a large number of specialist and trade directories generally for the professions that will give more background to a man's career and may well mention his time in the services. Professional directories are difficult to find and there are relatively few online.

USING PROFESSIONAL RESEARCHERS

There may come a time when you become stuck or bewildered by your research. One solution might be to employ a professional researcher to help sort things out. There are a number of specialists who can help. But before you contact them you need to be clear in your own mind what you expect them to do.

A list of such people can be found on TNA's website (look under the 'Help with your Research' menu). The Association of Genealogists and Researchers in Archives (AGRA) is also a professional association of reputable researchers, several members specialise in military research.

3

COMMON SOURCES

Many of the military records you will use are common to the armed forces. In part, this reflects the common sacrifice made by individual servicemen and women, but also the increasing homogeneity between the three services.

RESEARCHING OPERATIONS

Particularly if you are tracing men who saw active service, you may wish to research the operations or missions in which they took part. Unless they were a senior officer it is unlikely that individuals will be mentioned by name. Even so, such research can provide a fascinating insight into the world that your ancestors experienced.

Generally, it is best to start with an overview of the aspect of the war you are particularly interested in. There are many books and websites about the more famous battles and campaigns.

But occasionally, if you are interested in something that has not been much written about, you might want to consult the Official Histories, which was prepared by the Cabinet Office after the war to see what lessons could be learnt from wartime experiences. Larger libraries should have copies. In addition, TNA has a complete set in series CAB 101. Many have been republished by the Naval & Military Press.

For each service there are numerous series at TNA that contain planning files and analysis of actions, battles and campaigns. They are described in a number of research guides, including:

- British Army Operations of the Second World War
- Royal Air Force Operations
- Royal Navy Operations of the Second World War

Use these records for

- In-depth studies of the battles, campaigns and operations your ancestor took part in.

Pitfalls

- There can be so many files to go through that it is easy to get confused.
- Operations were almost always assigned code names, deliberately chosen so that they would not give a clue to the enemy. The best-known operation of the war was Operation Overlord, for the D-Day landings. It should, however, be fairly easy to discover the particular code name for the operation in which you are interested. But sometimes names were assigned to minor actions or the operation did not take place for one reason or another. If you find any mentions of Tube Alloys, this refers to Britain's contributions to the Manhattan project – building the first atom bomb.
- The file descriptions in TNA's online catalogue often leave a lot to be desired.

SERVICE RECORDS

Personnel records are kept for members of the three services. During the war, each of the three services maintained very different types of records, which reflected their needs and traditions. They are discussed in more detail in the appropriate chapters below.

In addition, the auxiliary services, such as the Home Guard and the Women's Land Army, also kept such records, although most have long been destroyed. Where they survive, the documents are generally not very illuminating. Again, they are described in the appropriate place.

For the army and the RAF you should expect to find:

- Personal details, including birth date, home address, faith, next of kin, details of next of kin or their spouse and children.
- Date enlisted and discharged.
- Units served with. This may include short periods when the individual was assigned to other units for training or time spent in hospital.
- Promotions and, occasionally, demotions, usually the result of some disciplinary offence.

- Medals awarded. Generally, they will be campaign medals rather than medals awarded for bravery or good service. (see below)
- Courts martial and other disciplinary matters, generally listing any punishment meted out, such as days of pay forfeited or, for very serious offences, a prison sentence. (see below)

Medical records may be redacted, as might be items relating to the security or operations of the armed forces (which usually means Special Forces).

Naval records normally only consist of lists of ships on which an individual served.

ORDERING SERVICE RECORDS

Service records for men and women who left the services before the end of 1963 are slowly being transferred to TNA. Others are still with the Ministry of Defence, while yet more are in transit.

At the time of writing (January 2025), **TNA** has records for non-commissioned officers in the army as well as ordinary soldiers. Few of the records, however, are yet available in the reading rooms or online. Where the individual is presumed to be deceased or was born more than 115 years ago, then you can request the service record from TNA by completing a Freedom of Information Request Form. This sounds daunting, but is actually quite simple. However, be aware that there may well be a charge for copying the file and sending it to you. Details on TNA's website at https://discovery.nationalarchives.gov.uk/mod-open-foi-request-step1

At time of writing the **Ministry of Defence** still has records for:

- Royal Navy (including Royal Marines)
- British Army (officers only)
- Royal Air Force
- Home Guard

You'll need to provide the person's full name, date of birth, and service number, if you know it. You do not have to provide a death certificate. However, without one, information may be withheld unless the person either died in service or died more than 116 years ago.

More details on how to 'Apply for the records of a deceased serviceperson' can be found on the UK government's website www.gov.uk.

The Ministry suggests that it may take up to a year to receive the service records, although in my experience the wait is rather less.

By the end of the decade, some 10 million personnel records from the three services will have been transferred from the Ministry of Defence to TNA at Kew. They are records for men and women who were born before the end of 1939. The vast majority are for individuals who served in the Second World War, although some are for men who took part in the First World War, Korea or undertook National Service in the 1950s and 1960s.

[The following paragraphs are based on material supplied by TNA, the Ministry of Defence and Ancestry.com and reflect the position in late 2024.]

> It will be the biggest and most complex transfer of public records in TNA's history. In an average year, TNA takes in about 1.5 linear kilometres of physical records from government departments. The service records are an additional 33 linear kilometres of physical records, so it is a huge undertaking.
>
> To begin, once the records are transferred TNA must ensure that all the material can be stored safely and to archival standards. In practice, this means removing them from their original packaging and placing them into specially made archival boxes that will keep the records free from any degradation or damage. In addition, the material is being indexed, so researchers can easily find the ones they are interested in. With almost 10 million records, this is going to be a significant task.
>
> As these are personnel records, they naturally contain a range of personal data, including medical information. This means that the records will not be produced until 100 years after the date of birth of the individual, so the records for a man born in 1929 will only become available in 2030. Some records may be closed for 115 years if they contain potentially distressing material, perhaps relating to court martials.
>
> In March 2023, TNA reported that it had already received over 4 million records and expects to complete the transfer of all army non-officer records within a year. It will then move on to RAF non-officer records in 2024–25. The whole transfer process will run until 2026.

The service records are being digitised by Ancestry and will be made available to Premium Subscribers as well as through their Library subscription service. The collections will always be free to read in the reading rooms at Kew.

The first four sets of records to be copied were British Army service records for non-commissioned officers and other ranks. This is about a third of the total material due to come to TNA. They are in various series:

- Approximately 54,000 service records of other ranks who served in the Royal Electrical and Mechanical Engineers (REME) during the Second World War. The REME was established in October 1942 and was responsible for the maintenance and repair of military equipment. It consisted of skilled tradesmen, many of whom had initially transferred from other units. The papers are now in series WO 420. These records are already available at Kew.
- Over 94,000 records, originally held at the Bournemouth Combined Manning Record Office, of soldiers from twelve smaller units/corps during the Second World War and immediately after, for those discharged as over-age personnel (WO 421). These records are already available at Kew.
- Over 830,000 records of other ranks discharged from the infantry of the British Army between 1921 and 1939. The majority of the service records relate to individuals who served during the First World War, and then opted to continue their service beyond 1921, but also include those who served only during the inter-war period and were discharged before the outbreak of the Second World War. However, these men may well have served in the Home Guard or the Civil Defence Service during the war. (WO 419)
- Over 2 million records of non-commissioned officers and other ranks who served in infantry regiments of the British Army during the Second World War and who were discharged from the armed forces as 'over age' before their time expired in the reserves after 1945. (WO 422)

The small collections of REME service records, along with those records of men who served in a variety of small units that were initially kept at the Bournemouth Combined Manning Record Office are now available online via Ancestry's premium service website called Forces War Records (sometimes known as Fold3).

The 830,000 service records for other ranks discharged between the wars and the 2 million records of non-commissioned officers (NCOs) and other ranks who served in the infantry will soon also be digitised.

These collections were chosen as they contain the largest proportion of open and immediately publishable records. They also include records of individuals from outside the UK who served in the British Army, particularly during the Second World War. Well over 100,000 men from Southern Ireland, for example, volunteered for the army.

Medical forms and disciplinary and conduct forms are not being digitised as part of this project as these records contain sensitive personal data.

Things will change dramatically as the project evolves. You should check TNA and gov.uk websites, genealogical blogs, social media and news stories in the family history press for updates.

OFFICERS OR OTHER RANKS

The personnel in the British armed services, in common with the forces of most nations, are divided into three: commissioned officers, non-commissioned officers and ordinary sailors, airmen and women, and soldiers. Royal Marines use army ranks, despite being part of the Royal Navy.

Officers receive a commission from the sovereign that is a formal document issued to an individual appointing them to a particular rank in the services and vesting them with the powers of that office. In practice, officers are leaders, managers and may also reflect the skills of experts. My father-in-law, for example rose to the rank of lieutenant colonel in the Royal Army Medical Corps, reflecting his abilities as a pathologist. Officer ranks in the army include lieutenant, captain and colonel; in the navy, lieutenants, commanders and captains; in the RAF, pilot officers, squadron leaders and group captains. Traditionally, officers came from the upper classes. During the Second World War, as the result of a deliberate policy to ensure that the best men received commissions, the vast majority came up through the ranks. About one in ten servicemen and women were commissioned officers.

Non-commissioned officers (NCOs) formed the backbone of the British armed forces, commanding small numbers of men, running the unit on a daily basis, providing training and running the stores. They also provided advice to officers, often based on years of experience. Men were chosen from the other ranks to become NCOs, although it was not unknown for them to return to the ranks because they did not like being separated from their comrades. In the army and RAF, NCOs were corporals (bombardiers in the Royal Artillery), sergeants, sergeant-majors and warrant officers. Lance corporals and lance sergeants were men temporally promoted to these ranks, but who received no extra pay. The Royal Navy equivalents are leading seamen, petty officers and chief petty officers.

Again, about 10 per cent of the armed forces were NCOs.

All others were privates (or sappers, troopers, gunners, or kingsmen etc.) in the army, aircraftsmen and women in the RAF, and ratings in the Royal Navy.

TEMPORARY PROMOTIONS

Occasionally you may come across individuals who were either promoted temporarily or on an acting basis.

Acting (abbreviation as A/ before the rank, i.e. A/Sgt) usually meant that an individual was promoted for a short period. Pay for the higher rank would only be paid 21 days after the person was promoted. Where this is the case, you find the abbreviation P/A as in P/A/Sgt, meaning paid acting sergeant.

Temporary (T/ in T/Lt) usually means an individual was promoted on a semi-permanent basis to a more senior rank. You may occasionally find the abbreviation W/S, which stands for War Substantive. This indicates an individual's permanent rank. If an officer has a war substantive rank of lieutenant, they may receive promotion to the next rank to become a temporary captain. If they leave that position, he or she will go back to their substantive rank.

In addition, there were lance corporals (L/Cpl) and lance sergeants (L/Sgt) who in effect were unpaid assistants to corporals and sergeants. It was usually the case that, if they were found suitable, they would be made up to higher rank.

ADDITIONAL MATERIAL FOR OFFICERS

For officers there are several additional sources:

THE *LONDON GAZETTE*

The *London Gazette* has been the UK's official public record since 1665. It therefore holds a range of official information on individuals (and companies) in the form of notices. There is also an edition in Edinburgh for Scottish notices, which also includes identical UK-wide military notices to those printed in the *London Gazette*. These notices can often be divided into one of four categories:

- Awards and accreditations – for all awards, state awards and military decorations and medals, including the New Year and Birthday Honours recipients.
- Insolvency – for all personal and corporate insolvency notices.
- Wills and probate – for all deceased estates and unclaimed estates notices.
- Companies – for all companies registered at Companies House.

Numb. 35306 5935

DIEU ET MON DROIT

SECOND SUPPLEMENT

TO

The London Gazette

Of FRIDAY, the 10th of OCTOBER, 1941

Published by Authority

Registered as a newspaper

TUESDAY, 14 OCTOBER, 1941

Title page for *London Gazette*. *Second Supplement to the London Gazette* No. 35306, 10 October 1941, p. 5935.

For our purposes, the *London Gazette* is of particular importance because it contains notices relating to:

- The appointment and promotion of officers in the three services – but NOT to non-commissioned officers or privates, seamen or airmen and women. Generally, the individual's name and initial is given together with the rank to which they are being promoted, the unit (and regiment in the army), as well as the date of the promotion. This date may vary slightly from that given in the service record. The date given in the *London Gazette* should be taken as the authoritative one.
- The award of honours, such as the Order of the British Empire (OBE), MBE etc., and gallantry medals, such as the Victoria Cross or the George Medal, to service personnel (both officers and other ranks) and, where appropriate, civilians.

INFANTRY.
R. War. R.
Ret. Off. re-empld.
Capt. H. S. Filsell, D.S.O. (14996), is restd. to the rank of Maj. 6th Sept. 1941.
R. Norfolk R.
Ret. Off. re-empld.
Maj. W. C. Parsley, O.B.E., M.C. (185646), ret. (late R. Norfolk R.), at his own request, reverts to the rank of Capt. whilst empld. during the present emergency. 1st Mar. 1941.

The undermentioned are placed on the h.p. list on account of ill-health:—
Somerset L.I.
Maj. (Qr.-Mr.) J. A. Trevelyan (36051). 16th Sept. 1941.
K.O.Y.L.I.
Lt. R. A. J. Warren-Codrington (69808). 12th Oct. 1941.

ROYAL ARMY SERVICE CORPS.
Maj. W. L. Biard, A.M.I.Mech.E. (14664), is placed on the h.p. list on account of ill-health. 15th Oct. 1941.

ROYAL ARMY MEDICAL CORPS.
The undermentioned Majs. to be Lt.-Cols. 13th Oct. 1941:—
(Temp. Lt.-Col.) F. R. H. Mollan, M.C. (5666).
G. O. F. Alley, M.C., M.D. (14138).

QUEEN ALEXANDRA'S IMPERIAL MILITARY NURSING SERVICE.
Matron Miss H. M. Jones, R.R.C., retires on ret. pay. 17th Sept. 1941.
Sister (temp. Matron) Miss S. A. Perry, to be Matron. 17th Sept. 1941.

An example of promotions and other personnel announcements found in the *London Gazette*.

Second Supplement to the London Gazette No. 35306, 10 October 1941, p. 5937.

Using the London Gazette

Every issue of the *London Gazette* is online. The indexing, however, is notoriously poor, but this advice might help:

> When searching for an individual, the best place to start is at the **all notices** page (aka home page) and use the text search on the left-hand side.
>
> In general, names used are surnames and initials, such as Churchill, W.S. or W.S. Churchill. Citations often use an individual's full name rather than his initials: Winston Spencer Churchill. However, because the *Gazette* is normally in two columns, it is possible that a surname is split into two lines with a hyphen to show the split, such as Church- or even Chur-.
>
> It can help to provide additional information. For example, searching by the approximate date that you think the award was gazetted, or adding an individual's service number or regiment as well as the name. For example, typing 'Apthorp Royal Norfolk Regiment' or 'Apthorp 56653' into the search box returns a mention in 1946, for Desmond Pretyman Apthorp.
>
> What does not seem to help, however, is to include details of the medal or decoration. This is because many awards, such as Mentions in Despatches or the Distinguished Flying Cross, may be awarded to large numbers of individual servicemen and women at once. As a result, lists of recipients can run multiple pages and the details of the actual award will only be mentioned at the beginning of the list.

ARMY, NAVY AND AIR FORCE LISTS

Lists of officers with details of the unit or branch where they were employed were issued by each of the services, generally quarterly. Going through various issues, you can build up some idea of an individual's career, promotions and for which organisations they worked. They do not contain anything about the award of medals.

To save space, only an individual's name and initials are given. It is likely that the officer will be listed in several places.

Sets are to be found in the reading rooms at TNA, the Imperial War Museum and the appropriate service museum. They are simple to use as they are well indexed.

More helpfully, they are also available online through the Digital National Library of Scotland and the Internet Archive. Of the two, the Internet Archive is by far the easiest to use, as you can easily do a keyword search by surname and initials.

More details about lists for each service can be found in the relevant chapters below.

MEDALS

Wartime medals offer a direct link to our parents and grandparents. There are two types of medals:

- Campaign medals awarded to everyone who participated in a particular campaign.
- Honours and awards that were made for particular acts of bravery or organisational achievement.

In addition, there are also medals awarded for good conduct and long service.

CAMPAIGN MEDALS

Service personnel who took part in particular battles or campaigns were issued with one or more medals. They were much prized by the individuals themselves as well as by their families. As Churchill said during a speech to the House of Commons in March 1944: 'The object of giving medals, stars and ribbons is to give pride and pleasure to those who have deserved them.'[1]

During the Second World War, every person who served as part of the British or Commonwealth armed forces, along with those part of auxiliary organisations such as the Home Guard and National Fire Service, would be awarded at least one campaign medal, depending on several factors. These campaign medals were issued as a recognition of service in a specific theatre of war or for service at home, at sea or in the air. Details of the exact medals awarded are often found in service records.

Veterans had to claim their medals after they had left the services. Only those men and women who were in the armed forces in 1947 received their medals automatically. Many people, however, did not claim them. It is still possible to submit a claim today. Medals can also be issued to the legal next of kin of deceased service personnel, but proof of kinship is required.

From left to right a row of campaign medals: the 1939–45 Star, the Burma Star, the Defence Medal and the War Medal. (Author)

Eight separate campaign medals were originally issued, although no more than five could be worn by an individual. An additional medal – the Arctic Star – was created in 2012 for service in the Russian convoys that went to Archangel and Murmansk.

Medals were not inscribed with the names of those who had been awarded them in order to reduce costs, but it was not uncommon for individuals to have inscriptions added privately after they had been given the award. British medals were made in copper-zinc alloy, although the equivalents issued by Commonwealth countries were in silver.

Each medal also has a unique ribbon. Their colours have symbolic significance and are believed to have been designed personally by King George VI.

The medals with descriptions of their ribbons are:

1939–1945 Star: This was generally awarded to men who had completed 180 days active (two months for aircrew) overseas. It was the only medal awarded to men who saw service in France and Norway in 1940 and Greece and Crete in 1941. Recipients were also eligible for other campaign stars if they served in other theatres of operation. Where appropriate recipients were also eligible for bronze clasps for service either during the Battle of Britain or in Bomber Command. The ribbon is three equal stripes of dark blue, scarlet and light blue representing the three armed services.

Air Crew Europe Star: Awarded to RAF crews who had had 60 days operational flying over Europe, including Italy and the Balkans. The ribbon is a broad central light blue stripe, black borders and narrow yellow stripes, for the sky, the night and searchlight beams.

Atlantic Star: This was generally awarded to personnel in the Royal and Merchant navies who had served in convoys across the North Atlantic for 180 days or longer, but members of the RAF and Army attached to these services also received it. The ribbon is three shaded equal stripes of dark blue, white and green.

Africa Star: Awarded for service anywhere in North Africa, Malta or Egypt before 12 May 1943. The ribbon is pale buff with a broad central scarlet stripe and two narrow stripes of dark blue (to the left) and mid blue (to the right).

Arctic Star: The medal was awarded to members of the British armed forces and the Merchant Navy for any length of operational service north of the Arctic Circle. On the ribbon the three colours represent the forces that were involved in the campaign, light blue for the air forces, dark blue for the Navy and red for the Merchant Navy, while the central white band, edged in black, represents the Arctic.

Burma Star: Awarded for service in India and Burma. The ribbon is a central red stripe and two narrower blue and yellow stripes on either side

France and Germany Star: Awarded for service in France, Belgium, Luxembourg, the Netherlands or Germany and adjacent sea areas between 6 June 1944 and 8 May 1945. The ribbon is equal width dark blue, white, red, white and dark blue bands. The colours are those of the Union flag and also of the national flags of France and the Netherlands.

Italy Star: Awarded for service in Italy, the Balkans and southern France between 11 June 1943 and 8 May 1945. The ribbon has equal stripes of red, white, green, white and red representing the Italian flag.

Pacific Star: Awarded for service in the Pacific to personnel who served in Hong Kong, Singapore and Malaya. The ribbon is dark green with scarlet edges, a central yellow stripe, a narrow dark blue stripe on the left side and a light blue one to the right.

Defence Medal: This was awarded to service personnel who served on non-operational duties in Britain and overseas, such as telephone operators at headquarters, in offices on training bases or as members of the Home Guard. Recipients had to have three years' service in the UK, one year if served in this capacity overseas, or 180 days where the location was subject to air attack, such as working during the Blitz. The ribbon is green (for the fields of Britain), with a wide central orange stripe (the flames of the Blitz) and two narrow black stripes either side (for those who lost their lives during the bombing).

War Medal: Awarded to anybody who rendered 28 days' service while in uniform or in an accredited organisation. The ribbon includes the colours of the Union Flag going from red to blue to white from each edge and a narrow central red stripe.

THE LANGUAGE OF MEDALS

Medals have a particular terminology and it can help you understand more about the medals that you might have. The key words are:

Bars: A gallantry medal can be won more than once, in which case a clasp of metal, known as a bar, should be affixed to the medal ribbon. Multiple bars on the same medal are used to indicate that the recipient has met the criteria for receiving the medal a second or third time. The term 'and bar' means that the award has been bestowed several times. Taking the example of Group Captain Leonard Cheshire, VC, OM, DSO and two bars, DFC, the 'DSO and two bars' indicates that the Distinguished Service Order was awarded on three separate occasions. Bars are usually shown by the use of asterisks, meaning 'DSO**' would indicate a DSO and two bars.

Citations: The published description of how a particular gallantry medal came to be awarded. They are often fairly bland. They are normally printed in the *London Gazette* and sometimes may also appear in local newspapers.

Clasp: A metal strip added to the ribbon to mark participation in a particular battle or campaign. Various clasps were issued during the war. The rarest of these was issued to aircrew who fought in the Battle of Britain. It was authorised for pilots, navigators and other aircrew who flew at least one operational sortie between 10 July and 31 October 1940.

Edge: The outside circumference of the medal that usually bears the recipient's name, rank and regiment. Second World War campaign medals do not have an edge.

Group: This means a group of medals awarded to one individual, which may be worn on formal occasions. There is a particular order in which they are displayed with gallantry medals to the left, as the viewer sees them. The two highest gallantry awards, the Victoria Cross and the George Cross, will always be on the extreme left. Campaign medals and other medals, such as long service and good conduct medals, will be towards the right.

Oak leaves: Soldiers of the British Empire or the Commonwealth of Nations who are mentioned in despatches are entitled to receive a certificate and wear a decoration. For the Second World War this was a bronze oakleaf, which was attached to the ribbon of the War Medal.

Obverse: The side of the medal that bears the sovereign's head. When wearing a medal this is the side that faces the viewer. Second World War campaign stars do not have an obverse, although the two medals do.

Post-nominal letters: The initials that could be used after an individual's name to indicate the award of one or more honour or award. For example, Leonard Cheshire's post-nominals were: 'VC, OM, DSO**, DFC', meaning that he was awarded the Victoria Cross, made a member of the exclusive Order of Merit, Distinguished Service Order and two bars, and the Distinguished Flying Cross. In addition, he was mentioned in despatches, but recipients do not use post-nominal letters.

Recommendations: These were normally made by the commanding officer of the unit in which the nominee served. They usually form the first draft of the citation.

Reverse: The opposite side to obverse. This generally bears a unique design or inscription, and sometimes both. When wearing a medal, this is the side that is hidden from the viewer.

Ribbons: Medals are worn suspended from their own specific ribbons. The colours used in them often have a symbolic significance, as detailed above.

THE RECORDS

There are no complete medal rolls for the services in the public domain. To claim medals, replace stolen or destroyed medals or find out whether an individual is entitled to medals you need to contact the MoD Medal Office. You will need to supply the service number, unit (Army and Marines) and branch or trade (RAF and RN), full name, date of birth, rank and date of discharge.

The exception is for the Merchant Navy, for which TNA has medal rolls in series BT 395, available through its website in a heavily abbreviated form. The archive records each seaman's name plus, usually, his discharge book number and date and place of birth as well as the medals, ribbons and clasps issued together with a reference to the long-destroyed medal papers file. The rolls do not include the Arctic Star, which was not awarded until 2012. If you think a family member is eligible for the Arctic Star, you need to contact the MoD Medal Office.

PAID PRIZE Z

NAME CLEGG R. W. | RANK or RATING and O.N. Ch. Cook. P/Kx 14746 | No: 35117

ADDRESS

Victorious X 53854

1939-45	Atlantic	A.C.Europe	Africa	Pacific	Burma	Italy	F.and C.	Defence	War Medal
✓	✓		✓ R	R	✓	✓			—

Service for 1939-45 Star

Issued 27/1/59 1948

Schedule No 3307

Formidable (Aircraft Carrier) 6-1-42 – 2-9-45

An entry from the medal roll for a Royal Navy rating. (Ministry of Defence)

Use the records for

- Finding a unique link with your ancestor.
- The medals will tell you roughly where an individual served.

Pitfalls

- Not every veteran claimed his medals.
- The information they provide is not very useful.

Further reading

These medals are described in the following sources:

- The gov.uk website, 'Medals: campaigns, descriptions and eligibility'.
- Wikipedia, 'The 1945 Star'.
- Peter Duckers, *British Military Medals* (2nd ed, Pen & Sword, 2021).

GALLANTRY MEDALS

There are also Honours (such as the Commander of the Bath (CB), the Order of the British Empire (OBE) etc., which recognise exceptional service, often providing support in its myriad forms to men at the front, and Awards (such as Victoria Cross, Distinguished Flying Medal etc.), which recognise individual acts of gallantry or leadership in combat. Each service had its own honours and awards, which are described in the appropriate chapter below.

There are usually two categories of honours and awards: First there were 'immediate awards', sometimes referred to as having been 'awarded in the field', which were bestowed for exceptional bravery – for example capturing an enemy position or rescuing a wounded officer.

However, many medals, perhaps the majority, were awarded for the exceptional performance of duties, such as ensuring essential supplies reached the front line in the midst of battle, or aircrew completing thirty bombing sorties flying over occupied Europe. They are often referred to as being 'non-immediate' or periodic awards.

Unless indicated otherwise in the following section, gallantry medals were only awarded to service men and women.

The **Victoria Cross** is presented to those who have shown the 'most conspicuous bravery, or some daring or pre-eminent act of valour or self-sacrifice, or extreme devotion to duty in the presence of the enemy', making it the most prestigious gallantry award available.[2] It was awarded 182 times during the Second World War. Just one man, New Zealander Captain Charles Upham, was honoured twice (that is he won the 'Victoria Cross and Bar'). According to the *London Gazette* in October 1941, Second Lieutenant Upham won his first VC for his actions in Crete, May 1941, during an enemy attack. Upham engaged an enemy machine-gun nests at close quarters with only his pistol and grenades. He then crawled to within 15 yards of another machine gun in order to kill the gunners, before rescuing his wounded men by carrying them away whilst under fire. Later, he ambushed an enemy force threatening Force Headquarters, shooting twenty-two enemy soldiers in the process.[3] Eighteen months later, during the First Battle of El Alamein, Upham received his second Victoria Cross. He destroyed a German tank, several guns and vehicles with grenades, despite being shot through the elbow. After his capture by the enemy, Upham was eventually imprisoned in the castle at Colditz after making numerous escape attempts from other PoW camps.[4]

War Office,
14th October, 1941.

The KING has been graciously pleased to approve of awards of the VICTORIA CROSS to the undermentioned:—

Second-Lieutenant Charles Hazlitt Upham (8077), New Zealand Military Forces.

During the operations in Crete this officer performed a series of remarkable exploits, showing outstanding leadership, tactical skill and utter indifference to danger.

He commanded a forward platoon in the attack on MALEME on 22nd May and fought his way forward for over 3,000 yards unsupported by any other arms and against a defence strongly organised in depth. During this operation his platoon destroyed numerous enemy posts but on three occasions sections were temporarily held up.

In the first case, under a heavy fire from a machine gun nest he advanced to close quarters with pistol and grenades, so demoralizing the occupants that his section was able to " mop up " with ease.

Another of his sections was then held up by two machine guns in a house. He went in and placed a grenade through a window, destroying the crew of one machine gun and several others, the other machine gun being silenced by the fire of his sections.

In the third case he crawled to within 15 yards of an M.G. post and killed the gunners with a grenade.

When his Company withdrew from MALEME he helped to carry a wounded man out under fire, and together with another officer rallied more men together to carry other wounded men out.

He was then sent to bring in a company which had become isolated. With a Corporal he went through enemy territory over 600 yards, killing two Germans on the way, found the company, and brought it back to the Battalion's new position. But for this action it would have been completely cut off.

During the following two days his platoon occupied an exposed position on forward slopes and was continuously under fire. Second Lieutenant Upham was blown over by one mortar shell, and painfully wounded by a piece of shrapnel behind the left shoulder, by another. He disregarded this wound and remained on duty. He also received a bullet in the foot which he later removed in Egypt.

At GALATOS on 25th May his platoon was heavily engaged and came under severe mortar and machine-gun fire. While his platoon stopped under cover of a ridge Second-Lieutenant Upham went forward, observed the enemy and brought the platoon forward when the Germans advanced. They killed over 40 with fire and grenades and forced the remainder to fall back.

When his platoon was ordered to retire he sent it back under the platoon Serjeant and he went back to warn other troops that they

Part of the citation for the award of the Victoria Cross to Second Lieutenant Charles Upham, New Zealand Army. *Second Supplement to the London Gazette*, No. 35306, 10 October 1941, p. 5935.

The civilian equivalent is the **George Cross**, the highest award bestowed by the British government for non-operational gallantry or gallantry not in the presence of an enemy. It is awarded for 'acts of the greatest heroism or for most conspicuous courage in circumstance of extreme danger, not in the presence of the enemy, to members of the British armed forces and to British civilians' and is equal in stature to the Victoria Cross.[5] Second to the George Cross, the **George Medal** was also established in 1940. The medal is awarded as recognition of 'acts of great bravery'. This award is primarily intended for civilians, but can also be presented to military personnel.

Also awarded to officers across the three services was the **Distinguished Service Order** (DSO). Some 4,880 DSOs were awarded during the war, with 947 men receiving it twice, 59 three times and 8 men receiving it four times (that is the DSO and three Bars).[6]

One of the eight was Brigadier Alastair 'Jock' Pearson, Parachute Regiment. Pearson was originally awarded the DSO for his actions in late January and early February 1943 in Tunisia. He was awarded again for actions during the Battle of Tamera in March. Pearson was awarded a another Bar for his contribution to the invasion of Sicily. In July 1943, the 1st Parachute Brigade was assigned to capture Primosole Bridge in Sicily. Due to high winds, intense flak, and poor flying, fewer than one in five of the 1,900 men of the brigade landed on target. However, the bridge was captured. German forces counter-attacked the following day and the paratroopers were forced to withdraw. Pearson helped to recapture the bridge by guiding the Durham Light Infantry in an attack on the flank of the Germans holding the bridge. A final Bar was awarded in February 1945 for his contributions during the Battle of Normandy.[7]

An unusual medal that was only awarded to military nurses for 'exceptional services in military nursing' was the **Royal Red Cross**.

The **Order of the British Empire** was established in 1917 to reward the men and women who worked tirelessly behind the scenes to support the service personnel at 'the sharp end'. There are two divisions: civilian and military, and five classes of the Order including MBE, OBE, CBE, KBE and GBE. We think of the medal now as a reward for celebrities, civil servants and lollypop ladies, who are appointed to the Civilian Division. Less well known is the Military Division. The vast majority of awards to military personnel were for meritorious service. A not untypical example was the award of an MBE in 1944 to Warrant Officer Cyril Uttley, York and Lancaster Regiment, who was responsible for supplying a tunnel being built under Japanese lines in Burma. The recommendation made by his commanding officer described how 'His outstanding organising ability and coolness under fire ensured order among what might have been confusion and that no single demand for food, ammunition or other supplies ... was unmet.'[8]

Despite the Order originally being awarded for meritorious service, during the war it was increasingly awarded as recognition of gallantry to both service personnel and civilians. This included the Merchant Navy, police, emergency services and civil defence. They were mostly British Empire Medals (BEM) and MBEs with a smaller number of OBEs and CBEs. These awards were intended to acknowledge gallantry that did not quite reach the same standards of the George Medal.

The least important gallantry award is the **Mention in Despatches** (MiD), which technically is a commendation for gallantry or meritorious service included in the final despatch, summarising the events of a particular campaign or battle, submitted to the sovereign by the commander in chief. Recipients received a certificate and wore an oak leaf device attached to the ribbon of the War Medal, but were not awarded a physical medal for their actions. It is the most common award: about 2 per cent of service personnel were mentioned in despatches.

CITATIONS

Grants for non-immediate service usually appear without any additional information about the reason for their award but there were often citations for awards made in the field. Citations are brief descriptions of the circumstances in which the medal was won. The date of the incident is never given and other details that might conceivably help the enemy are omitted. However, using other records, such as war diaries, it is occasionally possible to work out the exact date and the reasons for the award.

Miss Marjorie Joyce Foster was awarded the MBE in 1942. She was working in Canterbury's Food Control Office, which dealt with the issuing of ration cards, during an air raid. An unusually detailed citation in the *London Gazette* described the reasond for the award:

> Miss Foster immediately left her home and went to the Food Office. While the bombs were still falling and the roof of the premises was on fire, she forced the door of the Office and commenced to salve the essential records from the premises. Despite the danger from an adjoining wall which was likely to collapse at any moment, Miss Foster carried on and mainly through her efforts, records, papers and forms were salvaged. As a result of her action the Food Office was established in new premises early on the following morning and it was possible to carry on with the work of supervising the feeding of the civilian population.[9]

THE RECORDS

LONDON GAZETTE

There are various sets of records where can you find out more about the award of gallantry medals. The place to begin is the *London Gazette*. All gallantry awards, including Mentions in Despatches, are listed in the *Gazette*. If you can't find an entry for your ancestor, then he or she did not receive an honour or gallantry award.

Details of the men and women so honoured include name (sometimes just surname and initials), service number, rank and regiment, service and ship.

Honours and awards to Dominion, Colonial and Indian service personnel are also included.

Every issue of the *London Gazette* is online. More about the *Gazette* and how to get the best from the website can be found above.

REGISTERS

The Victoria Cross Register can be found in piece WO 98/8 and on TNA's website. It consists largely of proofs of the citations to be published in the *London Gazette*, often with notes about when and where the Cross was invested by King George VI.

There are also registers for the Distinguished Service Order (WO 390) and Military Cross (WO 389). Again, they can be downloaded from TNA's website. They contain much the same information as the VC register.

Registers for the Military Medal are in WO 326 and the Royal Red Cross in WO 145. Each record details name, rank, service number and unit of the recipient with the date the award was announced in the *London Gazette*. The records are not online, although an index to the Royal Red Cross is on Findmypast.

FILES AND DOCUMENTS

The National Archives has many files concerning the award of medals. A useful list of medals and related paperwork is in a TNA Research Guide: 'British Military Gallantry Medals'.

THE ARMY

In the Army, the Distinguished Conduct Medal (DCM) was the second highest award for gallantry and was awarded to non-commissioned officers and other ranks for 'distinguished, gallant and good conduct in the field'. The equivalent for officers was the Distinguished Service Order (DSO). In addition, the Military Cross and Medal (MC, MM) were awarded to officers and other ranks respectively for 'acts of gallantry and devotion to duty under fire'. The numbers of medals awarded during the war were: DCM 1,900, MC 10,892, MM 15,503.[10]

Series WO 373 contains surviving successful **recommendations** for gallantry medals forwarded from theatres of operations for awards to British Army personnel, both officers and other ranks, and for men serving in Commonwealth armies. The series also includes papers for 'non-immediate' awards.

Although the recommendations start in 1935, there are very few before early 1943 and almost none for Mentions in Despatches. For each individual, you are likely to find a typed memorandum describing the recommendation for a specific award. It is usually more comprehensive than a citation, together with signatures of superior officers approving the recommendation. There may also be a note about the award to be made. It is not uncommon for a lesser award to be made rather than the one

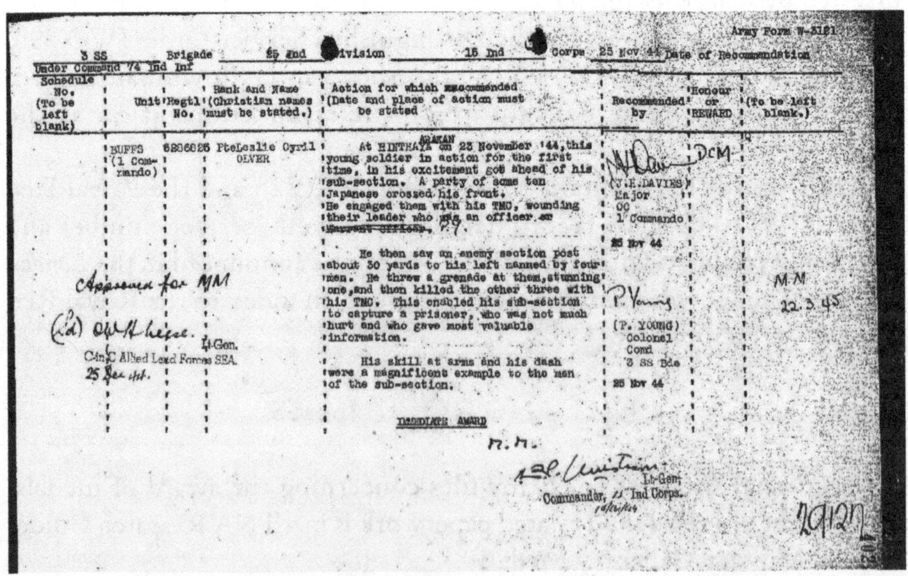

Army Form W-3121

3 SS Brigade 25 Ind Division 15 Ind Corps 25 Nov 44 Date of Recommendation

Under Command 74 Ind Inf

Schedule No. (To be left blank)	Unit	Regtl No.	Rank and Name (Christian names must be stated.)	Action for which recommended (Date and place of action must be stated	Recommended by	Honour or REWARD	(To be left blank.)
Approved for MM (Sd) O W H Leese. Lt-Gen. C-in-C Allied Land Forces SEA. 25 Dec 44.	BUFFS (1 Commando)	6286826	Pte Leslie Cyril OLVER	At HINTHAYA ARAKAN on 23 November '44, this young soldier in action for the first time, in his excitement got ahead of his sub-section. A party of some ten Japanese crossed his front. He engaged them with his TMC, wounding their leader who was an officer. ~~or Warrant Officer.~~ He then saw an enemy section post about 30 yards to his left manned by four men. He threw a grenade at them, stunning one, and then killed the other three with his TMC. This enabled his sub-section to capture a prisoner, who was not much hurt and who gave most valuable information. His skill at arms and his dash were a magnificent example to the men of the sub-section. IMMEDIATE AWARD	(J.H. DAVIES) Major OC 1 Commando 25 Nov 44 P. Young (P. YOUNG) Colonel Comd 3 SS Bde 25 Nov 44	DCM	MM 22.3.45

M.M.

Lt-Gen, Commander, 15 Ind Corps.

29127

The recommendation for the award of a Military Medal to Private Cyril Olver, 1 Commando. (TNA WO 373/26/271)

recommended. In November 1944, Private Cyril Olver, 1 Commando, was awarded the Military Medal for taking out a Japanese machine gun nest. His citation concluded that, 'His skill at arms and his dash were a magnificent example to the men of the sub-section.' He was nominated for an immediate DCM by the battalion commander, but this was later reduced to the MM. The award was published in the *London Gazette* without the citation.[11]

You can download individual recommendations on TNA's website. The indexing is pretty good so it should be easy to find the entry for the person you are interested in.

Unfortunately, there is no equivalent set of recommendations for the Royal Air Force or Royal Navy, although army awards were sometimes given to air force and naval personnel if they had worked closely with the army, for example, on liaison duties.

ROYAL AIR FORCE

Unique to the RAF was the Distinguished Flying Cross (DFC) for officers and Medal (DFM) for airmen and women. It was awarded for 'acts of valour, courage or devotion to duty whilst flying in active operations against the enemy'. During the war, 20,354 DFCs (with a further 1,592 with one or more bars) and 6,637 DFMs were awarded, with 60 bars for a second award. In most cases they were 'non-immediate awards' rewarding bomber aircrews who had completed a tour of thirty sorties over enemy territory.[12]

In addition, there was the Air Force Cross (AFC) and Air Force Medal (AFM) for officers and other ranks respectively, which was awarded for 'an act or acts of valour, courage or devotion to duty whilst flying, though not in active operations against the enemy'. During the Second World War, 2,028 AFCs and 259 AFMs were awarded.[13]

Recommendations are contained in many files at TNA. There are no indexes at Kew. However, one is held by the Air Historical Branch. You need to contact them at Air Historical Branch – email: ahb.raf@btconnect.com. You should provide the full name, service number and rank, and the squadron or other unit the individual served with at the time the award was made. (For more about RAF medals, see Chapter 5.)

ROYAL NAVY

In the Royal Navy, the Distinguished Service Cross (DSC) was awarded to officers 'in recognition of an act or acts of exemplary gallantry during active operations against the enemy at sea'. Most petty officers and ratings could be awarded the Distinguished Service Medal (DSM) 'for bravery and resourcefulness on active service at sea'. During the Second World War, 7,290 awards were made.[14]

Medal rolls for the DSM, BEM and other awards between 1942 and 1945 are in piece ADM 171/164, and on Ancestry. No rolls for 1939 to 1941 are known to survive. The Admiralty, however, largely recommended the award of the BEM, MBE and occasionally the OBE. They can be found in the *London Gazette*, usually with a short citation.

Recommendations for gallantry awards can often be found in the case files (in series ADM 199), but you have to know or be able to guess the circumstances in which the medal was won. (For more about the award of Royal Navy medals, see Chapter 6.)

OTHER SOURCES

- An individual's RAF or army service record will almost always indicate the award of any gallantry medal together with the date that the award was gazetted.
- The war diary – or the RAF or RN equivalents – may describe the circumstances in which the award was made as well as provide background information, such as regimental orders mentioning awards to infantry.
- It is worth checking records relating to a particular operation for which the award was made to see whether the award of the medal is mentioned, or the circumstances of the award is described. Generally, the best place to start is with a final report or summary, where one exists.
- The award of gallantry medals was often mentioned in local newspapers. Generally, the paper just gives the man's name and the award. If there is space, or the award justifies it, they may reproduce the citation and include additional information, perhaps about his family or his occupation. On 10 October 1947, the *Kentish Express* included a story about the presentation of the MM to Cyril Olver, by now an instructor sergeant, by the regimental colonel of the East Kent Regiment (Buffs). Why the presentation took place so long after the award is not known. The story also includes the full citation, which was very similar to the recommendation now in series WO 373.[15]

Use these records for

- Finding out about the heroism of ancestors.
- They can provide an insight into the histories of particular operations – for example an SAS raid in occupied Europe, as well as for individual military formations or the experience of civilians on the home front.

Pitfalls

- It can be hard to find details in the *London Gazette*.
- If there is no citation, the chances of tracing the reason behind the award becomes much trickier. It is particularly difficult to find details for individuals who were mentioned in despatches, which were almost all for exceptional work rather than for a specific act of gallantry.

Further reading

Max Arthur, *Symbol of Courage; Men Behind the Medal* (Pan Books, 2005)
Michael Ashcroft, *Victoria Cross Heroes* (Headline, 2006)
Peter Duckers, *A Pocket Guide to British Gallantry Awards* (Spink, 2009)
Peter Duckers, *British Gallantry Awards: 1855–2000* (Shire, 2001)
Peter Duckers, *British Military Medals: A Guide for the Collector and the Family Historian* (Pen & Sword, 2013)
Michael Maton, *Honour the Armies: Honours and Awards to the British and Dominion Armies During the Second World War* (Token, 2006)
William Spencer, *Medals: The Researcher's Guide* (TNA, 2006)
P.E. Abbot and J.M.A. Tamplin, *British Gallantry Awards* (Nimrod Dix, 1981)

An interesting series of articles about medals in general, including much about the Second World War, is on the Identify Medals website. More basic is another website: Medals of the World.

More about eligibility for medals can be found on the UK Government's gov.uk website (type 'medals' into the search box). Also useful are the British Campaign Medal pages on Wikipedia.

There are several useful TNA Research Guides on TNA's website about wartime medals and awards, which can help you work your way through the records.

Biographies of all VC and most GC winners can be found on the Victoria Cross Online website as well as on Wikipedia.

CASUALTIES

British casualties in the Second World War were considerably fewer than in the Great War; roughly a third of the total losses between 1914 and 1918. There are various reasons for this. For a start there was no equivalent to the month-long battles of Ypres, Somme and Passchendaele that saw the senseless slaughter of tens of thousands of men. The war was much more mobile and British commanders took care not to waste lives, particularly as they were very aware of manpower shortages at home and in the other services. General (later Field Marshal) Bernard Montgomery became notorious for his caution in this regard.[16]

That is not to say that there was not serious loss of life; the proportion of casualties during the advance through Normandy in June and July 1944 was as great as any First World War offensive. On 17 June 1940, the troopship *Lancastria* was sunk with the loss of up to 7,000 lives, but there are no precise figures, as she was evacuating British civilians and troops from St Nazaire in France. It was the worst maritime disaster in British history.[17]

Proportionally the greatest losses, however, were in Bomber Command. According to the Canadian Bomber Command Museum, the overall loss rate for its operations was 2.2 per cent, but loss rates over Germany were significantly higher; between November 1943 and March 1944, losses averaged 5.1 per cent. The highest loss rate (11.8 per cent) was on the Nuremberg raid at the end of March 1944.[18] The very high casualties suffered give testimony to the dedication and courage of Bomber Command aircrew.[19]

We tend to think of casualties as being deaths, but the term also includes service personnel who become ineffective due to wounds, desertion or being captured by the enemy. In Bomber Command for example, 55,573 were killed out of a total of 125,000 aircrew (a 44.4 per cent death rate), a further 8,403 were wounded in action and 9,838 became prisoners of war.[20]

COMMONWEALTH WAR GRAVES COMMISSION

The Imperial War Graves Commission was formed in 1917 to care for British and Commonwealth war graves and provide memorials for those men who had no known grave. Their beautifully maintained cemeteries contain row upon row of white gravestones and can be found all along the Western Front of Belgium and northern France, testifying to the shocking losses of the Great War.

The Second World War again saw the Commission record the details of the fallen and care for their remains. The Commonwealth War Graves Commission (it was renamed in 1960) now cares for the graves or memorials of 384,000 British men and women who lost their lives between 1939 and 1947, and another 200,000 graves and memorials for men and women from other Commonwealth countries.[21]

There are Commonwealth casualties from the war on every continent in the world, apart from Antarctica. As a result, new cemeteries and memorials were constructed, although few have the presence of those built after the 1914–18 war.

The largest cemetery is at Reichswald Forest in north-west Germany. Most graves here are for the air crew who died during the air war over Germany. Many other graves are for men who fell during the Allied advance into Germany in February and March 1945. In addition, many men here were originally buried in smaller burial sites across northern Germany but were moved – or 'concentrated' in the terminology – to a single large cemetery.

CIVILIANS

The Commission also cares for British civilian war dead, that is the 68,000 or so men, women and children who directly lost their lives as the result of enemy action.[22] The largest proportion are for those killed during the Blitz and other air raids on the UK. In addition, there are records for:

- British civilians who died during the Japanese occupation of Singapore, Malaya and Hong Kong.
- British civilians living in European countries who died during military action. This includes those deported to a concentration camp.
- Channel Islanders who were forced to work in labour camps on the Continent.

Memorials erected by local authorities to commemorate residents who had died during air raids can often be found in municipal cemeteries. Sadly, these are now often rather neglected. Gravestones might also be erected for individuals. You can search for the civilian war dead in exactly the same way as you would for military casualties.

The neglected memorial to the civilian war dead of Barnes and Mortlake in North Sheen Cemetery. (Author)

THE RECORDS AND HOW TO USE THEM

Details of all the casualties – both military and civilian – are available on the Commission's website. There is a powerful search engine, which allows users to search by name, place, date, cemetery or unit. It is perfectly possible, if you wish, to find all the men from Hull called Johnson who were killed on D-Day. The downside is that the search engine is tricky to use and is not entirely intuitive. Therefore, it is worth reading the briefing notes on the website before you begin:

- When you type in an individual's name (remember to put surname before forename or initials), you are provided with a list of people with the same or similar names. Scroll down to find the person you want. There will be basic information: name; unit; date of death; and location of cemetery or memorial. Don't forget to tick the Second World War box so that only results for that war are produced.
- For an individual, click on the More Details box. A new screen appears, with additional information. In particular, this may include the exact location of the grave or place on a memorial, details of parents and next of kin (usually the spouse) and peacetime address. For Wing Commander Brendan Eamonn Fergus 'Paddy' Finucane RAF – who died aged 21 – there are just the names of his parents: 'Son of Thomas Andrew and Florence Louise Finucane, of Richmond, Surrey'.

- If the family decided to include an inscription on the gravestone this is also given. Unfortunately, the epitaphs seem to lack the joyous eccentricity of many of those from the First World War: the Commission now only allowed certain sentiments to be expressed. For Squadron Leader Wilmot Pettit, 620 Squadron RAF, who was killed on D-Day it reads: 'Son of Harry A. and Kathleen Pettit, of Brantford, Ontario, Canada' and the personal inscription on his gravestone reads: 'lovingly remembered by father, mother, sisters and brothers'. Unusually, Pettit's entry also records the gallantry awards he had received (OBE and DFC).

The entry for Squadron Leader Wilmot Pettit. (CWGC)

- Make sure to scroll to the very bottom of the site, as there are links to pages from the CWGC Archives. These pages contain grave registration details, wording on the respective gravestones, and occasionally a record of where the individual was originally buried. After the war, the bodies of many men were moved from their original resting place to larger purpose-built war cemeteries. Wilmot Pettit and his crew were originally buried at Grangues, but their bodies were moved – concentrated was the phrase – to the larger cemetery at Ranvilles in August 1945. This might be a useful clue in discovering what happened to your ancestor. It is likely Pettit's plane crashed near the dropping zone, which was close to the village, killing its crew.[23]
- There is also the opportunity to print off a ceremonial scroll with the individual's details for your records.

GRAVES CONCENTRATION REPORT FORM

Report No 48 GCU/116/J/34.

2102

The following have/been concentrated here :-

Name of Cemetery RANVILLE BRITISH MILITARY CEMETERY

Full Map Reference France Sh 3A & 8 1/250,000 MR. U 110735

(1) Serial No	(2) Regt or Corps	(3) Army No	(4) Name & Initials	(5) Rank	(6) Date of Death	(7) K/A D/W or Died	(8) Plot	(9) Row	(10) Grave	(11) Date of Reburial	Previous Location of Grave Place & Map Ref	Report Number
37/174 1	591(Antrim) Para Sqn R.E.	14550031	REARDON-PARKER J.	Spr.	6-6-44	K/A.	II		195A	1-6-45	GRANGUES, France 252755 1/50,000 7F/2	J/26 3143
2	"	1877562	YOOELL. J. ~~Unidentified Airborne~~	SPR	"	K/A.	II		196A	"	"	"
3	"	2116526	EVANS. R.T.	SPR	"	K/A.	II		197A	"	"	"
4	R.A.F	UNKNOWN	UNKNOWN "	F/Sgt	"	K/A.	II		198A	"	"	"
5	"	"	" "	UNKNOWN	"	K/A.	II		199A	"	"	"
6	"	"	" "	"	"	K/A	II		200A	"	"	"
7 *	R.C.A.F.	J15517	PETTIT W.R. " (O.A.S., D.F.C.)	S/Ldr	"	K/A.	II		201A	"	"	"

Date...7.June.1945.

Previously registered as 'UNKNOWN' on report 3143.

Where a grave has not already been registered, a Registration [illegible] AF W3372 will be prepared, and attached to this FORM.

Captain. Commanding "J" Section 48 Graves Concentration Unit.

Major R.A. Commanding 48 Graves Concentration Unit

See 48 [illegible] /5/78. dated 2 August

One of the forms from the Commission's archives indicating where Wilmot Pettit was originally laid to rest. (CWGC)

THE MOD WAR DETECTIVES

The MOD War Detectives, officially the Ministry of Defence's Joint Casualty and Compassionate Centre Commemorations team, attempt to identify the remains of British service personnel found in battlefields across the world, identify and rededicate the grave of any former service man or woman originally buried as 'unknown', and organise the appropriate commemoration service for the bodies they have recovered, whether they can be identified or not.

Most bodies recovered are on the Western Front from the First World War, but they also find and identify men from the Second World War. Details of their current cases are on the gov.uk website, search for 'Joint Casualty and Compassionate Centre Commemorations'. They are always looking for help from the public to provide DNA samples and other information that could help identify those who have no known grave.

WAR MEMORIALS

Unlike for the First World War, there are relatively few local memorials specifically for the Second World War. In most places, names of the deceased were added to existing memorials. A typical case is the memorial in Basingstoke, which was dedicated in 1923 with 229 names for local men who did not return after the Great War and also has 108 names from the Second World War.[24]

Almost all British war memorials are described on the online War Memorials Register maintained by the Imperial War Museum. For most memorials there is a physical description, the location and often a photograph. It is also possible to search by name, although not all service personnel are named on memorials, or conversely individuals may be commemorated in several places. Similar details can also be found on the War Memorials Trust website.[25]

The Cenotaph in central London, where the Remembrance Sunday commemoration takes place each November, is the national memorial for the servicemen and women who died during the two world wars and other conflicts since 1914.

There are a number of other national memorials in London, particularly near Green Park, including the Bomber Command memorial, and memorials to service personnel from Canada, Australia and New Zealand who served in Britain during the two world wars.[26] Of particular note are the Memorial Gates near Hyde Park, which are dedicated to 5 million people from the Indian Sub-Continent, Africa and the Caribbean who served or lost their lives in the two world wars.[27]

The **Commonwealth War Graves Commission** maintains a number of memorials to those who have no known grave. Perhaps the most moving is the Runnymede Memorial, near Egham in Surrey, commemorating more than 20,000 servicemen and women of Commonwealth air forces who died during operations from bases in Britain and north and western Europe, and who have no known grave. At the Brookwood Military Cemetery near Woking can be found a memorial for nearly 3,500 men and women of the land forces of the Commonwealth who have no known grave. The Commission explains that the nature of their death meant that it was not possible to commemorate them on any one campaign memorial across the various theatres of war.[28] Details of all CWGC memorials can be found on its website.

The **National Memorial Arboretum** near Burton-on-Trent has 400 memorials to the men and women who served during the Second World War and other conflicts, including memorials to the Naval Services, Jewish servicemen and the Women's Land Army. Full details about the Arboretum and the memorial it contains can be found on its website.

The Jewish ex-service men and women memorial at the National Memorial Arboretum in Staffordshire. (Author)

Use these records for

- Confirming the dates of death of men and women killed during the Second World War for British and Commonwealth forces, the Merchant Navy and civilians in the United Kingdom killed by enemy action.
- Finding where the deceased are either buried or commemorated.
- Confirming the unit with which the individual was serving.
- Finding details of parents, spouse and home address.

Pitfalls

- The information provided by the CWGC is as accurate as humanly possible. If, however, you spot an error they will amend their records if you can prove conclusively that a mistake has been made.
- Names on local memorials may not be accurate. It is not unknown for local men and women to be missed off, or people added who seemingly have no obvious connection with the area. The spelling of names may be wrong and initials or forenames transcribed incorrectly.

OTHER SOURCES

The circumstances of the deaths of individual servicemen can often be found in the Unit War Diaries (British Army see Chapter 4) or Operations Records Books (RAF see Chapter 5). It is harder to find additional information about the deaths of Royal Navy and Merchant Navy personnel, although the convoy reports in series ADM 199 should list men lost at sea and there should be reports for incidents on individual ships (Chapter 6).

Unlike with the First World War, there are few private commemorative rolls or lists compiled of the war dead. In many places, the town hall, cathedral or parish church has memorial books listing men and women from the area who fell during the war. A few can be found on the Roll of Honour website. The names of 67,730 civilians from the Commonwealth, whose deaths were due to enemy action, are displayed in the Civilian War Dead Roll of Honour in Westminster Abbey.

If you can't visit the cemetery where your ancestor lies, the next best thing may be to obtain a photograph. At the time of writing the Commission is planning to add photographs of graves to the entries for individuals. Volunteers with the War Graves Photographic Project, however, already have photographs of gravestones for both world wars. You can download a low-resolution image from its website or order a high-resolution photograph for £4 (digital) or £6 (hardcopy).

Although it is more difficult to do than for the First World War, an interesting research project is to discover what happened to the men and women who appear on the local war memorial.

Further reading

- Commonwealth War Graves Commission: www.cwgc.org
- National Inventory of War Memorials: www.iwm.org.uk/memorials
- National Memorial Arboretum: www.thenma.org.uk
- Roll of Honour: www.roll-of-honour.com
- The War Graves Photographic Project: www.twgpp.org

Derek Boorman, *For Your Tomorrow: British Second World War Memorials* (Author, 1995). The book lists 700 plaques, including ones for individuals, schools and universities, churches, clubs and places of work, and military memorials.

Keith Lowe, *Prisoners of History: What Monuments Tell us About our History and Ourselves* (Collins, 2020)

David Stewart, *Basingstoke War Memorial 1939–1945* (Author) via Amazon.

MEDICAL TREATMENT

The organisation of medical care was based on the system that had proved very successful during the First World War. Men would be efficiently transported back through a series of casualty clearing stations, to base hospitals and, depending on the wound, be ferried back to specialist hospitals in Britain if required. The Queen Victoria Hospital in East Grinstead was one of these hospitals. During the war the hospital became a specialised burns unit, ran by Sir Archibald McIndoe. The hospital became renowned for providing pioneering treatment of RAF and Allied aircrew that had been badly burnt or crushed in action and subsequently needed reconstructive plastic surgery. The Guinea Pig Club was formed there in 1941, as a social club and support network for recovering aircrew and members of family. Another was the National Spinal Injuries Centre at Stoke Mandeville Hospital near Aylesbury, established in 1943, which helped servicemen with severe spinal injuries.

Partly as the result of the lessons learnt during the Great War, new treatments and techniques were available, notably blood transfusions and penicillin, which was used from 1944 onwards. Penicillin especially was in short supply at the time, making it highly valued throughout the war. The drug was so scarce that often patients already being treated had their urine collected, in order to isolate and reuse the remaining penicillin for other injured soldiers.

THE RECORDS

No medical records for individual service personnel are available, and will not be until 2044. Entries in service records will often indicate which hospital an individual was admitted to, although the reasons are rarely given. Bear in mind that patients generally spent longer in hospital in the 1940s than would be normal today. Even a fairly minor disease or procedure, such as tonsillitis, meant that a man could be away from his unit for several weeks.

Military casualty units and hospitals kept war diaries, which are now in series WO 177 – although not all survive. There are no lists of patients and very few of staff, although senior medical staff may occasionally be named. The arrival of large numbers of patients after a particular battle may be recorded. It is also worth checking any appendices as they may say something about the conditions at the hospital, even down to the food offered to patients.

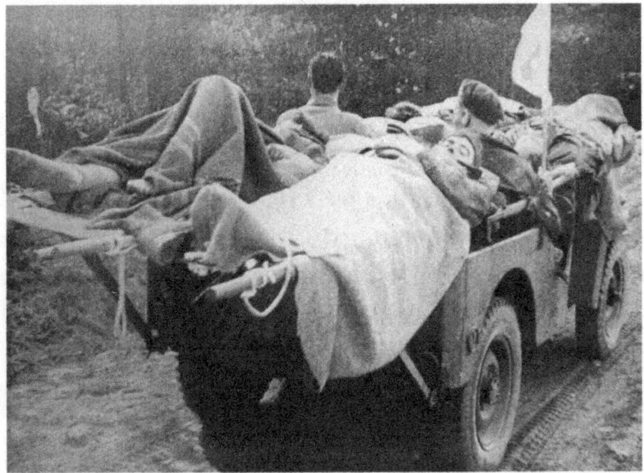

A casualty evacuation by Jeep, in France, 1944.(Archives and Manuscripts, Wellcome Library (ref RAMC 1637/6))

RESEARCHING MEDICAL STAFF

During the war, the Royal Army Medical Corps (RAMC) and the much smaller Army Dental Corps, RAF Medical Services and RN Medical Services, were responsible for maintaining the health of service personnel in the field and at home. To do so, they provided a range of hospitals, casualty clearing stations and other facilities, such as blood transfusion centres.

There were also separate nursing services for each area of the armed forces. The Army was supported by the Queen Alexandra's Imperial Military Nursing Service, the Royal Navy by the Queen Alexandra's Royal Naval Nursing Service, and the RAF by the Princess Mary's RAF Nursing Service.

THE RECORDS

Service records for medical personnel can be obtained from the MOD/ TNA in the normal way. TNA holds little information about the medical or nursing services in the Second World War, although there are informative research guides on researching military nurses and medical staff.

Most historical records of the RAMC are held by the Library of the Wellcome Collection in central London. However, there are no personnel records and relatively little about individual members of the corps.

Further reading

John Broom, *Faithful in Adversity: The Royal Army Medical Corps in the Second World War* (Pen & Sword, 2019)

Liz Coward, *Blood and Bandages Fighting for life in the RAMC Field Ambulance 1940–1946* (Sabrestorm, 2017)

Nicola Tyrer, *Sister in Arms: British Army nurses tell their story* (Phoenix, 2009)

QARANC is a website mainly devoted to Army nursing in the Great War, but there are a few pages about the Second World War.

Museum of Military Medicine: www.museumofmilitarymedicine.org.uk

PRISONERS OF WAR

During the Second World War, over 170,000 British prisoners of war (PoWs) were taken by German and Italian forces. Many were captured after a string of defeats in France, North Africa and the Balkans that took place between 1940 and 1942, others were aircrew who survived after their aircraft had been shot down, only to be found by the enemy. They were held in a network of PoW camps stretching from Nazi-occupied Poland through to Italy. A further 190,000 men were captured, mostly in Malaya, by the Japanese throughout the campaign.[29]

The experience of capture could feel humiliating and even traumatic. It was not uncommon for soldiers to feel a sense of shame after having been overwhelmed or forced to surrender on the battlefield. Airmen who had been shot down had first to experience the trauma of the crash and the potential loss of comrades, before being hunted down in enemy territory. In a similar way, sailors on a sinking vessel firstly had to survive themselves before dealing with the possibility that their fellow soldiers did not, before being dragged away by the enemy.

There was a set of regulations that laid out protection and standards of treatments for PoWs, known as the Geneva Convention. This was not always followed, but German and Italians for the most part behaved fairly towards British and Commonwealth prisoners. Despite this, conditions remained difficult for PoWs; many men had to survive on Red Cross parcels delivered from home because rations were so limited. Furthermore, men – excluding the officers – were forced to work, often involving some form of heavy labour. A few hundred prisoners were even sent to work at an electrical factory next to the concentration camp at Auschwitz.[30]

Most men quickly became resigned to their existence as prisoners, the only sustaining thought being when they could go back home. To add to this, prisoners faced a constant battle against boredom, often trying to overcome this by staging entertainments and even running education classes.

Things were very different in the Far East. Here, Japanese military philosophy held that anyone surrendering was beneath contempt. As a result, their treatment of captives was harsh. Conditions varied, but in the worst camps – such as those along the Thailand–Burma 'Death Railway' – prisoners suffered terribly. Of the 60,000 Allied prisoners of war who worked on the railway, 16,000 died.[31] Forced to carry out slave labour on a starvation diet and in a hostile environment, many died of malnutrition or disease. Sadistic punishments were handed out for the most minor breach of camp rules.

Most PoWs lived on a restricted diet of rice and vegetables in Japanese-occupied territory, which often resulted in severe malnutrition. Red Cross aid parcels were withheld from prisoners, forcing them to supplement their standard rations using anything they could trade or grow themselves. Matters were made worse by increasing food shortages across the region, which affected the guards themselves as well as local civilian populations.

Most men were so weak as a result of hunger and labouring that escape was simply not a possibility, only officers had the strength and capacity to consider the idea. Escapers were largely officers, senior NCOs who had the time and the inclination to dig their way under the wire. Any prisoners who did manage to escape imprisonment ran the very real risk of being shot, and escape was simply not a possibility in the Far East.

LISTS OF PRISONERS

Both Ancestry and Findmypast have extensive lists of prisoners of war. Ancestry's database is called 'UK World War II Allied Prisoners of War, 1939–1945' with a smaller 'British Prisoners of War 1939–1945' database, while Findmypast calls its list the 'British Prisoners of War 1715–1945' collection. Generally, only the man's name (usually just surname and initials), service number and unit are given. Sometimes there is the camp and other information.

Most of the information comes from the published lists prepared by the War Office: Directorate of Prisoners of War, found on TNA's website. These lists include British and Commonwealth prisoners of war from all three services as well as the Merchant Navy held in Germany and Italy. There are also lists of service personnel (not Merchant Navy) and some civilian internees held by the Japanese either in Japan or Japanese-occupied territory in September 1944.

Material was also included from an official publication, *Germany and German Occupied Territories: Imperial Prisoners of War: Alphabetical Lists* (HMSO, 1945), which listed details of approximately 169,000 British and Commonwealth prisoners of all ranks held in Germany and German-occupied territories.

Findmypast's collection also contains a lot of other miscellaneous lists and other material, not just from the Second World War but also for the First World War and the Napoleonic Wars. It can be hard to understand what the information is telling you, or indeed where it came from. There is a lot of potentially useful material here, but the way it is arranged and the lack of any kind of background briefing means that it can be very confusing. It is best to use this collection to trace the movement of men between various camps, although by the time that the information was received by the War Office it may be have been very out of date, particularly during the chaotic conditions experienced upon the collapse of Germany during the spring of 1945.

OTHER LISTS

The National Archives has a number of other lists and card lists. They were generally compiled by the country who looked after the prisoners. Increasingly, they are either being scanned or being indexed in TNA's Discovery Catalogue.

Lists of Royal Navy personnel interned in enemy PoW camps may be found in many of the files in ADM 1 (code 79) and ADM 116 (code 79), although the exact files are not identifiable from the catalogue.

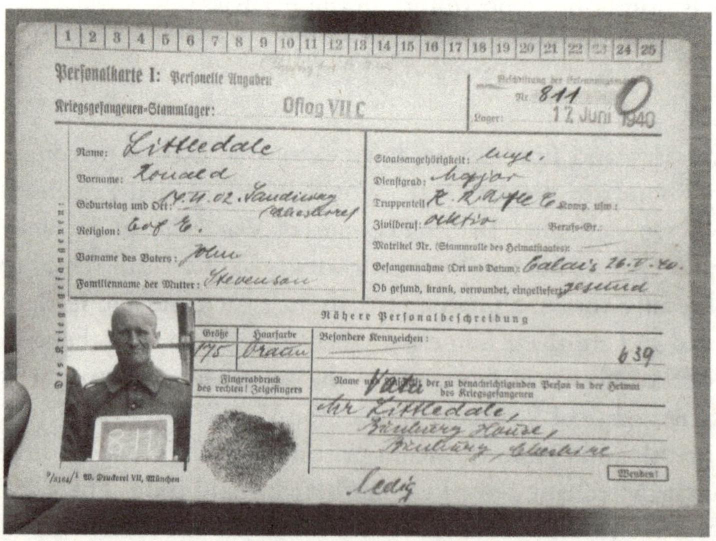

1 2 3 4 5 6 7 8 9 10 11 12 13 14 15 16 17 18 19 20 21 22 23 24 25

Personalkarte I: Personelle Angaben
Kriegsgefangenen-Stammlager: Oflag VII C
Nr. 811
Lager: 12 Juni 1940

Name: Littledale
Vorname: Ronald
Geburtstag und Ort: 14.11.02
Religion:
Vorname des Vaters:
Familienname der Mutter: Stevenson

Staatsangehörigkeit:
Dienstgrad: Major
Truppenteil: Komp. usw.:
Zivilberuf:
Berufs-Gr.:
Matrikel Nr. (Stammrolle des Heimatstaates):
Gefangennahme (Ort und Datum): Calais 26.V.40.
Ob gesund, krank, verwundet, eingeliefert: gesund

Nähere Personalbeschreibung
Größe: 175
Haarfarbe:
Besondere Kennzeichen:
639
Fingerabdruck des rechten! Zeigefingers
Name und Anschrift der zu benachrichtigenden Person in der Heimat des Kriegsgefangenen
Vater
Mr Littledale,
Ledig
Wenden!
Des Kriegsgefangenen:

Prisoner of war card for Lieutenant Colonel Ronald Bolton Littledale, who escaped from Colditz. (TNA WO 416/225/350)

PRISONERS IN GERMAN AND ITALIAN HANDS

Series WO 416 contains index cards for British and Commonwealth prisoners of war, and some civilian internees, compiled by the Germans. The information on the cards varies tremendously. A few contain photographs, fingerprints or medical records. Most, however, contain some personal details of the prisoner and their next of kin, date and place of capture and perhaps the camp where they were housed.

The cards are not online, but fortunately they have all been fully indexed in Discovery, so you rarely need to look at the original. For data protection reasons, cards for men who are under the age of 100 are not opened until they reach their hundredth birthday (even if they have been dead for many years).

The card for Douglas Bader, for example, indicates that the was kept at Oflag XC in Lübeck; that of Arthur Dodd just indicates that he was at Stalag VIIIB, Lamsdorf. However, the card for Lance Corporal Thomas McGrath, RASC, contains a photograph, and indicates that he was captured at St Valery, France, on 12 June 1940 and his camp was Stalag XXA at Thorn, Poland.[32]

JAPANESE

Prisoners of the Japanese are listed in index cards found in series WO 345 at Kew. They are also available on Ancestry (as part of its Allied Prisoners of War database).

There are about 56,000 pre-printed cards, although the reason for their creation is unknown. The information given for individual prisoners is in Japanese and/or English and may include personal and family details, a service number, the date of capture and the camp where the man was a prisoner. Other information can sometimes be found on the back of the card, which may include medical details. It is thought that the diagonal red lines across some cards could indicate the man's death.

Three registers in WO 367 record the names of some 13,500 Allied prisoners of war and civilian internees of British and other nationalities held in camps in Singapore. The registers give minimal information about each prisoner.

A number of transport ships carrying Allied prisoners of war were sunk with great loss of life. The greatest disaster was the sinking of the *Lisbon Maru* in October 1942 by an American submarine with the loss of over 800 British prisoners of war.

LIBERATION QUESTIONNAIRES

TNA has approximately 140,000 Liberation Questionnaires completed by former British and Commonwealth prisoners of war from camps in Germany and Japan. They were designed to uncover any mistreatment which had occurred while the individual had been a prisoner, identify collaborators, and record escapes and acts of sabotage. Not all men filled in these forms, but perhaps 90 percent, of those who had been liberated from camps at the end of the war did so. They are very interesting documents, but unfortunately they reveal very little about a man's time as a prisoner of war. It is clear that the majority of those who completed these questionnaires either wanted to forget their experiences as quickly as possible or had very little to complain about.

They are now available on Ancestry.

ESCAPE AND EVASION REPORTS

Prisoners of war were expected to try to escape. If they returned home they could rejoin the war and fight again as well as provide useful information about conditions in occupied Europe. Even those who didn't make it back to safety still helped the war effort by occupying large numbers of police, and soldiers who had to hunt them down.

However, with so little opportunity, less than 1,200 PoWs managed to escape to return to home soil. The journey to neutral territory – and then back to Britain – was uncertain and dangerous. Few spoke German or other languages except, perhaps, a little schoolboy French. Despite this, thinking about and planning potential escape methods could sometimes provide a distraction from camp life and a glimpse at what may follow. By 1943, aircrew were receiving basic training in escape and evasion techniques and were given compasses, maps and other aids to help them if they were shot down over enemy territory. Elaborate escape lines grew up to helped Allied airmen and soldiers find their way to freedom. Websites about several of them are listed below. The work was co-ordinated by MI9 in London.[33]

Men who either had successfully escaped from captivity or evaded capture in Europe were interrogated on their return to Britain or once behind Allied areas. This was to make sure that firstly, they were not enemy agents, and secondly to gain knowledge from their experiences and pass this on to other men. Detailed reports were made as a result, which include narratives, of widely varying lengths, that describe the individual's experiences on the run; they mention civilians who helped them along the way, other Allied personnel, and their experiences in the hands of the enemy.

The reports can be found in series WO 208. They do not appear to be complete. In particular, those for men in the Special Forces have often been removed. The reports are not online at present, although they have been indexed by name in TNA's Discovery Catalogue. Occasionally, individual reports can be found online. The Airborne Assault Paradata website, for example, has a number of such reports.

If escaping and evasion was difficult in Europe, it was almost impossible in Japanese-occupied areas, where cultural differences and the terrain conspired against Allied service personnel on the run. The British Army Aid Group helped military personnel and civilians who had escaped camps in Hong Kong reach Chinese territory.[34] Some records of the Group are in series WO 343 and can be downloaded from TNA's website. Other files are in series WO 203. There do not appear to be the equivalent to escape and evasion reports. The Gwulo website has a history of the Group.

THE INTERNATIONAL COMMITTEE OF THE RED CROSS (ICRC)

Delegates from the International Committee of the Red Cross in Geneva monitored PoW camps and reported on conditions. Their reports, in series WO 224, offer an interesting insight into the conditions endured by PoWs in both Europe and the Far East.

CONSTRUCTING A RESEARCH STRATEGY

If you are researching a man who ended up in a German camp it is best to start with the cards in WO 416 as they will give you some idea of his time in enemy hands. However, they do not give an idea of what happened to individuals once they were captured. Bader's card does not record his many escapes (or his time in Colditz), McGrath's card does not mention his successful escape from the Stalag, nor does Dodd's card mention his time at the Auschwitz work camp. The lists on both Ancestry and Findmypast can suggest the camps. If the person survived the war there should be a Liberation Questionnaire that might provide additional information.

The ICRC also acted as the exchange for information about the fate of servicemen and women (as well as civilian internees) from both sides. As a result, it can have correspondence and other material about individual prisoners and those thought to be missing. Because of the demand, the ICRC Archives deals with limited numbers of research requests each year.

Further reading

TNA's holdings are summarised in a Research Guide 'British and Commonwealth prisoners of the Second World War and the Korean War'.

The IWM also has many documents including memoirs from former PoWs and camp newspapers.

There are smaller collections at the National Army and RAF museums and at regimental museums.

There are many websites devoted to the experiences of PoWs.

EUROPE

A fascinating website devoted to Allied servicemen who escaped through Belgium and the Belgians who helped them is at www.belgiumww2.info.

Other websites dealing with escape and evasion include:

- Conscript Heroes: www.conscript-heroes.com/index.html
- WWII Netherlands Escape Lines: https://wwii-netherlands-escape-lines.com
- WW2 Escape Lines Memorial Society: https://ww2escapelines.co.uk

The Frank Falla Archive has fairly detailed histories of the PoW camps, labour and concentration camps to which individuals deported from the Channel Islands were sentenced. Small numbers of Islanders seemed to have been found in many camps in Nazi Germany and north-west Europe.

Further reading

Martin W. Bowman, *Escape from Hitler's Reich* (Air World, 2014)
Martin W. Bowman, *Voices in Flight: RAF Escapers and Evaders in WW2* (Pen & Sword, 2015)

Oliver Clutton-Brock, *RAF Evaders: The Complete Story of RAF Escapees and Their Escape Lines, Western Europe 1940–1945* (Grub Street, 2009)
Helen Fry, *MI9: A History of the Secret Service for Escape and Evasion in World War II* (Yale University Press, 2020)
Adrian Gilbert, *POW: Allied Prisoners in Europe 1939–1945* (John Murray, 2007)
The National Archives, *Captives: Prisoners of War and Internees 1939–1945* (The History Press, 2024)
Howard R. Simkin, *Home Run: Allied Escape and Evasion in World War II* (Casemate, 2022)

FAR EAST

- Far East Prisoners of War: www.fepow-community.org.uk
- Children of Far East PoWs: www.cofepow.org.uk
- Center for Research: Allied PoWs under the Japanese: www.mansell.com

Use these records for

- Researching men who became prisoners of war or had successfully evaded capture by the enemy.

Pitfalls

- As always, it may not possible to build up a detailed picture of an individual's experience as a prisoner. This is especially true for men in Japanese hands, where there is a paucity of records.

PLACES TO VISIT

The RAF Escaping Society Museum at Lincolnshire Aviation Heritage Centre, East Kirkby Airfield, Spilsby PE23 4DE, www.lincsaviation.co.uk/lots-to-see/exhibitions

4

THE BRITISH ARMY

SERVICE RECORDS

British Army service records are the key source for researching ancestors – both men and women – who served in the army during and after the war. You should obtain those for any soldiers on your family tree.

But at first glance they look very daunting and rather uninteresting. However, if you concentrate, their riches will be revealed. One problem might be that you find there's a lot of duplication, but persevere. They are not actually one simple form, but a collection of documents about the individual. The contents do vary somewhat as a result.

To make sense of what you have in front of you, it is a good idea to construct a timeline, that is putting all the information into chronological order. Or, if you prefer, use the form in Appendix 2 and adapt it as you see fit.

The records should tell you:

- Service (aka army or regimental) number and other personal details.
- Next of kin, often with date of marriage, where appropriate and, on occasion, the birth dates of any children born during the individual's army service. This was needed in order to calculate a widow's pension in case the worst happened.
- Date of enlisting and discharge. Often a man was discharged to the Reserve on leaving the army. This is referred to as Class Z in service records. In theory, he might be called up again in case of national emergency, but this only happened during the Korean War (1950–53), and then just for a few specialists.
- The units served with. In many cases, men and women were posted to a surprising number of units during their service. Many men, in particular, spent time in holding camps for weeks or months at a time before being posted to any regiment or corps where there was a shortage of personnel.

Individuals would be taken on strength (TOS) when they were posted to a unit and struck off strength (SOS) when they left, either on transfer elsewhere or through being incapacitated in some way.

- Departure to and return from overseas' postings. Occasionally, the transport ship or the port of arrival may be named. You may well come across mention of Python Leave (aka Python) or LIAP (sometimes called LILOP). Python Leave was for anyone who had served overseas continuously for longer than four years and nine months or a slightly shorter period if they were serving in Burma. They were granted six weeks' home leave followed by a posting in the UK before demobilisation. LIAP (Leave in Advance of Python) was six weeks' home leave awarded to individuals who had served overseas for three years. After this they returned to their units.
- Promotions (and demotions). This will include details if an individual was commissioned from the ranks as an officer.
- Training courses attended. The army was increasingly sophisticated, so most men would have received specialist training on new pieces of kit or how to fight while in the front line. New officers, in particular, would be sent on a variety of management courses.
- Court martials. Usually the date is given, but it is rare for the punishment (if any) to be included. (See below)

Awards of medals, both campaign and gallantry. (See Chapter 3)

Army service records normally come in three parts:

- Attestation form. This is basically a questionnaire completed when an individual joined up. There will be a physical description, details of his family, civilian employment and whether he had had any previous military service. There may also be a copy of the reference given to the soldier on his discharge. As might be expected, this was generally very positive if rather non-committal.
- Statements of Service. These provide details of the units an individual served in, including dates and what period of service had been overseas.
- Service and Casualty forms. This is the heart of the record providing rich information about the individual's service, including details of the units in which he served, promotions, demotions, training and where he was posted. Dates for each event are normally given, although it may be a few days between when somebody arrives overseas and subsequently joins their unit.

Use these records for

- A framework for researching an individual's army career. In particular, they give exact dates for when a person joined or left a unit, when they were promoted, and when they left and returned from overseas.
- They tell you which units they served with, training courses attended, and, if appropriate, where they served overseas.

Pitfalls

- They can be hard to read, partly because of the clerk's handwriting. In addition, entries may not always be in chronological order.
- The biggest problem concerns the large number of abbreviations you may come across; some are obvious, but many are deeply head-scratching.
- Inevitably, some service records are more detailed than others. Whether that is because the individual had an action-packed career (or was a complete duffer being passed from one unit to another), or whether the clerks back at the personnel centre were a sloppy lot, we may never know.
- To get a full picture of an individual's service you need to consult the war diaries, which describe what the unit did day by day. These are most useful for men who were in the front line; they might well, for example, describe the circumstances around a man's death or wounding in action, even if he is not always named. Even then, it may not always be possible to pin down the extract truth behind family stories.
- Detailed medical records have been extracted, although dates of admission to hospital and subsequent discharge are given.

ABBREVIATIONS

The biggest problem with these records is the use of abbreviations – for units, training courses and other events – that can be difficult to interpret. There is no complete list of abbreviations, in part because clerks back in the personnel centres who kept the service records up to date seemly made them up as they went along.

The Ministry of Defence used to send out a set of lists of abbreviations to accompany service records. Some online lists can be found on the Researching WW2 website.

The excellent WW2Talk mailing list has a list in the form of an Excel spreadsheet. But, for one or two abbreviations it may be best just to ask someone on the List. Somebody is bound to know!

If all else fails, Google may know – but don't forget to add 'WW2' after the search question to ensure the answers are relevant.

A list of some common abbreviations is in Appendix 3.

X AND Y LISTS

You may well also come across reference to X and Y lists. According to the King's Regulations, published by the Army Council, X lists relate to those who became non-effective, e.g. as a result of wounding, being missing in action or being taken prisoner of war. X lists were broken down as follows:

- X(i) refers to a posting to fill vacancies elsewhere.
- X(ii) refers to individuals evacuated on medical grounds beyond a Regimental First Aid Post. Personnel so evacuated cease to be on the effective strength of their units.
- X (iii) are for men who were either prisoners of war, declared missing, deserters, or in prison.
- X (iv) lists unposted reinforcements and incoming reinforcement drafts.
- X (v) refers to officers who are on training courses for more than twenty-eight days.[1]
- Y lists refer to personnel who for some reason are not where they were initially posted. In most cases this refers to those who had been in hospital for 21 days or longer.[2]

OTHER SOURCES: OFFICERS

Details of officers are given in the **Army Lists.** You can trace promotions and very broadly the branches they served in. They include women officers, but not non-commissioned officers or privates.

Copies can be found on the open shelves in the reading rooms at TNA and the Imperial and National Army museums. Regimental museums may also have sets. Most issues for the Second World War are also available online through the Internet Archive. You need to search for 'Army List' and click on the volume you are interested in. Then do a key word search. Officers are normally only identified by surname and initials. There may be several entries for each person.

Appointments and promotions of officers are also published in the *London Gazette* (see Chapter 3 for more details).

OTHER SOURCES: OTHER RANKS

Ancestry has a set of **Tracer Cards** for the Royal Artillery. The cards track the movements of gunners, that is privates, between Royal Artillery units. Compiling the cards was meant to answer the question 'where is that man right now?', saving the burden of administration and searching through many files. As well as units, there may be information about date of enlistment and discharge, and service number. A similar set of cards, although less informative for the Royal Engineers, is on Findmypast.

Findmypast also has a collection of miscellaneous material, including enlistment registers, for the Coldstream Guards.

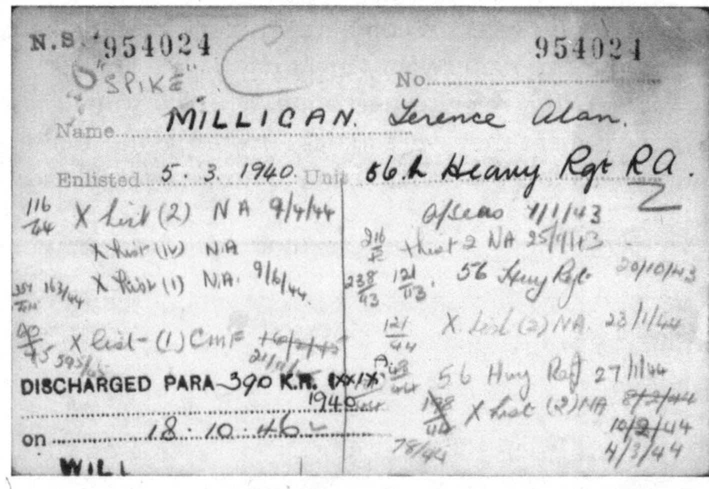
N.S. 954024 C 954024
"SPIKE" No.
Name MILLIGAN. Terence Alan.
Enlisted 5. 3. 1940. Unit 56th Heavy Rgt RA.
DISCHARGED PARA 390 K.R.
on 18. 10. 46.
WILL

Royal Artillery tracing card for the comedian and writer Terence 'Spike' Milligan. (Royal Artillery Archives/ Ancestry)

MEDALS

On Forces War Records, the supplementary subscription service run by Ancestry, there are 1.7 million medal cards for men and women who served in the Army. All the key information on the cards of individuals is included on the results page of the main Ancestry website.

These cards were completed by veterans when they applied for their campaign medals. The cards indicate which medals an individual applied for and the rank and service number they had at time of discharge. If a veteran did not apply for their medals, no card was created.

The records are not complete. In particular, there are no cards for the Royal Engineers, the Royal Army Ordnance Corps, the Auxiliary Territorial Service as well as many infantry regiments. However, although Ancestry says there are no cards for the Royal Army Medical Corps, there is a card for my father-in-law, who was a lieutenant colonel in the corps.

A few cards are closed for 100 years, or have had information redacted to protect the privacy of living people. This may have happened when applications were made by next of kin rather than the veterans themselves, and it was thought that the applicant might still be alive.

Another 750,000 cards are due to be added to Forces War Records in due course.

For army medals see Chapter 3.

CASUALTY RECORDS

The main series of casualty records are explained in Chapter 3. However, there are several sources unique to the British Army.

ARMY ROLL OF HONOUR

In 1947, the army compiled a Roll of Honour that listed all 174,000 officers and other ranks who lost their lives while serving in the army during the Second World War. The Roll provides some personal details about the deceased together with when and where they lost their lives. In practice, this is much the same information that you would find on the Commonwealth War Graves Commission website.

The original records are at TNA in series WO 304. However, it is much easier to use the copies available on both Findmypast and Ancestry.

Use these records

- As an alternative to the CWGC.

Pitfalls

- They do not include men who died of wounds subsequent to leaving the army.

ENQUIRIES ABOUT MISSING PERSONNEL

Series WO 361 at TNA contains files of enquiries into Missing Personnel made by the War Office during and after the war. A small team based at the Blue Coats School in Liverpool was responsible for tracing these missing men and women who could not be traced either as prisoners of war or as casualties. Most men who were reported missing had become prisoners of war, although it is not unknown for soldiers to have no last resting place. Years ago, I researched a man who disappeared after he tripped when on patrol in the Burmese jungle, falling into a fast-running stream.

The files contain correspondence with the person's family as well as with other organisations such as the Red Cross, eyewitness statements from comrades, and casualty lists. The records are arranged by unit.

Use these records for

- They are perhaps most use for men who became prisoners of war, particularly in the Far East, where it might have taken months for the paperwork to be received by the War Office.

Pitfalls

- The records are not complete.
- The chances of finding an individual is pretty small.

CASUALTY LISTS

The key sources that can be used for tracing casualties are the casualty lists. They not only list individuals who were killed in action or died of their wounds, but the lists also record service personnel who had been reported wounded (most of whom subsequently recovered), prisoners of war and those recorded as being missing – most of whom were eventually reported as captured by the enemy or deceased

Inevitably the lists are very inaccurate, so corrections were constantly being made as additional information arrived at the War Office. As a result, there are likely to be several entries for each man, perhaps the first when he was first posted missing, then subsequent entries when he was reported as being a prisoner of war and then having died in the camp.

Each entry gives the individual's name, rank, service number and the theatre of operations where they were stationed (for example, north-west Europe, Italy or Burma).

4192880 Fusilier D.I. Rowland, Royal Welch Fusiliers was posted missing after Dunkirk. A few months later there was a notification that he was a prisoner of war. Searching by his service number, it appears that there are two German prisoner of war cards for him as Idris Rowlands became a prisoner at the big camp Stalag VIII-B Lamsdorf in Silesia.[1] He survived the war, but as with many other veterans, he found it hard to settle down. In 1949, Rowlands is recorded as living in a hostel in Gloucestershire and was bound over for getting in trouble with another man's wife.[2]

The original Casualty Lists are at TNA in series WO 417. They are also available on Findmypast.

Use them for

- Providing additional information about dates of death, wounds and capture as prisoner of war.
- They can sometimes be used to identify other men from the same regiment who were killed or wounded in a particular incident. A tank commander, Sergeant Derek Rowland, MM and his crew, were killed when his tank was destroyed in the Tunisian desert on 7 April 1943. The casualty list on which Rowland appears also gives the names of four other men from his regiment – 3 Royal Tank Regiment – who were also killed on the day. They must be the other members of the tank crew.
- Another source of finding service numbers.

Pitfalls

- The information they contain is often provisional. As a result, the lists may be inaccurate. As more details reached the War Office they were likely to be updated, so you may need to check more than one list.

- They usually only give initials not full names (W. or W.S. Churchill not Winston Churchill), so unless you have a service number, or regiment, it is easy to pick up the wrong person.
- They are full of mistakes. Errors are normally picked up and corrected in subsequent lists.

WAR DIARIES

War diaries should be a key part of the research into your soldier ancestors, as they describe what the units they served in did day by day. They were compiled by all units in the British Army at home and overseas between the outbreak of war in September 1939 until the end of 1946. They were designed for the use of official historians writing the histories of particular battles or units. And, of course, they are now immensely useful for academic researchers, family historians and medal collectors.

War diaries were first kept during the First World War.[3] Those for the Second World War are very similar in look and content. The main change is that they are now largely typewritten and they more often contain appendices than those from the Great War. They are normally filed monthly in purpose-made file covers.

They were kept for official purposes, which explains why there are relatively few mentions of individual soldiers. Even junior officers might only be mentioned if they went on training courses. Compilers were reminded that the purpose of these diaries was twofold: 'to provide information from theatres of war in sufficient details and in such a form as to provide data upon which to base future improvements in Army training, equipment, organisation and administration… [and] to furnish an historical record of the war'.[4]

THE NARRATIVE

Printed inside the war diary was an explanation of what the writer was expected to write up in the 'narrative' (the war diary itself) daily:

> Account[s] of operations with notes of topographical and climatic factors affecting them. Note[s] of how orders were carried out … Note[s] of any administrative difficulties and action taken to overcome them … Intermediate movements of unit or formation. Note[s] of any important visits paid and received by commanders and senior staff officers.

In smaller units, the diaries were usually written by the officer in charge. In larger units, such as infantry battalions or tank regiments, they might be compiled by the adjutant, that is the junior officer responsible for the unit's administration, or the unit intelligence officer. They were checked and initialled by the officer commanding. Many large units might have detachments, companies and platoons stationed at some distance from battalion headquarters. Where this is the case, the diaries inevitably reflect the experiences of headquarters rather than of the components.

Although the diary writers had strict instructions about what to describe, the rules were rarely followed, largely because the subjects that should be included were irrelevant to the unit. As a result, the diarists, within reason, followed their own inclinations, which the historian today finds both a joy and a curse. Some are beautifully and graphically written, while others are little more than terse repetitions of visits made by superior officers to the unit, or, perhaps, the numbers of shells fired. It also seems to be the case that war diaries are fuller in units where morale was particularly high.

In all fairness it was often hard for diarists of those units that did much the same work day after day, such as petrol depots or anti-aircraft batteries, to write very much. Here the writer might only mention visits by senior officers and the amount of fuel stored or training exercises participated in during the month. More imaginative compilers might include results of football matches played by the unit football team or a note of air raids on area where the unit was stationed. In March 1942, the war diary of the 5th Hampshire Regiment, who were stationed in Thanet, recorded that 'an enemy agent reported landing on Margate Beach'.[5] As well as mention of the constant training exercises, the diary also describes weekly dances at the Foresters Hall in the town and a good attendance at *It's a Wise Child*, a play put on by ENSA.[6]

When the unit is in action, there may be entries in the narrative almost hourly, so at times readers can get a sense of battle and the confusion that often surrounds it. And even when they are resting or training there may be notes about sporting fixtures or film shows, permission given allowing troops to visit local cafes and the organisation of buses to take men away for a few days' leave.

In May 1944, for example, the war diary of the 2/4th Hampshire Regiment, which was fighting near Monte Cassino in Italy, recorded that between the 6th and 11th it was quiet, while they were preparing for an attack on enemy lines: 'Patrols removing booby-trapped machine guns and clearing mine fields'. And it was possible 'to see Germans lighting cigarettes and moving around.' At 2300 hours on the 11th: 'Artillery barrage commences. It is the most spectacular of the war and is a magnificent spectacle. The Battalion stands ready to move.' Unfortunately, the attack had only partial success with heavy casualties. 'The attack started off in brilliant moonlight, but after the barrage, the resultant smoke and dust kicked up reduced visibility on the river bank to a minimum.'[7]

APPENDICES

In the folder in which the monthly narrative is found there is often a number of appendices. At first glance they may appear to be either irrelevant or difficult to comprehend, but they are worth looking at. They may include:

- Strength and casualty returns
- Routine orders and administrative instructions
- Operational orders and instructions
- Reports
- Messages
- Location statements

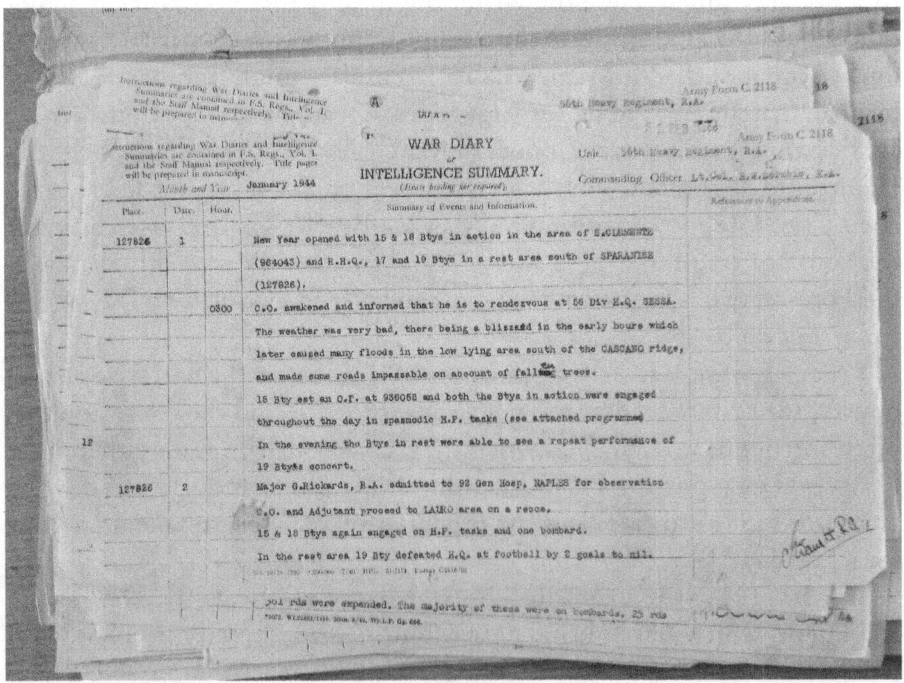

Instructions regarding War Diaries and Intelligence Summaries are contained in F.S. Regs., Vol. I. and the Staff Manual respectively. Title pages will be prepared in manuscript.

Army Form C. 2118

WAR DIARY
or
INTELLIGENCE SUMMARY.
(Erase heading not required).

Month and Year January 1944

Unit 56th Heavy Regiment, R.A.

Commanding Officer Lt.Col. [illegible], R.A.

Place.	Date.	Hour.	Summary of Events and Information.	References to Appendices.
127826	1		New Year opened with 15 & 18 Btys in action in the area of S.CLEMENTE (964043) and R.H.Q., 17 and 19 Btys in a rest area south of SPARANISE (127826).	
		0300	C.O. awakened and informed that he is to rendezvous at 56 Div H.Q. SESSA. The weather was very bad, there being a blizzard in the early hours which later caused many floods in the low lying area south of the CASCANO ridge, and made some roads impassable on account of fallen trees. 18 Bty est an O.P. at 936055 and both the Btys in action were engaged throughout the day in spasmodic H.F. tasks (see attached programme) In the evening the Btys in rest were able to see a repeat performance of 19 Bty's concert.	
127826	2		Major G.Rickards, R.A. admitted to 92 Gen Hosp, NAPLES for observation C.O. and Adjutant proceed to LAURO area on a recce. 15 & 18 Btys again engaged on H.F. tasks and one bombard. In the rest area 19 Bty defeated H.Q. at football by 2 goals to nil.	

... rds were expended. The majority of these were on bombards, 25 rds

Entries from early January 1944 in the war diary for 56 Heavy Artillery Regiment. The regiment was training in preparation to going into action in Italy. (TNA WO 170/903)

- Intelligence summaries
- Photographs, sketches, maps, and traces
- Ephemera, such as Christmas cards

Diarists were especially asked to include all important documents relating to operations. On the cover was a list of appendices to be included and the order in which they were to be inserted. For the higher echelons, such as divisional and corps headquarters, the war diary is likely to consist mainly of appendices, with only a very brief page or two of narrative.

The most common items found among the appendices are the weekly strength and casualty returns, which normally consist of weekly lists of officers, and another form detailing the strength of the unit indicating the number of roles filled and any vacancies. Although at first glance they are of little value, genealogically they are not uninteresting for it is possible to track the arrival and departure of officers. There is often a list of men 'particularly required for return to unit', that is individual soldiers and NCOs who were either in hospital or recovering from injuries.

Also of interest are the unit and movement orders, which detail actions that should be followed by members. They often include instructions on the clothing to be worn or rations and other items to be carried by individual soldiers. Occasionally, individual men might be mentioned if they were assigned to particular duties, such as joining an advance party.

For units engaged in battle (or on training exercises) there are often detailed orders with maps and traces, which would have been laid on maps to show where the battalion or regiment should be positioned at the time when the action began. Less common are photographs and items of ephemera, such as Christmas cards or unit newspapers.

SOURCES

The vast majority of war diaries are at TNA. There are separate series for each theatre of operations, so it is useful to know roughly at least where the unit your ancestor was a member of was serving. Providing you know the unit, a search in TNA's Discovery Catalogue, for say 5th Hampshire Regiment, should be enough. Sometimes, however, the description uses army abbreviations, particularly for the component parts of the Royal Engineers, Royal Army Medical Corps, Royal Army Ordnance Corps and Royal Army Service Corps. If you can't find the unit, often a search by the number on unit's name might be enough (5 or 5th), but here it is helpful to know the theatre of operations.

The main series of war diaries are:

- Home forces (based in the UK) WO 166
- British expeditionary force (France, 1939–1940) WO 167
- North-West expeditionary force (Norway, 1940) WO 168
- Middle East forces WO 169
- Central Mediterranean forces (Italy, 1943–1946) WO 170
- North-West Europe (1944–1946) WO 171
- South-East Asia command (Burma 1941–1946) WO 172
- British North Africa forces (Algeria, 1942–1943) WO 175
- Medical services WO 177
- Military missions WO 178
- Special services (i.e. SAS, Commandos) WO 218

Some war diaries are online through Ancestry. At time of writing, they largely consist of diaries for units in the Middle East. Incidentally, a few diaries have been transcribed, such the war diaries of various mounted units at the History of the British 7th Armoured Division website and for battalions of the Berkshire and Wiltshire regiments by the regimental museum The Wardrobe. Google should be able to tell whether any diaries for units you are interested are online.

Use these records for

- War diaries are a key source for finding more about the experiences of the men and women whom you are researching.
- Researching the history of a particular unit or units. Looking at all war diaries for units that took part in a particular action can build up a broader picture of what happened rather than just relying on the diary from one unit alone.

Pitfalls

- The National Archives set of war diaries is not complete. In particular, many war diaries for the Royal Artillery are missing. Fortunately, duplicate copies were kept and, where they survive, they should be with the regimental archives. (For more about regimental archives see Chapter 2.) In addition, the occasional month or run of months may also be missing. This is particularly the case during the retreat to Dunkirk in May 1940 when, because of the chaos, it was almost impossible to maintain the diary. Many were probably destroyed to prevent them falling into German hands. However, in many units an attempt was made to write up the events of May 1940 once the unit had reached safety and while the memory was fresh in people's minds.

- Many appendices have also been lost. Instructions for the liberation of the concentration camp at Belsen by the 63rd Anti-Tank Regiment, for example, were in 'Appendix J', which has long since been destroyed.[8]
- They rarely mention individual soldiers, although there are usually more entries for officers.
- War diaries are working documents, so they make few allowances for non-military readers. In general, this rarely presents a problem, but it may not always be easy to determine exactly where the unit was based, as locations often use a numerical map reference and without the map it is hard to work out exactly what is going on.

Further reading

TNA Research Guide: 'British Army Operations-Second-World War'.

COURTS MARTIAL

A court martial is a court convened to try an offence against military discipline, or against the ordinary law, committed by a person in one of the armed services. Surviving records are all at TNA. Most minor offences, such as returning to base drunk, would have been tried by the regiment itself. Where this is the case, any surviving records should be with the regimental archives. Occasionally, mentions of courts martial can be found in the unit war diary.

Registers of courts martial of soldiers accused of more serious crimes, such as desertion or striking an officer, are mainly in series WO 213. They will give brief details of the offence and the sentence awarded by the court, if any. The registers are not indexed, but are roughly arranged by the date that the paperwork arrived at the War Office in London. So it can be difficult to track a particular trial in the original documents. The registers, fortunately properly indexed, are also available through Ancestry's Fold3 service.

There is a selection of case papers in WO 71, mainly for the most important trials and generally relating to murder, treason, mutiny and, finally, cases considered to be of historic interest.

In addition, there are some miscellaneous records in WO 93, including details of death penalties carried out after 1941. Some records relating to individual cases of courts martial are closed for seventy-five years from the last date on each file. More information is given in a TNA Research Guide: 'Courts martial and desertion in the British Army 17th-20th centuries'.

Further reading

There are, of course, many memoirs and regimental histories, but here are two good general introductions to the army that soldiers experienced on a daily basis:

Alan Allport, *Browned Off and Bloody Minded: The British Soldier Goes to War 1939–1945* (Yale University Press, 2015)
Jeremy A. Crang, *The British Army and the People's War 1939–1945* (Manchester University Press, 2000)
George Forty, *The British Army Handbook 1939–1945* (Sutton, 2002)

Museums

National Army Museum
Royal Hospital Road
London
SW3 3HT
www.nam.ac.uk

Almost all corps and regiments have museums, which are well worth visiting. Details at www.armymuseums.org.uk

THE SECRET WAR

During the Second World War, a seemingly inexhaustible number of secret military organisations was set up. In recent years, they have come to prominence through a variety of books, films and TV programmes. Their dramatic stories have overshadowed the less showy but more effective parts of the British and Allied war effort, such as Bomber Command's strategic air offensive that destroyed Germany's industrial capacity.

A large number of separate organisations were involved in the Secret War. Some were short-lived groups formed for a particular mission or coalescing around a particular leader, such as Popski's Private Army, which operated in the Western Desert. But others were properly set up with hundreds, if not thousands, on the establishment.

They were created, in part, as the result of Churchill's fascination with irregular forces, whom he admired as a young officer and war reporter during the Boer War. This was coupled with the common desire, in the dark days of 1940, to take the war to the enemy. In Churchill's memorable words there was a desire to 'set Europe ablaze'.

In June 1940, Churchill told the Joint Chiefs of Staff to propose measures for an offensive against German-occupied Europe: 'Enterprises must be prepared, with specially trained troops of the hunter class, who can develop a reign of terror down these coasts, first of all on the "butcher and bolt" policy… '.[9]

It wasn't Churchillian rhetoric. He understood that, despite having left much of its equipment at Dunkirk, the lack of modern kit or an obvious strategy to win the war, the country wanted and needed to take the war to the Germans. The key units were:

The Commandos evolved from a small number of 'Independent Companies' which were set up during the summer of 1940 to conduct raids on the enemy. In a minute of a meeting on 18 June 1940, Winston Churchill said: 'There ought to be at least twenty thousand Storm Troops or 'Leopards' drawn from existing units, ready to spring at the throat of any small landings or descents. These officers and men should be armed with the latest equipment, tommy guns, grenades etc., and should be given great facilities in motor-cycles and armoured cars.'[10] Initially Commando units were formed by volunteers from the Army, but in early 1942 the Royal Marine Infantry battalions were reorganised as Commando battalions. They were small, highly mobile, surprise raiding and military reconnaissance forces. In addition there were smaller, more specialist, Royal Naval Beach Commando and RAF Servicing Commando units.

Most Commando operations against the enemy during the war were Combined Operations which involved other naval and air force units, transporting the Commandos or pummelling enemy strongpoints. They include the raids on St Nazaire in March 1942, and Dieppe in August 1942.

Government Code and Cypher School (GCCS), known as Bletchley Park.

Political Warfare Executive (PWE) is probably the least known of the various secret organisations set up during the Second World War. Under the inspired leadership of a former Foreign Correspondent, Sefton Delmar, PWE produced and disseminated propaganda in a variety of different media forms; from leaflets and fake stamps dropped over Nazi occupied Europe, to radio stations broadcasting to German soldiers. All of which sought to cast doubts about the Nazi regime among the Germans and to encourage resistance across occupied Europe.

Special Air Service (SAS) was formed in July 1941 by Major David Stirling to attack behind enemy lines with small raiding forces. The name was originally designed to persuade the Axis into thinking that there was a paratrooper regiment with numerous units operating in the Western Desert. It was particularly active across France after D-Day as small troops of men ambushed and harried German forces.

Special Operations Executive (SOE) was established in July 1940 to conduct espionage, sabotage and reconnaissance in occupied Europe and to aid local resistance movements. By the end of the war, SOE was present in all the theatres of operation and involved in a wide range of activities, including at one stage a monopoly of cigarette imports to Spain. It was the only part of the British armed forces where women directly fought in the front line, as a number of female agents were parachuted into occupied Europe.

The most successful contribution by the Commandos and related units to the war effort was probably Operation Biting, in February 1942, which captured a mysterious German radar installation at Bruneval in northern France. It led to improvements in British radar technology and the development of Window – thin strips of aluminium foil dropped by bombers that confused the Germany night defences.

The work of MI5 (the Security Service) and MI6 (the Secret Intelligence Service or SIS) during the Second World War remains shrouded in secrecy, although if you are interested it is well worth reading their official histories. Neither service, however, had a particularly good war. The historian Hugh Trevor-Roper later wrote: 'Of all the great intelligence triumphs of the war not one was directly or exclusively due to the Secret [Intelligence] Service proper.'[11]

Undoubtedly the most successful of all the secret organisations was the Code and Cypher School (now the Government Communications Headquarters (GCHQ)). Based at Bletchley Park, on the edge of Milton Keynes, the School ingeniously broke German codes. Churchill famously claimed that their work shortened the war by three years. Certainly, he was entranced by their work – receiving a daily summary from Bletchley Park, on which he often scrawled comments.[12] Whether Enigma did shorten the war has been debated by historians. Each of the major combatants could, to a greater or lesser degree, read each other's signals or had high-placed spies in each other's most secret organisations. Bletchley Park's greatest achievement was undoubtedly to read German naval code that enabled the Royal Navy to locate and sink the U-boats that were preying on the convoys carrying vital supplies to Britain. This was key in winning the Battle of the Atlantic.

FINDING OUT MORE

Service records

Service records for men and women who served in special forces can be ordered in the normal way (see Chapter 3). Service was entirely voluntary. Most men and women were recruited when they answered appeals in the regimental orders. Occasionally entries in service records are redacted and the occasional service retained if they went on to join MI6 after the war.

Service records for SOE personnel, both men and women, are in series HS 9 at Kew. Some records were destroyed after the war. Where no date of death is known, the file may still be closed to public access, but TNA will open the file on proof of death. These files can be quite informative, giving details of training and missions in occupied Europe (and their fate if they were captured), as well as comments about suitability for the work. There may also be passport-sized mugshots. If no file survives there may be an entry on a card in one of the card indexes to be found in series HS 12–HS 20.

The Code and Cypher School at Bletchley Park ultimately employed 9,000 people, 75 per cent of whom were women. In order to meet the ever-growing demand for signals intelligence, staff would work around the clock. They would decipher masses of enemy communications into understandable, actionable intelligence to eventually contribute toward an Allied victory. Brief details of those who served there are included on the Bletchley Park Museum's website.

All MI6 records are closed. This includes records for agents. It is, however, possible to get brief details from MI5 of wartime personnel, see their website. A number of carefully selected and heavily redacted MI5 files relating to wartime activities can be found under the KV letter code at TNA.

Medals

Campaign medals were granted in the normal way.

Citations for gallantry medals may be found in series WO 373, although there are many gaps, particularly before 1943. They can provide useful background both to why the medal was awarded, but also to the operations that the individual took part in.

Lieutenant Anthony Greville Bell, 2SAS was awarded a DSO, having been parachuted into Italy near Florence on 8 September 1943:

> with the object of disorganising enemy railways and communications. Despite two broken ribs and other injuries, he took command of the party as the other officer was missing after the drop. Despite great pain, he derailed one train in a tunnel on the Pistoia–Bologna line … Three weeks after dropping Lt Bell, on the way back through central Italy, organised a band of Italian partisans in telephone wire cutting and train wrecking … [he] showed outstanding powers of leadership and unfailing judgement in most difficult circumstances. He was an inspiration to the small force under his command.[13]

After the war, awards were made to resistance members and others who had helped the Allied cause, mainly in Western Europe. They include European members of SOE who were parachuted into occupied Europe to help the local resistance. The recommendations are in series WO 208 and have been fully indexed in TNA's online catalogue.

An unusual source of information are papers in series T 336, containing the recommendations or civilian awards for SOE agents like Eileen Nearne, Yvonne Cormeau, Pearl Witherington and Odette Sansom. These women were placed in enemy-occupied France in the role of wireless operators, helping to create a consistent method of communication between British intelligence and the French resistance. Their role would not likely be considered as civil, but they were put forward for civil awards instead of their military equivalents.

Operations

There is also a mass of files relating to operations undertaken by special forces, very little of which is online. The survival of operational records is patchy; after all, these organisations were extremely secretive by nature.

Most operations were assigned an operational name, which would be used in the files. Loyton, for example was used by SAS groups dropped into central France in the late summer of 1944, while Archway refers to SAS operations in north-west Germany and the Netherlands in March and April 1945. Look out in particular for reports submitted by SAS officers after each operation as they normally include a list of all men – including privates – who were on the mission. On occasion, this may be the only evidence that a man had served in the SAS.

Papers and war diaries relating to the SAS, the Commandos, the Long-Range Desert Group, GHQ Liaison Regiment and other units are in series WO 218. This is probably the best place to start.

There is some overlap with material in DEFE 2, which includes material relating to Combined Operations. Other files might be found in the defence intelligence material in WO 208 and the Headquarters papers for the various commands. Some papers for the Liaison Regiment are in WO 215.

Files relating to all aspects of the work of SOE are in the various series in the HS letter code. Material relating to PWE are in series FO 898. However, the indexing is rather poor and there are rarely mentions of individual agents.

The vast majority of decrypts of German signals are available at TNA in various series in the HW letter code. Fortunately, they are well indexed. They are probably of limited genealogical interest, but can make remarkable reading.

There are collections of personal and other papers at the Imperial War Museum, National Army Museum and at the Liddell Hart Centre for Military Archives, King's College London.

An excellent introduction to the history of Combined Operations is provided on the Combined Operations website.

THE FIRST AID NURSING YEOMANRY (FANY)

The First Aid Nursing Yeomanry, now formally the Princess Royal's Volunteer Corps, was set up in 1907 to provide medical support on the battlefield. It was, and remains, a volunteer unit for women, although with close links to the armed services.

For much of the Second World War, members provided drivers and welfare services to the army. Formally they were known as Women's Transport Service (WTS FANY) and members were often referred to being Free FANYs.

Despite pressure they managed to avoid being absorbed into the Army but continued to provide services alongside the Auxiliary Territorial Service (ATS) to which most women in the Army belonged.

At the beginning of the war in September 1939, twenty-three FANYs of No. 1 Motor Ambulance Convoy were amongst the first women in uniform to cross the Channel.

Today, the members are largely remembered for their clandestine role in the Special Operations Executive (SOE). Many worked in the Signals and Cipher departments. Others were agents on the ground in occupied Europe, receiving training as wireless operators and as 'silent killer'.

Thirty-nine of the fifty women parachuted into France were FANYs. They were expected to have perfect knowledge of France, very good (though not necessarily perfect) French, and few family ties. Twelve of whom were captured by the Nazis and subsequently murdered by them. Another member was killed on operations.

Other members became conducting officers who supervised agents' training and reported on their strengths and weaknesses. They also gave each agent a small token of humanity before their departure into the field, such as a compact, lipstick or perfume, as well as, of course, a deadly cyanide pill.

The corps' strength during the war was 6,000, of whom 2,000 served with SOE. Gallantry awards included: George Crosses to Odette Hallowes, Violette Szabo and Noor Inayat Khan; two George Medals; thirty-six Mentions in Despatches, as well as one CBE; six OBEs; twenty-three MBEs and ten BEMs.

FANYs who lost their lives in the service are commemorated on a memorial at St Paul's Church, Knightsbridge.

FANY's archives were recently deposited at the National Army Museum. They should be available online by the end of 2025. For those who served with SOE, an index in series HS 20 at TNA indicates where they were posted and provides basic personal details. In addition, surviving service records are to be found in series HS 9.

Further reading

More information about researching men and women who were in special forces can be found in Phil Tomaselli, *Tracing Your Secret Service Ancestors* (Pen & Sword, 2009).

There is a huge range of books on all aspects of the work of the special forces, the security services, and SOE during the Second World War. Most bookshops and libraries will have a selection. Books by Helen Fry, Ben Macintyre and Damien Lewis are particularly recommended.

If you are researching somebody who died while serving with the SAS, it is probably worth seeing whether you can find a copy of *The SAS and LRDG Roll of Honour 1941–47*, by 'Ex-Lance-Corporal X', which was published in 2016. The four-book box set is a comprehensive history of the SAS and Long-Range Desert Group with details of the wartime records of individual soldiers who fought and died during the war. Unfortunately, only 2,000 copies were printed.

For MI5 and MI6, the surprisingly readable official histories are a good place to start: Christopher Andrews, *The Defence of the Realm: The Authorised History of MI5* (Allen Lane, 2009) and Keith Jefferies, *MI6* (Bloomsbury, 2010).

A sceptical eye on these activities is provided by Max Hastings in *The Secret War: Spies, Codes and Guerrillas, 1939–1945* (Collins, 2015).

Websites

INTRODUCTIONS TO THE SUBJECT

- www.iwm.org.uk/history/secret-war-what-you-need-to-know
- www.nam.ac.uk/explore/special-forcesWW2
- https://en.wikipedia.org/wiki/British_Commando_operations_during_the_Second_World_War

There are several very informative websites that can help researchers. They are maintained by enthusiasts, and all the better for it. One of the best is the Special Forces Roll of Honour for many British, Commonwealth and American units. It includes brief details of soldiers and provides links to more specialist websites and books. It is particularly useful for the SAS. Unfortunately, there doesn't seem to be a website specifically dedicated to the men who served in the SAS during the war.

Another excellent site devoted to Combined Operations can be found at www.combinedops.com. Look out also for the Commandos Veterans website.

There are several useful sites for the Parachute Regiment including the Pegasus Archive and Paradata.

Museums

Bletchley Park is an excellent museum devoted to code-breaking on the site where it happened.

Bletchley Park
Sherwood Drive
Bletchley
Milton Keynes
MK3 6EB
www.bletchleypark.org

The **Military Intelligence Museum** is the regimental museum of the British Army's Intelligence Corps. It contains much about the work of the corps and on espionage in general. There is also a useful small archive devoted to the work of military intelligence, details at: www.militaryintelligencemuseum.org

The **Combined Military Services Museum** is a private collection of the equipment used by spies and special forces at: https://cmsm.co.uk

Imperial War Museum Duxford, near Cambridge, houses **Airborne Assault**, the successor to the Parachute Regiment and Airborne Forces Museum. You will find it in the Airspace Hangar.

5

THE ROYAL AIR FORCE

RAF PERSONAL RECORDS

RAF service records can be obtained from the Ministry of Defence in the usual way (see Chapter 3). By 2026, they should have been transferred to TNA and will be made available online via Ancestry by the end of the decade. Any medical records are closed to 2044.

These records are rather less informative than their army equivalents, but they contain the key information about an individual's career, including:

- Personal description, including next of kin.
- Trade, i.e. pilot, fitter, clerk.
- Ranks and promotions.
- Units served with, including dates of posting to the unit and subsequent departure. Entries might include hospitals to which the individual was admitted.
- Medals: gallantry, campaign and long service and good conduct.

Use these records for

- Tracing a man's RAF career.
- Dates when attached to a particular squadron or other unit can be followed up in the operations record books (see below).

Pitfalls

- There is some use of abbreviations that might not always be clear.

OTHER SOURCES: OFFICERS

Details of officers (female as well as male), together with the branch they served with (engineering, meteorological etc.) and details of promotions, appear in the **Air Force Lists**. Sets are in the Reference Room at Kew as well as at the RAF and Imperial War museums and possibly in other large reference libraries.

More usefully, most issues for the Second World War are also available on the Internet Archive. You need to search for 'Air Force List' and click on the volume you are interested in. Then do a key word search. Officers are normally only identified by surname and initials. There may be several entries for each individual.

Confidential lists were also produced with more detail and these can be found in series AIR 10. They are not online.

Submissions to the sovereign for approval of appointments are in series AIR 30. Many pieces concern honorary appointments for RAF personnel who were attached to the Royal Household.

FLYING LOG BOOKS

Pilots and flight engineers were expected to keep log books, recording flights undertaken and other incidents of note, such as accidents or mechanical failures. Often, they are annotated with drawings or photographs.

In 1958, aircrew were invited to claim their logbooks, but relatively few did. A small selection was set aside for permanent preservation at the Public Record Office (now TNA), which are in series AIR 4. Other log books may be found in private or family papers or donated to museums and archives.

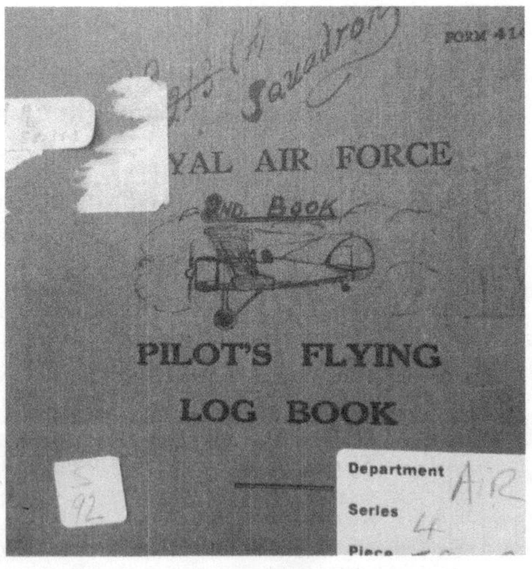

The log book, suitably annotated, for Squadron Leader B.J.E. Lane. (TNA AIR 4/58)

Further reading

Although somewhat dated, the best guides to using RAF records to trace your ancestor's service remain William Spencer's *Air Force Records for Family Historians* (HMSO, 2000) and Phil Tomaselli, *Tracing Your Air Force Ancestors* (Pen & Sword, 2007).

Short biographies of 3,000 men who flew with Fighter Command during the Battle of Britain can be found in K. Wynn, *Men of the Battle of Britain* (2nd edition, CCB Associates, 1999). Francis K, Mason, *Battle over Britain* (Aston Publications, 1990), also contains full details of all RAF Fighter Command flying personnel during the battle, and their subsequent service history.

Aircrew & Groundcrew Research is an excellent website with lots of information about RAF personnel. It contains much more than lists of names, such as brief histories of individual squadrons and units. The Air of Authority website contains heavily abbreviated biographies of senior members of the RAF at air commodore level and above, which is to be found behind a paywall.

MEDALS

For more about campaign medals and honours and awards see Chapter 3.

GALLANTRY AWARDS

Details of awards were published in the *London Gazette*. For non-immediate awards it was usual just for a man's name and rank to be included.

As with the other services, gallantry awards to RAF officers and other ranks were subdivided into two types: immediate (for single acts of bravery), or non-immediate, which were normally awarded at the conclusion of a tour of duty of between twenty-five and thirty sorties. The most common gallantry awards were the Distinguished Flying Cross (DFC) for officers and its equivalent for non-commissioned officers, which was the Distinguished Flying Medal (DFM). Just over 21,000 officers were awarded the DFC and 6,650 NCOs received the DFM.[1]

Surviving recommendations for gallantry awards are in series AIR 2 at Kew. The recommendations are not indexed, nor are they arranged in any logical way. For non-immediate awards the recommendations normally only indicate that it was made for completing thirty sorties. Fortunately, the excellent RAF Commands website has a searchable index to gallantry awards, including those for the military division of the Order of the British Empire (OBEs, MBEs etc.). Often entries include citations describing why the medal was awarded. For immediate awards they can be quite detailed. On 27 August 1943, for example, the *London Gazette* recorded the award of the Air Force Cross to:

> Acting Wing Commander Richard Godfrey SEYS, DFC (34130), RAF. Squadron Leader Fowler Morgan GOBEIL (Can/C.i2i), RCAF. Flight Lieutenant William Sydney LONGHURST (42852), RAF. These officers made the first tug-and-glider crossing of the North Atlantic from Canada to the United Kingdom, landing on 11 July, 1943. Wing Commander Seys and Squadron Leader Gobeil were pilot and co-pilot respectively of the glider and Flight Lieutenant Longhurst piloted the towing aircraft. Both aircraft carried useful loads, the cargo of the glider being nearly 1.5 tons and including serum and vital aircraft spares. The flight involved landings in Newfoundland, Greenland (an exceptionally difficult one) and Iceland. Adverse weather was encountered at times and, as the glider could not ascend higher than 13,000 feet, the aircraft were frequently buffeted about and might have broken adrift but for the skilful flying of the glider pilots. They also showed great skill in overcoming the difficulties of flying in clouds.[2]

There are no indexes to gallantry medals at Kew. There is one with Air Historical Branch. You should provide the full name, service number and rank, and the squadron or other unit the individual served with at the time the award was made. AHB will supply you with the old RAF file number, which you will have to match using the Discovery Catalogue to find the current TNA reference. Let us say, this isn't always easy!

Further reading

Nicholas and Carol Carter, *The Distinguished Flying Cross and How it Was Won 1918–1995* (2 vols, Savannah Publications, 1998)
Michael Maton, *Honour the Air Forces: Honours and Awards to the RAF and Dominion Air Forces During the Second World War* (Token, 2006)
I.T. Tavender, *The Distinguished Flying Medal: A Record of Courage 1918–1982* (2nd edition, Savannah Publications, 2004)
I.T. Tavender, *The Distinguished Flying Medal Register for the Second World War* (2 vols, Savannah Publications, 2000)
www.rafcommands.com/database/awards

CASUALTY RECORDS

Flying was a dangerous business. About 70,000 RAF personnel were killed, the vast majority of whom had served in Bomber Command. In addition, many thousands of lives were lost in flying accidents, whether during training or perhaps as the result of engine failure during a flight.

The deaths of men and women in the RAF are commemorated by the Commonwealth War Graves Commission (see Chapter 3). The Air Forces Memorial at Runnymede near Egham in Surrey commemorates over 20,000 men, British and Commonwealth, who failed to return from operations from bases in the United Kingdom and north and western Europe, and who have no known graves. This memorial was designed by Sir Edward Maufe with sculptures by Vernon Hill. It was unveiled by HM Queen Elizabeth II in October 1953.

In Green Park, London, can be found the Bomber Command memorial, which was dedicated by the Queen in June 2012. It marks the sacrifice of 55,573 aircrew who served in the Command from Britain.

The national Battle of Britain Memorial is at Capel-le-Ferne overlooking the English Channel near Folkestone in Kent.

AIRMEN DIED IN THE SECOND WORLD WAR, 1939–46

Details about airmen (both officers and other ranks) can be found in the 'Airmen Died in the Second World War, 1939–1946' dataset, which is available on both Ancestry and Findmypast. Nearly 129,000 airmen and airwomen are commemorated here. To a large extent, the information here duplicates that provided by the Commonwealth War Graves Commission, but there is often a brief description of how the individual lost their life.

ROLLS OF HONOUR

A roll of honour for men and women of the RAF who lost their lives during the war can be found at Central Church of the RAF St Clement Danes on the Strand in central London. A visit to the church can be a very moving affair. The roll records the name and rank of the deceased, together with their date of their death.

Rolls of honour for Bomber Command groups are displayed in the following cathedrals: Lincoln: 1 and 5 Groups; York Minster: 4 and 6 Groups, and those members of 7 Group who died while serving in Yorkshire; Ely: 2, 3, 8 and 100 Groups. The RAF Museum holds copies of the rolls except the one for 2 Group. The National Archives has a roll of honour for 5 Group in piece AIR 14/2091.

CASUALTY FILES

During and after the war, the RAF spent considerable time investigating crashes, both of the aircraft themselves (these records are largely at the RAF Museum) and the personnel who were flying them. The case files, known as Casualty Packs, are in series AIR 81 at Kew. At the time of writing, they are available for the period between September 1939 and the end of 1943. Later files are slowly being transferred to TNA, although it may be some years before everything is available. As well as for aircraft that crashed in Europe, there are reports on accidents that occurred in training or over the UK.

Fortunately, the records are well catalogued with the file titles including all the aircrew involved in the accident or crash, their unit and where the incident took place.

The content of each file varies greatly. You may find correspondence with the next of kin, and sometimes there may be lists of possessions returned to the family. In addition, there can be correspondence with the squadron and station where the man was based, with the civil authorities in Europe (generally the local mayor) after the war about the burial of RAF aircrew, together with exhumation and reburial forms.

Use these records for

- Finding out more about the fate of pilots and their crews in Europe and at home.
- Correspondence with the families of the deceased and the missing.

Pitfalls

- Each file varies greatly in content.
- The files for 1944 and 1945 are not yet available, but will be in due course.

BOMBER COMMAND LOSSES DATABASES

Most lists and databases of casualties essentially reproduce the information that is found on the Commonwealth War Graves Commission website. They are nice to know about but they don't really add much to a researcher's knowledge.

An exception is the International Bomber Command Centre Losses Database, which records details of over 58,000 Bomber Command deaths during the twenty-two years of its existence between 1936 and 1968. The vast majority of entries are for men who died during the Second World War, during which Bomber Command crews suffered an extremely high casualty rate: 55,573 men were killed out of a total of 125,000 aircrew (a death rate of 44 per cent). Another, 8,400 were wounded in action and nearly 10,000 became prisoners of war. In other words, a Bomber Command crew member was more likely to die than any other British serviceman during the war. The nearest comparable casualty rates were for the Army during the fighting in the six weeks or so after the Normandy landings. In addition, about a quarter of merchant seamen became casualties.[3]

The database is a genuinely impressive piece of work. It includes an ever-increasing amount of biographical information and photographs. Volunteers have cross-referenced an impressive range of sources, including the authoritative Volumes of Bomber Command Losses prepared by W.R. Chorley in the 1990s; many rolls of honour; the records of the Commonwealth War Graves Commission; Squadron Association records; and material relating to prisoners of war. There are almost 5 million individual pieces of information. In addition, there are also links to Squadron Record Books, which provide details of the aircraft that men were in on the date of their death as well as names of other crew members, and a description of the operation in which the aircraft was taking part in.

MUSEUM

The International Bomber Command Centre on the outskirts of Lincoln is well worth visiting.

Use this for

- Researching Bomber Command aircrew who were killed during the war.

BOMBER COMMAND LOSS CARDS

The RAF Museum has a set of Loss Cards. For every aircraft that failed to return from an operational flight, Bomber Command created a card. These cards were then used in order to try to identify methods that could reduce the number of losses. The data recorded on the cards normally includes the names of the crew, their fate, the route taken and bomb load. In some cases, information from survivors has also been added. In practice, these cards rarely add anything to the Bomber Command Losses Database.

There are no equivalent records for other commands.

WEBSITES

As well as the CWGC, there are several other databases listing casualties, although inevitably there is a lot of overlap with the Commission's records. The best is provided on the RAF Commands website. The Aircrews Remembered website provides photographs of graves and memorials.

As the name suggests, the excellent Dutch website WW2 Allied Aircraft Crashes in The Netherlands, North Sea & English Channel has details of nearly 2,000 aircraft that crashed on Holland, although understandably there is much less information for the hundreds of aircraft that met their fate in the seas around Britain.

Further reading

Patrick Bishop, *Air Force Blue: The RAF in World War Two – Spearhead of Victory* (Collins, 2017)

W.R. Chorley, *RAF Bomber Command Losses* (4 vols, Midland Publishing, 1992–1998)

Len Deighton, *Bomber* (Penguin, 1970) – a brilliant novel telling the story of a single mission over Germany in mid-1943 told from both the British and German sides.

N.L.R. Franks, *Fighter Command Losses* (3 vols, Midland Publishing, 1997–2000)

Max Hastings, *Bomber Command* (Michael Joseph, 1979)

Ross McNeill, *Coastal Command Losses 1939–1941* (Midland Publishing, 2003)

David Price, *The Crew: The Story of a Lancaster Bomber Crew* (Head of Zeus, 2020)

Biographical details of some 1,200 fighter aces (that is pilots who shot down five or more enemy aircraft) are given in C.F. Shores and C. Williams, *Aces High, the Fighter Aces of the British and Commonwealth Air Forces in World War Two* (2 vols, Grub Street, 1994, 1998)

Short biographies of 3,000 men who flew with Fighter Command during the Battle of Britain can be found in K. Wynn, *Men of the Battle of Britain* (2nd edn, CCB Associates, 1999)

Another book, Francis K. Mason's *Battle over Britain* (Aston Publications, 1990), also contains full details of all RAF Fighter Command flying personnel during the Battle of Britain, and their subsequent service history.

RAF PRISONERS OF WAR

Most RAF men who fell into enemy hands had survived being shot down over Germany, France or the Low Countries. Both officers and other ranks were housed in camps known as Stalag Luft because they were run by the German Air Force – the Luftwaffe. In comparison to servicemen from other countries, particularly Russians, they were reasonably well treated.

As well as the sources given in Chapter 3, there are a number of other places to look for RAF prisoners.

TNA holds an alphabetical list of British and Dominion Air Force PoWs in German hands in 1944–1945 in piece AIR 20/2336. Nominal rolls of prisoners in German camps are in AIR 40/263–281 and AIR 40/1488–1491. A roll for Changi prison in Singapore is in pieces AIR 40/1899–1906.

A substantial quantity of material concerning prisoners of war, although there aren't many lists of names, can be found in the Bomber Command papers in series AIR 14 and in the Air Ministry Intelligence Papers (AIR 40).

Reports on many individual RAF servicemen taken prisoner in occupied Europe, with the circumstances of their capture, are in AIR 14/470–471. Reports on the condition of British and Dominion prisoners in German and Japanese camps towards the end of the war are in pieces AIR 40/2361 and 2366.

A number of airmen either escaped or evaded capture. On their return to Britain they completed escape and evasion reports, which are in AIR 40/1874, or for the Far East AIR 40/2462. These reports and other material form the basis of Graham Pitchfork, *Shot Down and on the Run: The RAF and Commonwealth Aircrews Who Got Home from Behind Enemy Lines, 1940–1945* (TNA, 2003).

Further reading

Oliver Clutton-Brock, *Footprints in the Sands of Time – RAF Bomber Command Prisoners of War in Germany 1939–1945* (Grub Street, 2003) lists all RAF PoWs who served in Bomber Command.

The story of the RAF's Air Sea Rescue Service, which rescued hundreds of men stranded in the seas around Britain, is told in Graham Pitchfork, *Shot Down and in the Drink* (TNA, 2005).

RAF OPERATIONAL RECORDS

OPERATIONS RECORD BOOKS

Put simply, Operations Record Books (ORBs) record daily happenings in RAF units. They are undoubtedly the most important records – and some of the most interesting – you will come across when researching men and women who served in the RAF.

They were formally introduced in 1936, although some unofficial ORBs were kept during the First World War.

The purpose of the books was to record the history of the unit so far as was possible, so that they could be used by the official historians when writing the history of the RAF in wartime. Naturally, the intelligence officers or adjutant compiling the diary took different approaches. Some volumes, particularly bomber squadron record books, are very detailed, but entries in many smaller units may be sparse. Often, they just record visits to the unit and training courses attended by officers.

For some reason, the records generally become fuller in 1942. Inevitably, records for squadrons who flew in the Battle of Britain are sometimes scrappy – just listing when aircraft took off and landed. And sometimes records are missing entirely, for example, for units in Malta that were under continual air attack. ORBs for smaller units do not all survive.

As well as official happenings, such as visits by members of the Royal Family or the arrival of a new commanding officer, less-formal events may well be recorded, such as Christmas festivities, dances and inter-unit sporting matches.

Technically there were two parts to the ORB:

- Form 540 A daily narrative of events.
- Form 541 Details of work carried out.

Form 540s are probably the best place to start as they provide a summary of the day's events. For most units and RAF stations this might take the form of a monthly summary recording key events, from visits by senior officers to station dances and the arrival and departure of members on training courses. ORBs for the larger and more important RAF stations might include brief reports from the heads of each of the trades based there, such as the aircraft engineers, meteorologists and air traffic control.

Form 540s of squadron record books tend to be more detailed. There may be amusing incidents and mild grumbling. Most squadron messes were close-knit communities of young men. But death was ever present, therefore it is not surprising that ORBs record the loss of aircrew. Normally there is just a note that an aircraft was missing. Occasionally, there is an eyewitness account describing how an aircraft had been observed in flames over Germany or France. When Flight Officer Edgar Innes-Jones failed to return from a nuisance raid over France on 13 July 1942, the war diary for 602 Squadron – a fighter squadron – noted: 'Six aircraft to patrol and search the Channel…but could not find him.'[4]

A few days later, when the squadron transferred from RAF Redhill, near London, to RAF Peterhead in Aberdeenshire, the pilots flew up. However, this option was not available to everybody. The Squadron Record Book noted that:

> The ground party consisting of 3 officers and 129 men boarded a special train at 1625. After slowly wending its way round London, via Barnes Bridge, it finally got a move on, stopping at Peterborough at 2110 for tea. Coaches were then attached to ordinary [train] to Edinburgh arriving at 0620 for more tea…arriving at Peterhead at 1320 hours. Even the Scotsmen from Glasgow found this too far north in the wilds for their liking. On arrival at Peterhead the usual muddle ensued.[5]

Generally, the **Form 541s** only survive for squadrons, where they summarise flights undertaken by individual aircraft (and their crews). If it was a routine patrol there might be nothing other than the time the plane took off and when it landed plus a few words describing the reason for the flight.

R.A.F. Form 540 — OPERATIONS RECORD BOOK — Page No. 1

See instructions for use of this form in K.R. and A.C.I., para. 2349, and War Manual, Pt. II., chapter XX., and notes in R.A.F. Pocket Book.

of (Unit or Formation) 602 SQUADRON — No. of pages used for day

Place	Date	Time	Summary of Events	References to Appendices
Redhill	1.7.42		2 more ground crew proceeded to Kenley by road. 2 Czech and 1 Polish Squadron arrived at Redhill, the latter taking over 602 Dispersal. Practise flying only.	
	2.7.42		Red Section scramble to Beachy Head took off 1935 hrs - landed 2105 hrs. Blue section patrol off Hastings took off 2040 hrs - landed 2145 hrs. Green Section took off 2110 hrs - landed 2240 hrs. Scramble of Hastings at 25,000'.	
	3.7.42		One M.T. driver (Echelon Waaf) proceeded to Kenley.	
	4.7.42		Black Section took off 0510 -landed 0650 hrs on convoy patrol off Hastings. Green Section on same patrol took off 0510 hrs - landed Friston 0735. Took off Friston 1145 - landed Kenley 1200 hrs. Sgt Lethbridge and F/Lt Bocock took off 0750 hrs and landed 0800 hrs. F/Lt Fifield and F/Lt Niven on Convoy Patrol due south of Shoreham took off 1840 - landed 2035 hrs.	
	5.7.42		Sgt Strudwick and P/O. Sampson patrolled Beachy Head - took off 1645 hrs and landed 1820 hrs. P/O. De-la-Poype and P/O Rippon patrolled Hastings at 25,000' took off 2100 hrs and landed 2210 hrs. Sgt Sanderson and Sgt Francis took off 2150 and landed 2310 on same patrol.	
	6.7.42		F/Lt Fifield and Sgt Francis took off on a patrol at 0950 hrs - landed 1030. 2 sections of 2 aircraft each took off on a Roadstead Anti-flak. Blue took off 1300 hrs - landed 1435 hrs. Green took off 1355 hrs - landed 1545 hrs.	
	7.7.42		6 aircraft took off on a Roadstead, Anti-flak at 0720 hrs. 3 aircraft landed at 0835, 2 aircraft landed 0840 and 1 at [illegible], Kenley 0900. Blue and Green sections scramble to Shoreham took off at 1355 hrs - landed 1450 hrs. Black and Red sections scramble to Shoreham took off 1405 hrs - landed 1425 hrs.	
	8.7.42		At 1100 hrs all the pilots and aircraft flew back to Redhill. All the ground staff returned by road by 1600 hrs. All very pleased to be back.	
	9.7.42		Practise flying only.	
	10.7.42		Released - rained all day.	
	11.7.42		Security patrols, Beachy Head from 0830 to 1155 - relays of two aircraft. At 1410 hrs P/O De-la-Poype and Sgt Strudwick proceeded 20 miles off Le Crotoy on "Rhubarb" where it became cloudless so returned to base, landing 1450 hrs.	

The Form 540 in the Squadron Records Book for 602 Squadron for 12–17 July 1942. TNA AIR 27/2076/13

The most detailed entries are almost always for bomber squadrons. They often seem to be summaries of interviews with aircrews by the squadron intelligence officer immediately on their return home. After bombing Düsseldorf during the evening of 2 November 1944, Flight Officer S.J. Sisson, of 166 Squadron, and his aircrew reported: 'Bombed at 16.16½ hours from 18,000 feet on centre of red T/Is [target indicators] burning on ground, markers were well placed and bombing well concentrated across them. Fires were seen for over 70 miles on the return to base.'[6]

On the evening of 5 June 1944, the Form 541 for 620 Squadron recorded the time that individual planes took off between 2330 and 2345 hours, returning between 0250 and 0520, to drop parachutists in preparation for the D-Day landings. In addition, for each aircraft (with its call letters), members of crew are listed with their rank and service numbers. The three aircraft that did not return are noted as being missing.

In this case the Form 540, however, provides more details:

Date	Aircraft Type & Number	Crew	Duty	Time Up	Time Down	Details of Sortie or Flight	References.
13-7-42	BM.325	P/O.R.W.Sampson	Patrol	1415	1525	- Newhaven. Flew sea level for 18 minutes and then climbed to Abbeville aerodrome, reading 17,000'. On way out some FW 190s were seen. 602 squadron turned to assist another sqmadron but no pilots fired. F/Lt Bocock, leading, saw 25 enemy aircraft waiting above and avoiding the trap turned for home. F/O.Innes-Jones did not turn up at base and nothing further has been seen or heard. 11 aircraft landed at 1525 hrs.	
	EP.280	SGt. E.H.Francis	"	1415	1525		
	EP.113	F/O.E.D.Rippon	"	1415	1525		
	EP.110	F/Lt.E.P.W.Bocock	"	1415	1525		
	BM.157	Sgt.W.U.Lethbridge	"	1415	1525		
	BM.182	F/O.E.Innes-Jones	"	1415	-----		
	BL.575	P/O.P.D.Davey	"	1415	1525		
	BM.136	P/O.R.P.R.De-la-Poype	"	1415	1525		
	BM.128	Sgt.N.T.Whitmore	"	1415	1525		
	BM.402	F/Lt E.P.Bocock	"	1715	1825	At 1715 hours 6 aircraft took off to patrol and search the channel for F/O.Innes-Jones - landed 1825, but could not find him.	
	BM.157	Sgt.W.U.Lethbridge	"	1715	1825		
	BM.136	P/O.De-la-Poype	"	1715	1825		
	BM.128	Sgt.N.T.Whitmore	"	1715	1825		
	BM.204	F/Lt.J.B.Niven	"	1715	1825		
	BM.355	F/O.E.D.Rippon	"	1715	1825		

The Form 541 in the Squadron Records Book for 602 Squadron for 13 July 1942. (TNA AIR 27/2076/14)

> Twenty-three Stirlings were detailed for operations over the Caen area, and successfully dropped elements of the 6th Airborne Division and their equipment. The weather on the outward trip was excellent, with full moon shining above 8/10th cloud. Visibility over the target area was also good, and no low cloud was encountered. Enemy opposition consisted of moderate light AA fire, and no enemy aircraft were seen. The airborne troops were successfully dropped in an area clearly indicated by lights. Three aircraft captained by S/L W R Pettit OBE, DFC. F/O L N Causkey and F/S Barton failed to return to base from this operation. The remainder carried out their missions as detailed. Four aircraft were slightly damaged by light AA fire.[7]

Record Books are now found in bound volumes with rather attractive covers in RAF blue. There may be one or more volumes each year for squadrons, commands and groups. However, for smaller units, half-a-dozen or more books may be bound in a single volume.

Originally, there seems to have been appendices, containing orders, intelligence summaries, maps and photographs. They have largely been destroyed but occasionally they survive bound with the Form 540s and Form 541s. The position is reversed, however, for groups and especially commands, where there are full appendices with only minimal narratives.

Using the records

Operations Record Books are held by TNA in the following series: Commands AIR 24, Groups AIR 25, Wings AIR 26, Squadrons AIR 27, Stations AIR 28, Units AIR 29.

Squadron Record Books (AIR 27) for the period of the war can be downloaded from TNA's website. This is a bit cumbersome as you have to download both the Form 540 and the Form 541 for each month. That is up to twenty-four downloads for a whole year. Fortunately, downloads are free.

Squadron Record Books are also available to view on Ancestry and The Genealogist. If you already have a subscription, it may be easier to use their sets as you can go through complete years. In addition, Ancestry has indexed the volumes for 1940 by name so you can search by individual aircrew. There are, for example, eighty-eight entries for Finucane; most if not all are for 'Paddy' the air ace. It might, however, be more difficult to identify men with common names.

Occasionally, transcripts of ORBs can be found online, so it may be worth doing a Google search.

Use these records for

- Gaining an understanding of what your ancestor experienced or witnessed during their service in the RAF.
- There may well be additional information about the loss of aircrew either on missions or in accidents to that found on the Commonwealth War Graves Commission website.
- Researching the service of individual aircraft.

Pitfalls

- Groundcrew are never mentioned.
- Some ORBs from small units and stations do not survive.
- They are not always very informative.

Further reading

TNA Research Guide: 'Tracing the life of a Unit: Operations Record Books'.
J. Foreman, *Fighter Command War Diaries, 1939–1945* (5 vols, Air Research Publications, 1996–2004)
M. Middlebrook and C. Everitt, *The Bomber Command War Diaries* (Viking, 1985)

Summaries of squadron histories are also given in:

P. Moyes, *Bomber Squadrons of the RAF and their Aircraft* (Macdonald, 1976)
J. Rawlings, *Fighter Squadrons of the RAF and their Aircraft* (Crecy Books, 1993)
J. Rawlings, *Coastal, Support and Special Squadrons of the RAF and their Aircraft* (Jane's, 1982)

The key reference guide remains Ken Delve, *The Source Book of the RAF* (Airlife, 1994)

COMBAT REPORTS

Combat reports were compiled by pilots after shooting down an enemy aircraft. They are a simple form containing the pilot's description of the action and where and when it took place.

Not all combat reports survive. Where they do, several pilots may claim that they shot down a particular aircraft, so they should not always be taken as definite proof of a man's skill or heroism.

The reports are largely to be found in series AIR 50 at TNA, and can be downloaded from its website. They are only for combats over Britain and North West Europe. No others are known to exist. Ancestry also has a collection, although it is only for the period of the war to May 1941.

PLANNING AND ANALYSIS

The strategic conduct of the war was divided between the Air Ministry and various RAF commands, of which Bomber Command was the best known. The records are largely at TNA.

Material is sparsest for the first two years of the war, but by mid-1944 there is a multitude of reports and files on almost every aspect of the war

264 Squadron 28.8.1940.

At 0835 hours 12 machines of 264 Squadron were ordered to take off from Rochford and patrol Dover at 1200 feet. At 15,000 feet over Dover 20 He.111s were sighted heading due North over Dover. Red, Yellow and Blue Sections attacked from the port side.

As soon as the attack had developed, the Squadron were set on by 25 Me.109s, which appeared from all directions. The majority of the Me.109s had bright yellow cowlings.

Owing to the Me.109s attack, the Squadron was only able to deliver one attack on the He.111s. Evasive action became necessary and Squadron returned to base. The escort of Me.109s, which was very large, was being engaged by Spitfires and Hurricanes.

The following enemy casualties are claimed:

P/O Carnaby) P/O.Ellery)- Red 2)	1 He.111 destroyed. Machine seen to start breaking up in the air.
Sgt.Lauder) Sgt.Chapman) Blue 3	1 He.111 damaged. Pieces seen to come off and 1 engine cowling.

A combat report for 264 Squadron for 28 August 1940. (TNA AIR 50/104/192)

in the air. TNA's online catalogue offers a fairly painless way to find papers on a certain operation, raid or technical development. Researchers should be warned that the titles of the files found in the catalogue may have only a tangential relation to the actual subject of the file itself. This is the legacy of the hurried transfer of files to the archives in the early 1970s. Many file titles only use operation code names, such as Husky for the invasion of Sicily in 1943, and abbreviations, like H2S for an airborne radar system.

Series AIR 41 contains historical studies prepared by the Air Historical Branch after the war and may be a good place to start if you are looking at 'the big picture'. They cover most of the campaigns and theatres of the Second World War with the exceptions of the strategic air offensive and the Atlantic. British air defence and the Middle East campaign are described extensively.

The most useful Air Ministry series are:

- AIR 2 Air Ministry Registered Correspondence
- AIR 8 Papers of the Chief of Air Staff
- AIR 19 Private Office Papers, Secretary of State for Air
- AIR 20 Air Ministry Unregistered Correspondence
- AIR 34 Central Interpretation Unit (reconnaissance photographs)
- AIR 37 Allied Expeditionary Air Force (north-west Europe 1944–1945)
- AIR 40 Directorate of Intelligence

The papers of commands are divided thus:

- AIR 13 Balloon Command
- AIR 14 Bomber Command
- AIR 15 Coastal Command
- AIR 16 Fighter Command
- AIR 17 Maintenance Command
- AIR 23 Overseas Commands (largely those outside north-west Europe)
- AIR 32 Training Command
- AIR 38 Ferry and Transport Command
- AIR 39 Army Co-operation Command

A basic research strategy is given in the TNA Research Guide 'Royal Air Force Operations'.

COURTS MARTIAL

The RAF was, in general, a pretty disciplined service, although inevitably there were cases of bad behaviour, petty crime, and ill discipline. Where this was serious, the accused would appear before a court martial. When a court martial was summoned, there may be a brief account in the appropriate operations record book, listing the accused, his offence and the names of the officers on the panel.

AIR HISTORICAL BRANCH

Any serious researcher into RAF history may need to contact the Air Historical Branch (RAF) at some stage of their studies. The Branch is a small department within the Ministry of Defence that works to preserve the historical memory of the RAF and to provide the public with a better understanding of RAF and air power history. The Branch has a large archive that holds classified policy and operational documents. An index of RAF casualties from 1939 onwards, aircraft accident record cards dating from as early as the inter-war years, and a photographic archive are all also maintained as part of the Branch.

The Judge Advocate General's Courts Martial Registers are in AIR 21. These give the name and rank of each prisoner, place of trial, nature of charge and sentence. The proceedings of district, general and field courts martial of officers and men of the RAF from 1941 are in AIR 18. Petitions to the sovereign in court martial cases are in AIR 30.

No records are online, although names of officers dismissed from the service might be found on the *London Gazette* website and in the *Air Force List*.

AUXILIARY AIR FORCE AND RAF VOLUNTEER RESERVE

In common with the army and the Royal Navy, the RAF had its own units of part-time airmen, known as the Auxiliary Air Force (AAF) and the RAF Volunteer Reserve (RAFVR).

By September 1939 the Auxiliary Air Force was well equipped, including aircraft such as Hurricanes and Spitfires, as well as forty-seven balloon squadrons and a total of twenty flying squadrons. The AAF quickly earned itself a reputation for both glamour and danger, thanks to the likes of Sir Douglas Douglas-Hamilton and Flight Lieutenant Pat Gifford, who provide an idea of the type of volunteers the service attracted, largely from wealthy families.

In August and September 1939 and throughout the war, the AAF was embodied within the RAF. The AAF squadrons were essential support in some of the war's largest air battles. In the Fighter Command for the Battle of Britain, the AAF comprised fourteen of the sixty-two squadrons, a significant number. These additional teams actually produced almost a third of all recorded enemy 'kills' of aircraft.

The RAF Volunteer Reserve was formed in July 1936 to provide a reserve of aircrew to draw upon in the event of war. Initially, the RAFVR was composed of civilians recruited from neighbourhood reserve flying schools. When the Second World War broke out in September 1939, the RAFVR comprised 6,646 pilots, 1,625 observers and 1,946 wireless operators. During the war, the Air Ministry used the RAFVR as the principal means of entry for aircrew to serve with the RAF as the men were only enlisted for the duration of the war.

THE RECORDS

For all practical purposes, the records for personnel and the auxiliary units they served with are identical.

RAF STATIONS AND AIRFIELDS

During the war, hundreds of airfields large and small were built across Great Britain. Most were constructed to house aircraft and the facilities needed to maintain them for the Bomber offensive on Germany or for units in Fighter and Coastal commands. Particularly in eastern England, they were largely used by the Americans and Canadians, although technically they remained under RAF control. No more than dozen are still in use by the RAF. The majority have become light industrial estates or have returned to agricultural use, although some remain as airfields catering for light aircraft.

Detailed information about many former airfields, including photographs and lists of units stationed there, can be found on the excellent Airfields of Britain Conservation Trust website. Wikipedia also describes individual RAF stations in some detail.

There may also be published histories of individual airfields and bases or websites devoted to them, particularly for the larger and more important places.

It is possible to build up a history of individual airfields, and RAF stations, from Station Record Books in series AIR 28, together with the Operation Record Books for squadrons and other units based at the airfield. It is much more difficult to find anything about the construction of airfields. Despite the fact that hundreds were built, almost no records appear to survive about their construction.

Further reading

C.G. Jefford, *RAF Squadrons* (Airlife, 1988) records the airfields and aircraft used by individual squadrons, and also includes maps indicating the locations of major airfields where these units have been based.

General histories for many airfields and bases are given in a series of books from Amberley Press and Countryside Books.

Former RAF stations occasionally house museums devoted to their history. Local museums may also have displays about life on airfields in their area.

RAF AIRCRAFT

There are huge numbers of books and websites devoted to aircraft design, construction and the flights they made, particularly for the famous planes ('warbirds' in the jargon) such as the Lancaster, Mosquito and Spitfire. The most correspondence we received when I was editor of *Family History Monthly* was when I wrongly captioned a photograph of a Westland Whirlwind, one of the more obscure aircraft flown by the RAF during the war. One reader even sent in a complete history of the individual aircraft and listed those who had flown it. There are some very knowledgable people out there!

Warbird Registry is a useful general website giving aircraft specifications and the locations of any surviving machines.

AIRCRAFT MOVEMENTS AND CODES

RAF units can often be linked to the individual aircraft they were allocated to, along with information on the causes of any accidents the aircraft may have been involved in. Operation Record Books can tell you more about the sorties a plane flew.

For each aircraft within the RAF, an Aircraft Movement Card (Air Ministry Form 78) was created, which kept a record of the units the aeroplane was allocated to and noting when it was damaged and repaired. The surviving cards are kept by the Air Historical Branch, but the RAF Museum has copies on microfilm and can supply prints for a fee. Most cards are detailed, but for certain aircraft sent to areas such as the Middle and Far East the records are limited. These cards instead record the basic information of the aircraft's arrival to its destination and no more.

M.J.F. Bowyer and J.D.R. Rawlings, *Squadron Codes 1937–56* (Patrick Stephens, 1979) gives the two-letter codes used by each squadron, flight or other unit to identify its aircraft. Codes are also listed in Ken Delve's *Source Book of the RAF* and on Wikipedia.

Bomber Command History is an excellent website with much about individual aircraft of all kinds.

AIRCRAFT CRASHES IN THE UK

English Heritage estimates that more than 10,000 aircraft from both the Allied and Axis sides crashed in Great Britain and Northern Ireland during the war. RAF Bomber Command alone lost 1,380 aircraft within the UK and nearly 4,000 aircraft in non-operational accidents. The Luftwaffe is known to have lost 1,500 aircraft in and around the UK.

The main source of information for determining crash site locations and basic data are found in contemporary records, although the quality of this information is variable. In general, very little remains of these sites. During the war itself, where possible, crashed aircraft were quickly removed for salvage. Since the war, archaeologists and souvenir hunters have excavated many other wrecks.[8]

Air Ministry Form 1180 was used throughout inter-war period, the Second World War and the post-war period to record RAF aircraft accidents. These forms are available on microfilm at the RAF museum, sorted by type and date, often providing further information about the aircrew. To trace a specific accident, it is essential to know the date and the aircraft type – there are no indexes for location, unit or crew names.

Details of missing aircraft and aircrew are often listed in the squadron and unit record books.

Information on individual crashes was also recorded locally by civil defence and the police and is usually held in local archives. Newspapers can also be a good source of information, but in wartime were subject to heavy censorship. For fatal crashes involving British or Commonwealth aircrew, the registers of the Commonwealth War Graves Commission are also particularly useful.

Further reading

Details of air crashes in the north-east of England are available on the North East Aviation Research website. There are several other websites, but none that cover a whole region.

WOMEN'S AUXILIARY AIR FORCE

The Women's Auxiliary Air Force (WAAF) was formed in June 1939 to take over some of the duties previously carried out by men. Their most famous roles were as plotters in operational control rooms directing aircraft during the Battle of Britain. Numbers grew from about 1,700 members at the outbreak of war to approximately 180,000 by 1943. Service records can be accessed in exactly the same way as those for their male colleagues. WAAF activities are recorded in the appropriate ORB in AIR 28 (for stations) or AIR 29 (units).

The WAAF Association's website has a comprehensive bibliography and other information about the force.

Further reading

Beryl E. Escott, *The WAAF* (Shire Publications, 2003)
Beryl E. Escott, *Women in Air Force Blue: The story of women in the RAF from 1918 to the present day* (Stephens, 1989)

AIR TRANSPORT AUXILIARY

The Air Transport Auxiliary (ATA) was a most unusual body consisting of civilian pilots who ferried aircraft from factories to the squadrons where they were needed. What's more, many members of the ATA were women, which, inevitably, led to complaints.

The view taken by C.G. Grey, editor of *Aeroplane*, was typical of the sentiment of the time:

> We quite agree ... that there are millions of women in the country who could do useful jobs in war. But the trouble is that so many of them insist on wanting to do jobs which they are quite incapable of doing. The menace is the woman who thinks that she ought to be flying in a high-speed bomber when she really has not the intelligence to scrub the floor of a hospital properly, or who wants to nose around as an Air Raid Warden and yet can't cook her husband's dinner. There are men like that so there is no need to charge us with anti-feminism. One of the most difficult types of man with whom one has to deal is that which has a certain amount of ability, too much self-confidence, an overload of conceit, a dislike of taking orders and not enough experience to balance one against the other by his own will. The combination is perhaps more common amongst women than men. And it is one of the commonest causes of crashes, in aeroplanes and other ways.[9]

By the early part of 1940, there were twenty-six women pilots. The women's Ferry Pool at Hamble delivered Spitfires from many differrent factories, along with two- and four-engine aircraft, throughout the war. By September 1941, the ATA pilots were ferrying all types of operational aircraft. By the time war was over, they had delivered 200 different types of aircraft, 309,011 in total.

The ATA was comprised of 1,152 men (including two of my cousins) and 600 women, including 166 pilots and flight engineers, during the war years. Women pilots performed exactly the same duties as their male counterparts, but were not given equal pay and rights until late 1943.

Personnel records for pilots and flight engineers, including some log-books, are at the RAF Museum. They are available to next of kin only. Other ATA records are to be found in series AVIA 27 at TNA.

A large collection of material relating to the ATA is at the Maidenhead Heritage Centre. It includes over 140 logbooks of ATA pilots, together with various diaries and memoirs of personnel. In particular, the museum holds a complete list of all ATA employees. It reveals that my cousin, Dennis Percy Lead, was a pilot first officer with the unit between March 1942 and July 1945.

Further reading

Diana Barnato Walker, *Spreading My Wings* (Grub Street, 2003)

ATA Museum Collections: https://atamuseum.org/collection

6

THE ROYAL NAVY

SERVICE RECORDS

OFFICERS

Service records for the vast majority of commissioned officers who served with the Royal Navy during the war are still with the Ministry of Defence, but will be transferred to TNA by the end of the decade.

Some records for officers who were born before 1900 – that is, they would have had to have been in their forties to serve during the Second World War – are at Kew in series ADM 340. Pieces 1–150 – mainly for the First World War – are fully indexed and can be downloaded via the Discovery Catalogue. But, the later cards, at least at the time of writing, are not indexed to the same degree, nor are they downloadable.

NAVY LISTS

If you are researching naval officers, including the nursing and women's services and the reserves, then a key source is the published Navy Lists, which provide basic details about an individual's carer. However, they do not include petty officers or ordinary ratings.

Career details include officers' surnames, forenames (in some cases initials only) rank, seniority, branch and specialisation, decorations and post-nominals, language qualifications and the ship or establishment that the officer was serving in at the time of every annual publication. They also list officers on board individual ships or at shore establishments.

A similar publication, 'The Navy List of Retired Officers Together with Emergency List Officers', provides information on commissioned officers who were no longer in service but remained alive in the year of publication, and on those who had passed away since the previous edition.

Copies of the List are available on the shelves in the reading rooms at TNA and the Caird Library at the National Maritime Museum. Most issues for the Second World War are also available online at the Internet Archive. You need to search for 'Navy List' and click on the volume you are interested in. Then do a key word search. Officers are normally only identified by surname and initials. There may be several entries for each individual.

It is also worth looking at the confidential Navy Lists, which contain additional information that might be of value to the enemy. They indicate where individual officers were serving, with the names of ships and establishments. A complete list of all ships in the Royal Navy is included, together with details of tonnage and armament. They are in series ADM 177. They can be downloaded via TNA's Discovery Catalogue.

OTHER RANKS (RATINGS)

The Royal Navy has no service records for petty officers or ratings for the period of the Second World War, which is most odd considering how useful they could have been to the bureaucracy at the time (and to genealogists today).

The main record of service is the Certificate of Service (form S 459) which records name, next of kin, postings, rating, etc., and provides a potted account of each member's entire service. The original document was handed over to the individual on their discharge from the navy. There is no duplicate on file. You may also find a Trade Certificate (S 1246F) and or a Discharge Certificate (S 542).

If you don't have the S 459 and you apply for your father's or grandmother's records, you will just be sent a list of ships (including shore stations) that they had served on with the dates they were there. The record is compiled from pay and victualling books, still in the care of the Ministry of Defence, which list the personnel on each ship and the ships in which they had served previously and where they were posted at the end of each commission (that is, when the ship was paid off at the end of the voyage).

For the foreseeable future these records can still be obtained from the Ministry of Defence. Presumably, the muster books will be transferred to TNA.

A few records for ratings and petty officers who had enlisted before 1928, and were still serving during the Second World War, are already at TNA. They can be downloaded from its website via the Discovery Catalogue.

NAVAL RESERVES

Unlike in the other services, the several naval reserve forces were not fully absorbed into the Royal Navy and maintained something of a separate nature. There were two reserves: the Royal Naval Reserve and the Royal Navy Volunteer Reserve. Lieutenant Commander Thomas Shaw, who served in the Royal Naval Reserve during the Second World War and afterward, gave a useful summary of the perceived distinctions between these services. Writing to the Ministry of Defence in 2013 he noted that:

> There were three classes of naval officer then. The regular Royal Navy (RN) whose officers wore straight gold stripes with a plain curl on their cuffs; Royal Naval Reserve (RNR) officers, all Merchant Navy officers who wore two thin gold stripes intertwined with the corresponding curl above; and Royal Volunteer Reserve officers (RNVR) who wore a thin gold wavy stripe. The latter were mostly from civil occupations who had been granted Commissions … The RN was still class conscious then and looked with disdain on the RNR, but tolerated the RNVR, as most, if not all, of the latter were then considered to be 'gentlemen' at least. There was a popular saying then: RN – gentlemen and seamen; RNR – seamen but not gentlemen; RNVR – gentlemen trying to be seamen. I am afraid this feeling prevailed then and the RNR was not without fault as well, looking on the RNVR as bloody amateurs. The war proved otherwise and as time went on respect began to develop for each other's qualities and acceptance of each other as equal.[1]

THE ROYAL NAVAL RESERVE (RNR)

The RNR was made up of men and officers from the Merchant Navy; as a result, many of the records are to be found in the Board of Trade (BT) series of records at TNA.

Service records for men who served in the RNR are on microfilm in piece BT 377/77 at TNA. The records are arranged in service number order and indexed on TNA's Discovery Catalogue.

An important section of the Reserve was the Royal Naval Patrol Service (sometimes nicknamed 'Harry Tate's Navy') recruited largely from fishermen who manned small naval vessels such as minesweepers. They served in all theatres of operations. Their story is told on the Harry Tate's and the Royal Naval Patrol Service websites.

MUSEUM

There's a fascinating small museum, the Lowestoft War Memorial Museum, devoted to the Patrol Service at Sparrow's Nest. Sparrow's Nest was officially the shore establishment HMS *Europa* and the service's headquarters during the war.

Sparrow's Nest
Whapload Road
Lowestoft
NR31 1XG

THE ROYAL NAVAL VOLUNTEER RESERVE (RNVR)

The RNVR included men from all walks of life, who trained with the navy at weekends in peacetime. During the war, the majority of officers who joined the Royal Navy were granted temporary commissions in the Reserve. By 1945 there were 43,805 officers in the RNVR who were primarily assigned to anti-submarine warfare/convoy escort, amphibious warfare and the Coastal Forces division. These areas of the naval service were most suitable for employing temporary officers, who could be quickly trained in specific areas of expertise. There were also various branches for specialists, including chaplains, accountants and engineers.

Medals

The system of the awards of medals both for campaign medals and gallantry honours and awards is discussed in Chapter 3. Captain's reports and courts of enquiry investigating incidents, such as enemy attacks on individual ships, often include lists of men recommended for a gallantry award. They are generally found in series ADM 1, ADM 116 and ADM 199. However, the indexing is very poor and you will need to have a good idea why an individual received a medal and when this occurred.

Casualties

Casualties are recorded by the Commonwealth War Graves Commission in exactly the same way as for the other services (see Chapter 3). Most men who served at sea have no known grave and are commemorated on memorials at Chatham, Plymouth and Portsmouth.

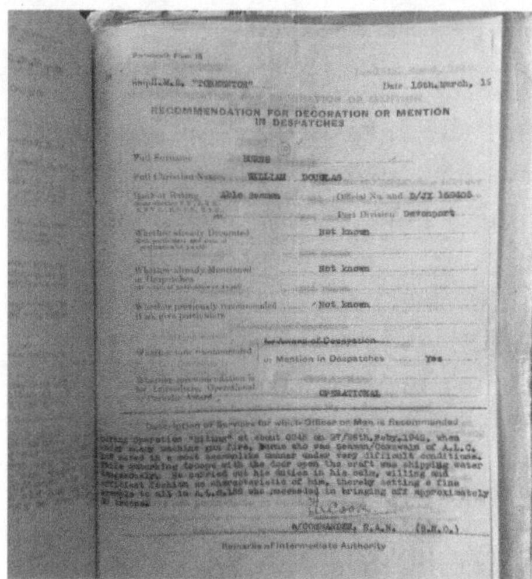

Date 10th March, 1[illegible]

RECOMMENDATION FOR DECORATION OR MENTION IN DESPATCHES

Full Surname: BURNS

Full Christian Names: WILLIAM DOUGLAS

Rank or Rating: Able Seaman

Official No. and D/JX 159405

Port Division: Devonport

Whether already Decorated: Not known

Whether already Mentioned in Despatches: Not known

Whether previously recommended: Not known

or Mention in Despatches: Yes

OPERATIONAL

Description of Services for which Officer or Man is Recommended

[illegible]

A/COMMANDER, R.A.N. (R.N.O.)

Remarks of Intermediate Authority

Recommendation for a decoration or Mention in Despatches for William Douglas Burns, HMS *Forester*, for his work ferrying Commandos on shore during the Bruneval Raid. (TNA ADM 1/29468)

After 1945, the memorials to the missing of the 1914–18 war were extended to include the names for those men who had no known grave as a result of the war. As well as sailors from the First World War, the Naval Memorial at Chatham now also commemorates 10,098 sailors of the Second World War. The one in Portsmouth marks the passing of almost 15,000 men. That in Plymouth records the loss of 15,933 men. It also commemorates sailors from many Commonwealth countries.

Lists of casualties arranged by surname and by date can be found on the Naval History Net. Brief details of the individual, the ship they were on and the cause of death, such as MPK (missing presumed killed), are given. They nicely complement entries on the Commonwealth War Graves Commission website. The information is based on two typescript lists at the Imperial War Museum: 'Names of Officers who Died during the Period beginning 3rd September 1939 and ending 30th June 1948' and the 'Register of Deaths (Naval Ratings) 3rd September 1939 to 30th June 1948'. A set is also held by the library of the National Museum of the Royal Navy in Portsmouth. More information can be found in the detailed histories of individual ships also found on the Naval History Net website.

Reports of deaths, other than that from enemy action, of individuals are to be found in series ADM 104/105–107, 127–139 (ratings only) arranged by ship at TNA. Again, details of service number, ship, and place and date of birth and death (and its cause) are given.

A list of RNR officers killed or wounded during the war is in BT 164/23. Details of RNR and RNVR medical officers who were killed between 1939 and 1946 are in ADM 261/1.

Casualty records

Surviving records of the Admiralty Casualty Branch are in series ADM 358. The files contain internal correspondence and letters with the next of kin. They can be searched by name or by ship through the Discovery Catalogue, although the files themselves are not online. However, only a selection of files appears to have survived. For example, there are papers for only one Fowler, out of the twenty-nine men with the surname who died while serving in the Royal Navy during the war.

Surgeons' journals, compiled by doctors on board ships and some at hospitals, can be found in ADM 101. These journals contain accounts covering the treatment of medical and surgical cases, and often a copy of the daily sick list, statistical abstracts of the incidence of diseases, and general reporting on the overall health and activity of those on the ship.They are arranged by ship or shore station. However, for data protection reasons, the vast majority have not yet been released to the public. ADM 261/1 also includes reports of medical treatment to survivors of RN ships either sunk or badly damaged by enemy action.

Further reading

Stephen Howarth, *The Royal Navy's Reserves in War and Peace 1903–2003* (Leo Cooper, 2003)

Brian Lavery, *In Which They Served: The Royal Navy Officer Experience in the Second World War* (Conway, 2008)

Glyn Prysor, *Citizen Sailors: The Royal Navy in the Second World War* (Penguin, 2012)

The Naval History Net has much about the Royal Navy in the Second World War.

OPERATIONS RECORDS

Operation records can be found in three series of records at TNA. The most important of these is series ADM 199, which contains material relating to various naval activities from convoys to captain's reports on damage done to individual ships. Also of use are two more general series of records: ADM 1 and ADM 116, which has more secret and important papers. In practice there seems to be no hard and fast rule about which

NATIONAL MUSEUM OF THE ROYAL NAVY

The **National Museum of the Royal Navy** is a confederation of half a dozen historic ships and museums scattered across England. The largest museum is located in Portsmouth Historic Dockyard. It has a superb collection of material relating to the Second World War.

Portsmouth Historic Dockyard
HM Naval Base (PP66)
HM Naval Base, Portsmouth
PO1 3NH

The extensive archives are largely held at the main museum in Portsmouth Historic Dockyards. An increasing proportion of the collections – mainly artefacts – have been scanned and can be viewed on the museum's website. There is also a library catalogue.

There is restricted physical access to the collections. If you would like to view the items in person, the research rooms are open as follows:

Storehouse 12, Portsmouth Historic Dockyard – Fridays.
Cobham Hall at the Fleet Air Arm Museum, RNAS Yeovilton, Ilchester – second & fourth Thursday of the month.

Booking must be made and confirmed at least one week in advance. Please include your preferred dates, though specific slots cannot be guaranteed.

A recent innovative move is that the museum offers introductory virtual reading room appointments, allowing you to discuss your research needs with a member of staff. These are chargeable at £20 for an appointment over Zoom for up to forty minutes.

More about the museum and its collections can be found at www.nmrn.org.uk

records are to be found where, although it is best to start by going through ADM 199. Fortunately, TNA online catalogue makes searching much simpler than was once the case. It now includes detailed indexes to a number of records including details of convoys, and the ships that sailed in them.

More information can be found in the TNA Research Guide: 'Royal Navy: Operational Records: Second World War, 1939–1945'. The U-boat Net website has many pages devoted to the role of the RN in the North Atlantic. Another invaluable source is the Naval History Net, although it is not terribly well organised.

RECORDS OF SHIPS

The best place to start researching naval ships is through Wikipedia, which has entries for many ships, although they are often short. There are also detailed histories for almost a thousand Royal Navy ships, with some for Canadian and Australian naval vessels and a few from Allied navies, on the Naval History Net.

Surviving ships' logs are in ADM 53, although those for ships smaller than cruisers do not appear to have survived, apart from for the early months of the war. It's easy to find out which logs have survived by typing the name of the vessel into TNA's online catalogue. They are basically nothing more than navigational and weather records and rarely include other details.

Ship's movements can be traced in a series of lists: the most useful are the Pink Lists in ADM 187. The others are Blue Lists (ADM 209), Red Lists (ADM 208), and the Green Lists (ADM 210).

Captain's letters and reports of proceedings contain information relating to the activities of naval vessels in the form of letters from the commanding officer (Captain's Letters) or Reports of Proceedings (R of P), submitted to the Admiralty. These are probably the most informative source if you are researching a particular incident. Unfortunately, they are not found together in a single source, but are scattered through ADM 199 (and to a lesser extent ADM I and ADM 116). You may find them arranged by ship or by operation or convoy.

A court martial to investigate the cause and make recommendations about preventing similar incidents in the future was held after the loss of a ship, and these records are for the most part in ADM 1.

The Caird Library, at the National Maritime Museum, has a large collection relating to the retreat from Dunkirk in 1940. In particular, it has 'The Dunkirk List (Dunkirk Withdrawal: Operation Dynamo

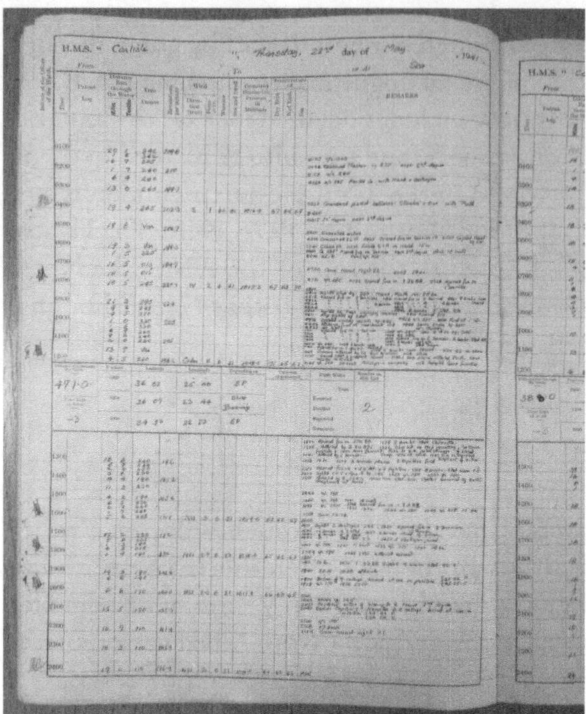

A page from the ship's log for HMS *Carlisle*, 22 May 1941. (TNA ADM 53/113833)

May 26–June 4, 1940: Alphabetical List of Vessels Taking Part, With Their Services)', which was compiled by Lieutenant Colonel G.P. Orde immediately after the evacuation, using all available sources, official and private, including numerous interviews with survivors.[2] Details of ships that were present during the evacuation can also be found on the Association of Dunkirk Little Ships' website.

CONVOYS

Perhaps the most important role of the Royal Navy during the war was to protect convoys made up of parties of merchant ships crossing the Atlantic. The supplies and Allied servicemen transported in these ships were vital for the survival of civilians in Britain and ultimate victory.

Convoys were described by a letter and number code. The letters normally stand for the port of departure and the port of destination; the number was given to the convoy as it left port. The major codes were: HX Halifax to Liverpool; ON Liverpool to Halifax; SC Sydney (Nova Scotia) to Liverpool; and SL Freetown (Sierra Leone) to Liverpool. The HX series was the longest-running Convoy series, starting in September 1939 with HX 1 and finishing with HX 358 in May 1945.

The average convoy consisted of between six and nine columns of ships with five ships in each column. HX 300, however, had 167 ships sailing in nineteen columns.

THE RECORDS

There is nothing online, although Google may well come up with material for a particular convoy or ship. The records are largely to be found at TNA. The best place to start is the reports of the proceedings completed by the Commodore of the Convoy, the civilian officer responsible for the convoy. They are in series ADM 199. They have been indexed by convoy code, which makes them easy to find. There are also a number of files about shipping losses and even some first-person accounts from survivors of shipwrecks. Unfortunately, they haven't been indexed to the same degree. 'Convoy Packs', in series ADM 237, include Reports of Proceedings, Commodores' Reports and other papers, although many records have been lost. There's some overlap with the material in ADM 199.

Any merchant vessel losses are also covered in the Daily Casualty Registers (series BT 347). The registers recorded daily ship casualties, most frequently as result of enemy action but also include other more routine instances of loss at sea that may have affected Allied merchant fleets during the war. Each incident recorded names the class of vessel, the ship's name, nationality of the ship, date and time, cause and approximate position, voyage details and cargo and any recent information available.

Websites

The aforementioned Naval History Net includes a day-by-day diary of events, statistics of losses and U-boats sunk.

Another key website is U-boat Net. It has many webpages devoted to convoys – including a complete list of the convoy codes – and to the Allied navies that sought to protect them. There are brief histories of the naval ships involved as well as a database containing brief details of British and Allied seamen who lost their lives at sea.

Useful background can be found on the Naval Encyclopaedia website.

Further reading

Martin Middlebrook, *Convoy: The Greatest U-boat Battle of the War* (Cassell, 2003)
Richard Woodman, *Arctic Convoys: 1941–1945* (John Murray, 2004)

Museums

HMS Belfast is the last surviving light cruiser from the period of the war. It took part in the D-Day landings and is now moored on London's South Bank.

South Bank
The Queen's Walk
London
SE1 2JH
www.iwm.org.uk/visits/hms-belfast

The **National Maritime Museum** has a huge range of collections relating to the British relationship with the sea: mercantile and naval. The Caird Library is a very good research area and the holdings are well described in the online catalogue.

Romney Road
London
SE10 9NF
www.rmg.co.uk/national-maritime-museum

Caird Library
www.rmg.co.uk/collections/caird-library

ROYAL MARINES

The Royal Marines – that is, soldiers who serve at sea – can trace their history back to 1664. Traditionally, small companies of Marines were responsible for maintaining discipline on board ship and participated in raiding parties on enemy ships and on land, most famously on the raid on the submarine pens at Zeebrugge on St George's Day 1918.

Because of their traditional role in mounting swift raids on enemy targets, they were a natural choice to become Commandos during the Second World War.

A small group of Royal Marines first landed ashore at Namsos in April 1940, taking control of the approaches into the Norwegian town ahead of an Army force arrival a couple of days later. In 1942, the infantry battalions of the Royal Marine Division were reorganised as Commandos, and became a part of the British Army Commandos. Nine Royal Marine Commandos were raised during the war. They were numbered 40 to 48 and were part of 1 to 4 Commando brigades. 43 Commando was among the first units to land on D-Day. Less notably, but equally important, two-thirds of all the landing craft which took troops across the Channel were crewed by Royal Marines.

After the war all British Commando units were disbanded apart from those made up of Marines.

THE RECORDS

Service records are still held by the Ministry of Defence and will eventually be transferred to TNA.

War diaries for Royal Marine units, including the Commandos, are in ADM 202 at TNA. There is some overlap with war diaries for combined operations in DEFE 2. Some files about the award of gallantry medals to Commandos are in ADM 1.

Much information about the history of the corps is found at the Library of the National Museum of the Royal Navy. It also has an extensive collection of photographs, operational war diaries and other reports.

Further reading

The Royal Marines History website has a useful page on the Marines service in the Second World War. The Combined Ops website has excellent material about 45 Commando.

FLEET AIR ARM (FAA)

After two decades of bitter infighting, the Fleet Air Arm was finally transferred from the Air Ministry to the Admiralty in May 1939. In September 1939, the FAA comprised 20 squadrons and 232 aircraft on strength. The war brought about a new impetus for naval flying that gradually altered naval tactics. Instead of the traditional ship-versus-ship format, aircraft-versus-ship conflict became standard practice, with devastating effects. One of the most significant FAA successes during the war occurred at Taranto Harbour in 1940. Swordfish biplanes holding torpedoes carried out a night attack on the Italian fleet, resulting a decisive and destructive defeat. However, this was not their only success, the FAA served in nearly every theatre of the war. This included the battles of France and Britain; the Battle of the Atlantic; Russian convoys; the invasion of Madagascar; North African and Libyan campaigns; the invasions of Italy and southern France; D-Day; the Pacific and the planned invasion of Japan.

The FAA served as one of the primary weapons of defence against the U-boat. FAA aircrew were also adept at aerial combat, meaning the FAA itself had many air aces and received a range of honours including two VCs, and many DSOs, DSCs, DSMs and Mentions in Despatches.

By September 1945, the Fleet Air Arm service consisted of 59 aircraft carriers, 3,700 aircraft, 72,000 officers and men and 56 air stations across the globe.

SERVICE RECORDS

Personnel records are with the Ministry of Defence and will be transferred to TNA in due course.

MEDALS

An (incomplete) list of honours and awards made to Fleet Air Arm personnel can be found in William Chatterton Dickson, *Seedie's List of Fleet Air Arm Awards 1939–1969* (Ripley Registers, 1990).

Some FAA personnel received RAF awards. The records are in series AIR 2 and AIR 30.

CASUALTIES

The National Museum of the Royal Navy has a computerised database of FAA losses that is available for public consultation in its library in Portsmouth.

OPERATIONAL RECORDS

Fleet Air Arm squadrons were numbered in two blocks, 800–899 for first-line and 700–799 for second-line squadrons. The key squadrons are, however, Nos 800 to 809 – fighter squadrons in carriers; Nos 810 to 819 – Torpedo bomber squadrons in carriers, and Nos 820 to 859 – Spotter reconnaissance squadrons.[3] Detailed histories of many squadrons can be found on the RN Research Archive website.

Many squadrons compiled unofficial line books, which are well worth looking at. These are a less-formal record of a squadron's activities and mishaps, enlivened by photographs, cartoons and so on. Most are held by the National Museum of the Royal Navy, Yeovilton.

Combat reports compiled by pilots are in AIR 50 at Kew, and online on TNA's website. TNA also has squadron diaries, which are less-detailed versions of the RAF's operation record books, in series ADM 207, with a few in AIR 27.

Reports of Proceedings about missions and operations compiled by commanding officers are with those of ships and squadrons in ADM 199 and elsewhere.

No Aircraft Carrier Flying Log Books are known to have survived.

Further reading

A TNA Research Guide, 'Fleet Air Arm Personnel', provides basic guidance.

Much useful information about the Fleet Air Arm and its squadrons can be found on the Royal Navy Research Archive website.

Other useful sites include:

- Imperial War Museum: www.iwm.org.uk/history/fleet-air-arm-during-the-second-world-war
- Fleet Air Arm Officers Association: www.fleetairarmoa.org/fleet-air-arm-history-timeline

Books

Kev Darling, *Fleet Air Arm Carrier War: The History of British Naval Aviation* (Pen & Sword, 2009)
Ray Sturtivant and Theo Balance, *The Squadrons of the Fleet Air Arm* (Air Britain (Historians) Ltd, 1994) provides a brief history for each FAA squadron, listing aircraft types flown, and where it was based.
Ray Sturtivant, *Fleet Air Arm at War* (Ian Allan, 1982)
David Wragg, *The Fleet Air Arm Handbook 1939–1945* (Sutton, 2001)

Museum

The Fleet Air Arm Museum based at Yeovilton in Somerset is well worth visiting.

THE SUBMARINE SERVICE

As in most navies, there were two types of submarines in the Royal Navy: the big ocean-going vessels and the coastal- and medium-range types. Smaller submarines were more economical, and therefore produced en masse during the war, based on models determined in 1937 and 1942 (Class S and Class T). These submarines served primarily in the Mediterranean Sea, launching attacks on Italian shipping lines and supply convoys in the aftermath of the French defeat. They also served as submarine hunters across the Atlantic.

The smaller S and T classes were also well suited as stealth transports, to transport officers working with the resistance or important individuals, such as the British ambassador in Belgrade who had to leave in a hurry when the Germans invaded Yugoslavia in April 1941. However, losses were still severe – on occasion the result of misunderstandings with other submarines, escorts or even Allied aviation.

THE RECORDS

In general, records for submarines and submariners are very similar to those of the rest of the navy. Submarine logs are in ADM 173, which record all wheel, telegraph and depth-keeping orders, and details of battery charges, torpedo firing and navigation. They were kept by crew members otherwise engaged in steering or depth keeping, and contain many abbreviated references. Some logs are annotated humorously with notes and drawings. War patrol reports and associated records, arranged by boat, are in ADM 236, with some records in ADM 199.

The National Museum of the Royal Navy has substantial archives of papers, both official and private, relating to the service. Of particular interest is the material relating to individual vessels. Also of use are the Movement Record Cards for ratings for the two world wars and the inter-war period, which indicate which boats a man served on.

Naval History Net records the loss of individual submarines,

Also of use is John Atkinson, *Royal Navy Submarine Service Losses in WWII* (Galago, 2004), a comprehensive record of the names of all the men who lost their lives at sea. The book includes details of each submarine lost (from HMS *Oxley* in 1939 to HMS *Porpoise* in 1945), the reason, date and the commanding officer, together with each member of the crew who died, his name, rank and any decorations awarded.

Museum

The highlight of the Royal Navy Submarine Museum in Gosport is the chance to explore HMS *Alliance*, the only remaining British submarine from the period. You can walk the decks and narrow corridors, look through the original periscope, and hear the stories of those who served on board. But it is not for the claustrophobic.

MERCHANT NAVY

Although often forgotten, merchant seamen played a key role in the Allied victory. They crewed the ships of the British Merchant Navy, which kept the United Kingdom supplied with raw materials, arms, ammunition, fuel and food. They suffered great hardship and many losses, evidenced by a casualty rate that was considerably higher than nearly every other branch of the armed services. As the historian, John Keegan wrote in his book *The Second World War*, published in 1989:

> The 30,000 men of the British Merchant Navy who fell victim to the U-boats between 1939 and 1945, the majority drowned or killed by exposure on the cruel North Atlantic, were quite as certainly front-line warriors as the guardsmen and fighter pilots to whom they ferried the necessities of combat. Neither they nor their American, Dutch,

> Norwegian or Greek fellow mariners wore uniform and few have any memorial. They stood nevertheless between the Wehrmacht and the domination of the world.[4]

The Registrar General of Shipping and Seamen calculated that 144,000 merchant seamen were currently serving on British-registered merchant ships at the beginning of the Second World War and that an additional 185,000 men were serving in the Merchant Navy.

As well as crew members from Britain, large numbers of Indian, Chinese and West African seamen – traditionally known as lascars – served on board, generally as seamen or stewards, rather than as officers. Additionally, it was not uncommon to find men from the Dominions and other European countries in crews.

Before the war, women worked on board ocean liners and larger passenger-carrying vessels, usually as chief stewardesses, stewardesses or assistant stewardesses in laundries and in nursing. But as most liners were converted to troopships, the numbers so employed fell away. A few served as radio operators.

In 1939, a man signed on to sail aboard a ship for a voyage or succession of voyages and after being paid off at the end of that period of service, he was free to sign on again. In 1941, the Merchant Navy Reserve Pool was established, to ensure that seamen would always be available to crew vessels. For the first time, continuous paid employment instead of casual work was provided. Any individual who had served at sea in the last five years, along with those who intended to serving during the war itself were required to register. When leaving a ship, a seaman was informed of how much leave he was entitled to, on what date he must return and the location of the port he had to report to in order to return to sea. In turn, seamen were guaranteed a wage that covered time spent shipwrecked in lifeboats or as prisoners of war, and it provided for two days' paid leave per month.

THE RECORDS

It is helpful to know whether the person you are researching was an officer – that is, masters, mates, first, second and third officers, skippers, engineers and cooks.

There are no service records, as traditionally there are for the armed forces, as men were paid off after each voyage. Instead, there may be certificates of competence for officers, and entries in the Central Registry for sailors.

Wartime poster promoting the Merchant Navy. (Wikimedia Commons/ TNA INF 3/127)

There are several useful research guides to help you understand the records, which are well worth consulting before you start as they are not always easy to use. In particular, there is the National Maritime Museum's research guide C10 'Merchant Navy World War Two' and two guides from TNA: 'Officers: Merchant Navy' and 'Merchant Seamen Serving Since 1918'.

Findmypast has records for seamen up to about 1941, when the Reserve Pool was established. Ancestry has records of campaign medals and a roll of honour for casualties. Otherwise most records are at TNA. These are not online.

Service records

OFFICERS

There are several series of certificates of competency on Ancestry, although they finish in 1938. However, they may be useful if your ancestor was already a Merchant Navy officer when war was declared. In TNA series BT 352 are microfiched indexes to certificates awarded between 1910 and 1962. The original cards recorded the name, date of birth, place of birth, certificate number, grade, date of passing and port of examination for each certificate gained.

Lloyd's Captains' Registers were compiled from the record of certificates issued to foreign-going masters. They list the name of each master or mate; the place and year of birth; the date, number and place of issue of the master's certificate; the name and number of each ship; the dates of engagement and discharge as master; the destination of each voyage; casualties; and special awards. The registers include men from across the Commonwealth. An incomplete set of Captains' Registers is on microfilm at TNA. Sets are also available at the Caird Library.

SEAMEN

There are two series of records that you may need to consult, so it is reasonably important to know when your man left the service:

The **Fourth Register** (Central Indexed Register), was started in October 1913 and continued until 1941. If a man left before May 1941 he should be found here. The records are available through Findmypast.

A new **Central Register of Seamen** (known as the Fifth Register of Seamen), was established in 1941. Cards for seamen who were still serving in 1941 were removed from the old Fourth Register, placed in pouches (BT 372) or files (BT 364) and their details added to the new register in BT 382. The Fifth Register was maintained until 1972.

An incomplete set of seamen's pouches are in BT 372. They consist of an individual's papers filed together in paper envelopes known as 'pouches'. The contents vary from single registry cards to ID cards, photographs, letters, applications forms and other ephemera, and date between 1913 and 1972, though few have contents dating further back than the 1930s. They are indexed by name in Discovery. Some information, particularly National Insurance numbers, may be redacted for data protection reasons.

Medals

CAMPAIGN MEDALS

Series BT 395 at TNA contains a database to the Second World War medals issued to merchant seamen between 1946 and 2002 and includes both medals claimed and those actually issued. It gives details of the ribbons and medals issued to individual seamen for their service. The data records each seaman's name with, usually, his discharge book number and date and place of birth as well as the medals, ribbons and clasps issued together with a reference to the medal papers file. Individual entries can be downloaded from TNA's website. The records do not include the award of the Arctic Star, which was announced in late 2012, nearly seven decades after the end of the Second World War, to be awarded to those who served on the Arctic convoys during that time.

GALLANTRY MEDALS

Lists of men who were awarded gallantry medals, together with service number and the date the event was gazetted, are listed in the *London Gazette*.

Series T 335 contains files about the award of gallantry medals and commendations for bravery, such as OBEs MBEs and BEMs, made to mercantile marine and fishing fleet personnel. The records are fully indexed in TNA's Discovery Catalogue. However, more information including descriptions of the actions deserving recognition, can be found in the files themselves.

Series BT 261 contains registers and papers that deal in the main with awards for acts of gallantry at sea, recommendations for and consideration of awards, and accounts of actions leading to the presentation of awards. The series is not online, nor has it yet been indexed by name.

Details of the award of Albert and George medals can be found on Ancestry up to the middle of 1943. Series MT 9 contains many files relating to various awards, including the Board of Trade Medal for Gallantry in Saving Life at Sea, the Sea Transport Medal, the George Medal, Lloyd's Medal for Gallantry at Sea and the Polish Cross of Valour. HO 45 also includes some papers relating to the award of the Albert Medal. The records are indexed by name.

The Albert Medal was instituted in 1866 to be awarded for saving life at sea. A similar medal, the Edward Medal, was established in 1907 for acts of bravery by all industrial workers in factory accidents and disasters. Both were subsumed into the George Cross after the Second World War.

The Lloyd's Medal for Gallantry at Sea was instituted by the Committee of Lloyd's in December 1940, to be awarded to officers and men of the Merchant Navy and Fishing Fleet in cases of exceptional gallantry at sea in time of war. All in all, 541 medals were awarded, including four for women. Recipients are listed on Wikipedia, see the entry for the medal.

Records of Merchant Navy personnel who received naval gallantry awards during the Second World War can be found in code 85 in series ADM 1 and ADM 199.

Further reading

TNA Research Guide: 'Merchant Seamen: Medals and Honours'.
Seedie's List of Awards to the Merchant Navy for World War II (Ripley Registers, 1997)

CASUALTIES

About a quarter of the men and women who served in the Merchant Navy during the Second World War lost their lives: 36,749 seamen were lost to enemy action, 5,720 were taken prisoner and 4,707 were wounded – a total of 47,176 casualties, including 50 women. The sacrifice made by merchant seamen during the war, particularly during the Battle of the Atlantic and in 1942 and 1943, has sometimes been overlooked.

Ancestry has details of men's deaths in their 'UK Merchant Seamen Deaths, 1939–1953 collection'. The cards roughly contain the same information as might be found on an ordinary GRO Death Certificate. In most cases, the cause of death is given as 'Missing Supposed Drowned'. Findmypast has Registers of Deceased Seamen in their 'British Armed Forces Overseas Deaths and Burials' collection, which contains much the same information.

Merchant seamen who died at sea are recorded by the Commonwealth War Graves Commission in the same way as other seamen.

The names of 24,000 seamen and women who lost their lives are commemorated on the Tower Hill Memorial in the City of London (nearly opposite Tower underground station). The Memorial Register, listing everybody who appears on the memorial, may be consulted in the Trinity House offices, Trinity Square. A memorial to the men who lost their lives during the Battle of the Atlantic overlooks the Mersey at the end of James Street in Liverpool.

Several series of a roll of honour for men who lost their lives were compiled after the war by the Board of Trade; it is now in series BT 339, arranged both by individual and by ship. It is also available on Ancestry, although normally only the man's name is given together with the ship he served on. Occasionally their occupation or trade is given, such as Master or Donkeyman.

PRISONERS OF WAR

There is an extensive collection of records in series BT 373 at TNA, giving the circumstances of capture and the eventual fate of British and Allied Asian merchant seamen captured during the Second World War. The series also includes details of ships captured or lost due to enemy action. These contain miscellaneous papers relating to the circumstances of loss/capture. You can search by individual prisoner or by ship.

Pieces BT 382/3232–3249 consist of an alphabetical series of printed cards relating to merchant seamen prisoners. The cards normally give details of: camp and PoW number; surname and full forenames; date and place of birth; discharge A number and rank/rating; details of ship; next-of-kin and relationship; and home address. In addition, some include dates of death, exchange, repatriation and arrival back in the United Kingdom. They are not online. However, some records in the series are available in the Prisoner of War Collections on Findmypast.

Of the 5,000 Allied merchant seamen captured by the Germans, 4,500 were at some time held at Marlag und Milag Nord camps at Westertimke, near Bremen, Germany (Marlag held Royal Navy personnel and Milag Merchant seamen). A camp history is in WO 208/3270. Milag was primarily for members of the merchant marine who had been captured aboard ships carrying Allied ordnance or military-related supplies, as well as holding Western European civilian internees.

RECORDS OF SHIPS

The basic source of information is the annual **Lloyd's Register of Shipping**. The register describes, classifies and registers vessels according to certain criteria of physical structure and equipment, to enable underwriters, shipbrokers and shipowners to more easily assess commercial risk and to negotiate marine insurance rates. It is published mid-year and covers ships registered between 1 July and 30 June of the previous year. Some ships, however, had too short a time at sea to be included, and some foreign-registered vessels were omitted from the register because of the difficulty of gathering information in wartime. Copies are available on the Lloyd's Register Foundation Heritage and Education Centre website.

An introduction to the register and how it can be used is available through the Mariners Mailing List website.

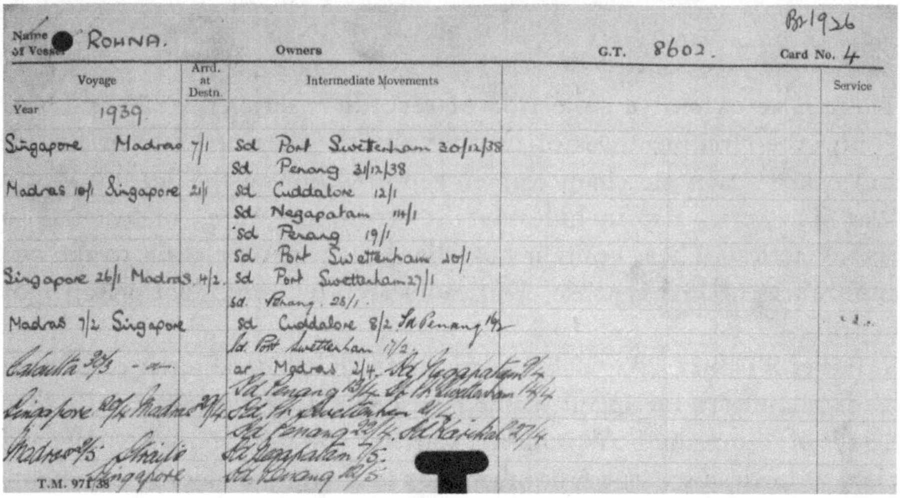
Name of Vessel ROHNA. Owners G.T. 8602. BT 1926 Card No. 4

Voyage	Arrd. at Destn.	Intermediate Movements		Service
Year 1939				
Singapore Madras	7/1	Sd Port Swettenham 30/12/38		
		Sd Penang 31/12/38		
Madras 10/1 Singapore	21/1	Sd Cuddalore 12/1		
		Sd Negapatam 14/1		
		Sd Penang 19/1		
		Sd Port Swettenham 20/1		
Singapore 26/1 Madras	4/2	Sd Port Swettenham 27/1		
		Sd Penang 28/1		
Madras 7/2 Singapore		Sd Cuddalore 8/2 Sd Penang 14/2		
		Sd Port Swettenham 17/2		
Calcutta 3/3 –		ar Madras 2/4 Sd Negapatam 9/4		
		Sd Penang 13/4 Sd Pt Swettenham 14/4		
Singapore 20/4 Madras	27/4	Sd Pt Swettenham 21/4		
		Sd Penang 22/4 Sd Karikal 27/4		
Madras 9/5 Straits Singapore		Sd Negapatam 7/5		
		Sd Penang 10/5		

T.M. 971/38

The movement card for SS *Rohna*, which was sunk with great loss of life, mainly of American soldiers, on 26 November 1943. (TNA BT 389/25/72)

Ships' movement cards in BT 389 record the movements of both British-registered and Allied vessels engaged in the war effort. They do not contain details of any passengers or crew. Each set of records includes the following information: name of the ship (and former name if appropriate); size (tonnage); to whom ship was registered; the ship's destination and date of arrival; and cargo carried. The cards also show if the ship was torpedoed, mined, damaged or sunk. They can be downloaded from TNA's website. More information about the cards is in a TNA Research Guide: 'Merchant Shipping Movement Cards 1939–1945'.

Crew lists and agreements list all members of the crew. Log books list daily occurrences and may include telegrams and other paperwork. Unfortunately, these records were often destroyed when a vessel sank as the result of enemy action. TNA holds all the surviving crew lists and agreements between 1939 and 1950. Search by ship's official number in series BT 380, BT 381 and BT 99. BT 387 has agreements and crew lists of Allied foreign ships requisitioned or chartered by the British government in the Second World War. The records contain details of UK merchant seamen who served on the ships. There is also an index to Second World War log books, agreements and crew lists in BT 385.

Ships' official numbers can be found in Lloyd's Registers.

Use these records for

- Researching individual seamen.
- Researching ships.
- Researching convoys.

Pitfalls

- The records may only give a partial insight into a person's career in the Merchant Navy.
- The records are slightly different for officers and seamen.
- It may be hard to trace which ships a man served on.

Further reading

More about the life of British Merchant seamen during the war can be found in an unusually comprehensive Wikipedia entry. It is well worth reading to understand the life your ancestor experienced in the Merchant Navy.

Brian James Crabb, *Beyond the Call of Duty: The Loss of British Commonwealth Mercantile and Service Women at Sea during the Second World War* (Shaun Tyas, 2006)

Bernard Edwards, *The Quiet Heroes: British Merchant Seaman at War* (Leo Cooper, 2002)

Peter Elphick, *Life Line: The Merchant Navy at War (*Chatham Publishing, 1999)

Tony Lane, *The Merchant Seamen's War* (Manchester University Press, 1990)

7

THE HOME FRONT

Every man, woman and child – unless they were very young or very old – was expected to play a part in the war effort. For the most part they willingly did so. As well as holding down jobs or running the family home, citizens were encouraged to volunteer in their leisure hours. Had they not done so, it would have been impossible for there to have been effective assistance during air raids and other civil defence emergencies. Old soldiers might join the Home Guard, while men and women might sign up for the Auxiliary Fire Service (AFS), become Special Constables or Air Raid Wardens. Many women joined the Women's Volunteer Service (WVS) or Red Cross working parties knitting or darning socks. Faith Buckley in Hampton, Middlesex, described the volunteering she did for the Red Cross in a series of amusing letters to her daughters in Canada, which were published by the local history society. In August 1940 she wrote:

> My salvage depot is still going strong. People bring in all sorts of things and we refuse nothing. If it is not fit for melting down to make munitions, we find another use for it. There are Red Cross depots everywhere where people take all the things they do not want and they are sold to someone who does want them and the money goes to the Red Cross. I send a lot of things from my depot to theirs – children's books, silver tableware, table linen. We have had some cutlery brought in and that has been sent to hospitals, but to-day when I arrived and saw in the window – to my horror – a set of false teeth!! What would you suggest I do with them?[1]

Many volunteers enjoyed their work. In 2001, for the Spartacus Educational website, Stella Hughes remembered:

> I joined the Voluntary Nursing Service working from the Chingford post most evenings and at weekends in order to do my bit, so to speak, in the war. Five days a week I made soldiers' uniforms working for Rego in

> Edmonton, north London, and then nursed at Whipps Cross Hospital in east London, travelling there by bus. Along with my 'indoor and outdoor' uniforms, which I was given, I was issued a tin hat (which I had to pay for) but all this made me feel great.[2]

For older volunteers (and the lonely) there was a sense that they were still needed and that they could make a vital contribution to the war effort.

Gardeners were encouraged to 'Dig for Victory'. Much of the green space in towns was turned into allotments. Pig clubs used scraps of food to feed porkers, and many families raised chickens. The fresh produce helped to supplement family rations and could, of course, be swapped for other items.

RATIONING

Rationing was introduced in January 1940 and became increasingly severe as the war progressed. However, the most severe rationing occurred after the end of the was in 1946, when even bread was rationed for a period. It was not finally abandoned until 1954, with sweets being the last item to come off rations.

The system was administered by the local offices of the Ministry of Food. Every man, woman and child was given a ration book with coupons, which they used at shops with which they had registered. The ration book had to be handed over to the shopkeeper, and the appropriate coupons cut out, before rationed goods could be purchased. Coupons were used to buy basic foodstuffs such as sugar, meat and fat.

Much else, including tinned goods, biscuits and clothing, were rationed using a points system. The number of points allocated changed according to availability and consumer demand. Priority allowances of milk and eggs were given to those most in need, including children and expectant mothers. Workers doing heavy

The cover of a ration book issued in 1942. (Wellcome Library)

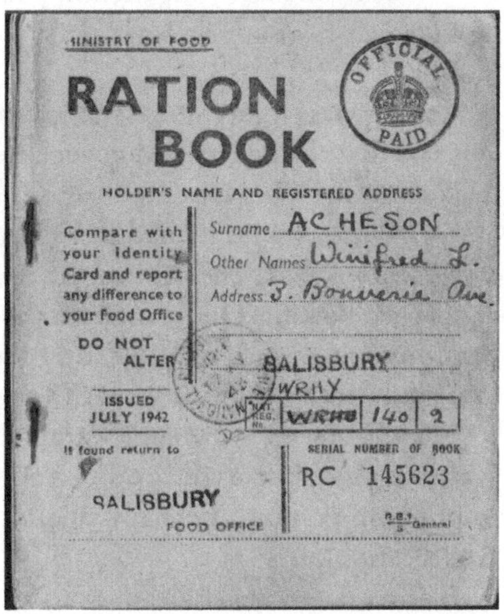
MINISTRY OF FOOD
RATION BOOK
OFFICIAL PAID
HOLDER'S NAME AND REGISTERED ADDRESS
Compare with your Identity Card and report any difference to your Food Office
DO NOT ALTER
Surname ACHESON
Other Names Winifred L.
Address 3. Bouverie Ave
SALISBURY
WRHY
ISSUED JULY 1942
WRHU 140 2
If found return to
SALISBURY FOOD OFFICE
SERIAL NUMBER OF BOOK
RC 145623

labour were entitled to larger rations than other adult workers; children received smaller rations but relatively higher proportions of fats and proteins, and nursing or expectant mothers were entitled to larger allotments of milk and other animal-source foodstuffs.

Not all foods were rationed. Fruit and vegetables were never officially rationed but were often in short supply, as was beer (much watered down), whiskey and other spirits. There were always queues, particularly when the rumour went round that there some rare delicacy had appeared in the shops. Famously, bananas, were almost impossible to obtain and came to be seen as being a very rare treat. And even when items weren't rationed, they might well be in short supply. Faith Buckley wrote to her children that:

> One no longer goes out with a shopping list all cut and dried. You think to yourself I'll have lamb this weekend and onions and sausages for supper. You go ahead and find that the butcher is indulging in a beef week and doesn't know what a sheep is. Sausages also are non-existent that week, will rabbit do? Knowing your husband's dislike of rabbit you smile and say no thank you and rush to the fishmonger for halibut or hake – he is indulging in an orgy of herrings, so herrings it is. The greengrocer smiles in a most superior manner and says: 'Not onions this week Madam but leeks!' It's all most confusing but comes out right in the end! If you don't decide the leeks pretty quickly someone else has them and you are left with turnips and carrots!
>
> When you meet your friends, you no longer say, 'How are you?' but 'Look what I've got – a lemon.'

Rationing was largely successful and designed to provide nutritious meals. It is said that the British had never been so healthy as they were during the Second World War. Despite the best efforts of food nutritionists working at the Ministry, who turned out a huge range of recipes to encourage the housewife to make the best use of the rations, the diet was at best boring and lacked flavour. Oddly, one dish widely eaten in the war years remains very popular – apple crumble, originally designed to reduce the use of fat and flour, both of which were in very short supply.

There were several ways to supplement the rations. The most obvious was to grow your own food or to know somebody who did and who might help you out, perhaps an allotment holder, farmer or a generous American soldier.

All but the most honest must have occasionally bought some little treat on the black market. The popular image was of sharply dressed 'spivs' whispering to potential customers on street corners with access to a seemingly inexhaustible range of good from tinned peaches to petrol, cigarettes to cognac. Although there were organised gangs, the most common way to get around the rations was by shopkeepers keeping 'something under the counter' for favoured customers or those they were certain could afford to pay. Despite the best efforts of the authorities, it was impossible to eradicate. In a debate in the House of Commons in February 1945, members claimed that 'the whole turkey production of East Anglia had gone to the black market' and 'prosecutions [for black market activities] were like trying to stop a leak in a battleship.' It was also said that the official prices given to such foods were set so low that their producers were forced to sell their produce on the black market in order to charge higher prices; one such tactic (in operation at markets in Diss, Norfolk) involved the sale of live poultry to members of the public, but each purchaser would first sign a form stating that they were buying the birds in order to breed them, before taking them home to eat instead.[3] The Minister of Food responding for the government limply replied that it wasn't worth the effort of officials to stamp out the practice.

Restaurants were not affected by rationing, but they were restricted in what they could serve and the most they could charge for a meal was 5 shillings. The grander restaurants got round this with a variety of additional surcharges. Wartime diaries of the rich suggest that they were hardly affected by these restrictions or rationing in general.[4]

In 1940 the Ministry of Food established canteens. These British Restaurants were sustained and ran on a non-profit basis by local authorities, with the aim of providing good meals for those unable to cook at home. For example, people who had lost their homes to German air raids or factory workers on long shifts may have struggled to cook for themselves.

A main course normally cost 9*d*; a sweet was 2*d*, bread 1*d*, soup also 2*d*, and a cup of tea 1½*d*. Bread was often in short supply, so to encourage people to eat potatoes, these were provided free with the soup. It was cheap and cheerful and provided a nutritious if not, by today's standards, particularly tasty meal.

Larger factories provided canteens for their workers. Schools too began to offer meals to pupils in much greater numbers then had been the case before the war.

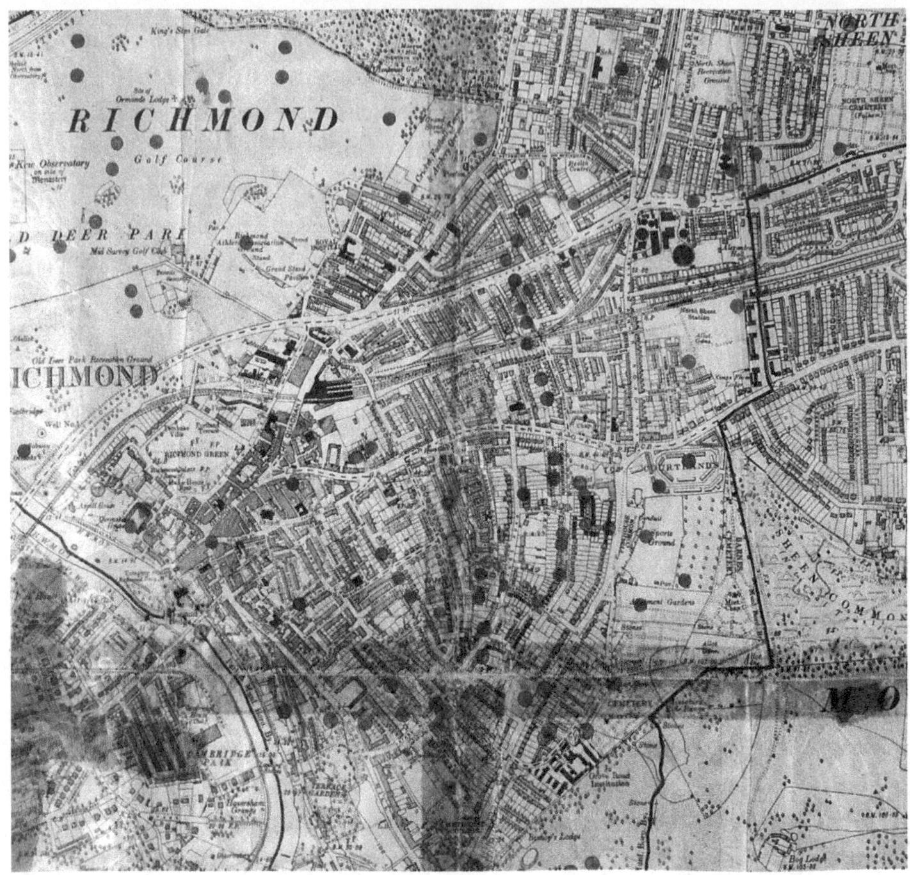

The bomb map for Richmond, Surrey, showing where bombs dropped in the centre of the town. (Richmond Archives and Local Studies)

Finding out more

It is surprisingly difficult to find out very much about the experiences of individual civilians during the war. The best place to start is by going through any family papers such as letters and diaries. It is safe to assume that all official material relating to the administration of rationing, conscription and much else about everyday life, including records relating to the war factories and the men and women who worked there, have long been destroyed. The major exception is the **1939 Register**, which was compiled at the end of September 1939 to allow identity cards and ration books to be issued (see Chapter 2).

In general, the best sources are **newspapers**. Despite shortages of newsprint and vigorous censorship, they are full of stories about the lives of ordinary people: getting married, winning vegetable shows or appearing in court of petty infringements of the law (see Chapter 2).

In addition, **county record offices** and local studies libraries should have material of interest, such as photograph albums, lists of volunteers and even people's wartime diaries. Local council minutes and papers might well contain lists of volunteers, such as air-raid wardens or secretaries of local allotment committees. There are likely to be lists of bomb-damaged houses and other property, bomb maps showing where bombs fell, and possibly lists of people killed during raids.

If you know where your ancestors worked, it is possible that company records survive. The most interesting source here is likely to be staff magazines, which may include obituaries of staff members who were casualties, letters from members in the forces and other stories. There is a plaque at the National Westminster branch in Richmond to two employees who lost their lives during the Second World War. Short obituaries were published in *The Westminster*, the bank's house magazine:

> Flying Officer Victor Crawford Parker RAFVR died on 5 February 1945 as the result of an aircraft accident. His obituary reads that 'he had joined the bank at Leigh on Sea in 1938 and came to Richmond in October 1940, remained at the branch only a few weeks, having volunteered for the RAF in the early days of the war. During the short period he was at Richmond he endeared himself to the whole staff.'[5]

Of Flight Sergeant Robert Lionel Vince, RAFVR *The Westminster* wrote that he was:

> Last heard off flying from Malta to the Middle East, and had been missing for six months. He joined the Richmond Branch in 1936 and his career seemed full of promise when he entered the RAF in August 1940. He was one of the brightest and most capable members of the Staff and was very popular with his colleagues so his loss will be deeply felt.[6]

TNA's Discovery Catalogue will tell you the location of company records. If the business is still trading it may be worth checking whether it has any wartime records.

With the exception of the 1939 Register, relatively little is online. However, some records for Berkshire connected to evacuation, civil defence, the Home Guard and more are available on Ancestry. Ancestry also has a register of men enlisting in the Home Guard in Surrey (which seems to mean Croydon and the surrounding area) and similar records for parts of Lancashire.

Use these records for

- Finding out more about men and women who fought on the home front.

Pitfalls

- The survival of records is very patchy, so unless you are very lucky you may not find much.

MEDALS

Civilians who performed acts of bravery during the war were entitled to be honoured in some way. The Blitz, in particular, saw many actions of heroism by the rescue services as they sought to find people buried in the rubble. It was dangerous and painstaking work. However, these acts often went unrecognised – the real reward was successfully saving a person's life.

Most men and women so recognised received a letter of commendation, but a few were awarded a gallantry medal. The most important award was the **George Cross**, the premier award given for non-operational gallantry or gallantry not in the presence of an enemy, awarded for acts of the greatest heroism or of the most conspicuous courage in circumstances of extreme danger. The George Cross is the civilian equivalent to the Victoria Cross. The **George Medal** is awarded for conspicuous gallantry not in the presence of the enemy.

Both medals were awarded to service personnel and civilians and could be issued posthumously. Brief accounts of why these honours were awarded can be found in the citations given in the *London Gazette* (see Chapter 3). Biographies of George Cross winners are on Wikipedia.

Civilians could also receive the Order of the British Empire (OBE), Member of the Order of the British Empire (MBE) or British Empire Medal (BEM) for heroism. For example, three members of Twickenham's Fire Brigade were awarded several gallantry medals for bravery during an air raid on Hampton. Chief Fire Officer William Woods received a George Medal, while Section Officer Ernest Stevens and Fireman Ernest Weller were each awarded a BEM. The citation read:

> On the occasion of a serious bombing incident when a number of houses and shops were wrecked [these men] were occupied for nearly three hours in rescue work, obtaining access to trapped inmates through a small hole in the debris. All the time there was the greatest likelihood that tons of masonry would collapse on them. Much of this was only supported by a few bricks.[7]

CASE 578.

Mrs. Lillian HALLE - 95 years.

95, Chesterton Road, North Kensington, W.10.

Civilian - Kensington.

Dealing with an incendiary bomb at Chesterton Road, W.10. on 11th January 1941.

Recommended by: Mayor of Kensington.

No.5 (London). Regional Commissioner Recommends: Commendation.

Documents: (1) Letter from Mayor of Kensington.
(2) Press extracts from "Evening Standard".

CASE CONSIDERED BY COMMITTEE: Jan. 21st. 1941. RECOMMENDATION: Commendation

TREASURY RECOMMENDATION: GAZETTED.

Copy of Letter of R.C. Jenkins, Mayor of Kensington, 17th January 1941.

I should like to bring to your notice the following act of resource and courage of an old lady of 95 during the air raid on Saturday 11th January.

She is Mrs. Lillian Halle of 95, Chesterton Road, North Kensington W.10, and she lives on the first floor at this address. During the raid she went out of her room and saw a blaze on the top floor from an incendiary bomb. She took upstairs sand and later water, and proceeded to put out the fire. Only when it was out did she go to the street door and ask for help. The other occupants of the house were in the basement and the communicating door was locked.

I feel this old lady showed great bravery and presence of mind and set all of us a splendid example. If her deed could in any way receive official recognition or commendation it would be a well deserved and popular reward.

(Sgd.) R.C. JENKINS.

Recommendation for an award to 95-year-old Lillian Halles of North Kensington, who received a letter of commendation. She was probably the oldest person on either side to be officially recognised for bravery during the war. (TNA T 336/13)

Ancestry has records relating to the awards made to civil defence personnel (that is, members of the police, fire services, air raid precautions and volunteer helpers) in its collection: 'World War II Civil Defence Gallantry Awards, 1940–1949'. These awards were primarily aimed at those involved in civil defence, such as ARP officers, rescue party workers, fire fighters and casualty and medical service workers. But they also recognised vital work carried out by the gas workers, electricians, train drivers and dockyard workers to keep Britain going during the Blitz. The collection contains evidence submitted to the Inter-departmental Committee on Civil Defence Gallantry Awards and its recommendations to the Chatfield Committee in Whitehall. The original material is in series T 330 at Kew.

There is another series – T 336 – with additional information. It has been re-catalogued to give brief details about each recipient. There's an interesting blog post on the re-cataloguing and what was uncovered during the 'Cataloguing T 336: Civilian gallantry awards in the Second World War' exercise on TNA's website.

The evidence can include the name and age of the person being recommended, the date and details of his or her actions of merit, lists of supporting documentation and possibly copies of correspondence from individuals who made the initial recommendation. In most cases it is not known exactly what award, if any, was made to an individual, but most men and women appear to have received a Letter of Commendation signed by the Home Secretary.

William Woods and his colleagues are also mentioned here, with rather more detail than the information provided by the *London Gazette*. During a raid on Hampton in Middlesex on 11 October 1940, Mr and Mrs Tuffin (as well as their dog), became trapped by debris after a high-explosive bomb had dropped nearby, killing four people. Mr Tuffin was found 'pinned down by a large dining table on its side across his legs and a huge slab of concrete on his back and his chest wedged between the back of the chair'. His wife, meanwhile, was buried in debris up to the waist under the table, where the couple had been sheltering. Mr Woods and his colleagues, working in the pitch black, 'had first to cut an aperture in the table top to make contact. This was very difficult, owing to the close proximity of Mr Tuffin and the small space to work in, then to relieve the pressure from his legs, the major portion of the debris had to be lifted with a 5-ton jack.'

To release Mrs Tuffin, 'it was necessary to remove with the hand, and lying on the stomach, about a yard of debris'. One witness reported how Mr Woods had held the hand 'sympathetically of a half-buried but still living victim'. At the same time, the crew was in danger of having tons of masonry collapse on them. The rescue took nearly three hours. But it was successful. Eventually, the Tuffins were pulled free and taken to hospital, where they recovered from their traumatic experience. Mr Woods' bravery, and that of his crew, was reported by several eyewitness to Twickenham's town clerk, who recommended Woods and his colleagues for the award. The awards were picked up by the local newspaper for the area. It is based on the citation but gives the name of the couple who had been rescued.[8]

More about the award of gallantry medals can be found in Chapter 3.

OPPOSITION TO THE WAR

The war was overwhelmingly supported by the vast majority of the British people. The Ministry of Information carried out regular surveys of public opinion, which normally revealed that people wanted the war to be more aggressively prosecuted. More importantly, there was very effective censorship of newspapers and the other media. Film, radio, photojournalism, comics and advertising were all used in propaganda that, for the most part, was based on the truth so that it could be trusted by those who received it. Occasionally, there were press stories about individuals who had been fined or imprisoned for spreading anti-war rumours.

INTERNED FASCISTS

The most obvious opponents of the war – Sir Oswald Mosley and his followers in the British Union of Fascists together with other known fascist supporters – were interred in the summer of 1940 under Defence Regulation 18B. About a thousand men and a few women were interned. By the end of 1943, as the war turned decisively in the Allies favour, most were released.

Files about a number of interned individuals are in series HO 45. As well as fascists, other undesirable aliens were interred, such as the notorious gangster Darby Sabini, who vehemently protested that he had never been to Italy.

CONSCIENTIOUS OBJECTORS

Unlike in the First World War, it was possible for pacifists to appeal against military service provided they were willing to serve in a civilian capacity. Some 60,000 British men declared themselves conscientious objectors. This represented about 1 per cent of men who were conscripted into the forces and proportionally more than the 16,000 who objected to service during the First World War. Most, but not all, objected on religious grounds and were from middle- or upper-class backgrounds. Most were still willing to work for the war effort. Conscientious objectors had to appear before an appeal tribunal. The tribunals were heard by a civilian judge and included representation from trade unions, a very different experience to those tribunals in the First World War. Actual incarceration was very rare. Only 3 per cent of those men who appeared before the tribunals – in comparison to one-third of those in the First World War – were given a short prison sentence, typically the result of refusal to engage with the process of the tribunal entirely In Richmond, Charles Fisher endured a number of prison sentences for his beliefs. In early 1943, for example, he was jailed for two months for failing to appear before a Labour Exchange. Another man, John Horton, was sentenced to six months' hard labour by Richmond Magistrates Court in May 1943 for refusing to take up land or civil defence work.[9]

No records of the tribunals appear to survive. There are records about the treatment of conscientious objectors at TNA and some local archives may have material as well, but it will be difficult to find much about individual pacifists. The best place to start is with newspaper reports, although these tend to be for the men who refused to undertake non-combatant work.

The Friends Library in London has some material, including records for the Friends Ambulance Unit that many objectors joined.

An excellent background article 'Conscientious Objectors in The Second World War: Little-Known Stories of Pacifists Plagued by Doubt but Willing to Risk Their Lives' by Linsey Robb is on The Conversation website.

INDUSTRIAL RELATIONS

The main civilian protests against the war were strikes in mines, docks and factories. It should be stressed that this was less about the direction of the war itself and more about pay and conditions. Once the Soviet Union entered the war in June 1941, communist influence in the trade unions switched to supporting the war effort. Even so, industrial action remained of great concern to Churchill and his ministers.

There were many strikes, local and national, large and small, during the Second World War. They might be covered to an extent in local newspapers. There is also much in the Ministry of Labour records (letter code LAB) records at TNA. Undoubtedly, MI5 kept a wary eye on trade unionists and strike leaders, but apart from a small collection of papers at TNA (letter code KV) most records have apparently been destroyed.

Further reading

Mark Crail, *Tracing Your Labour Movement Ancestors: A Guide for Family Historians* (Pen & Sword, 2009)

HOME GUARD

The Home Guard consisted of volunteer, unpaid and part-time soldiers, formed into units to defend local communities, airfields and vital infrastructure and traffic routes. In short, this was an armed civilian militia prepared to defend the country in the event of invasion.

On 14 May 1940, the Secretary of State for War, Anthony Eden, made a speech to the nation on BBC radio. He called for volunteers:

> We want large numbers of ... British subjects between the ages of 17 and 65 to come forward and offer their services ... You will not be paid but will receive uniforms and will be armed. In order to volunteer, what you have to do is give your name at your local police station.

Even before the broadcast was at an end, police stations were besieged by volunteers. The government expected 150,000 men to volunteer for the Home Guard. Within the first month, 750,000 men had joined, and by the end of June 1940, the total number of volunteers was over 1 million. The membership of the Home Guard did not fall below 1 million until they were stood down in December 1944.

Eight hundred local men in Richmond alone responded to the appeal. Most were veterans of the First World War, and even the Boer War, who were too old to join the army but not too old to fight. In the words of their commander Lieutenant Colonel A.E. Redfern they were all 'very much out of date, a bit short in the wind, and very rusty [but this was compensated] by their enthusiasm and eagerness to get going'.[10]

It was the beginning of the Local Defence Volunteers (LDV), soon to be renamed the Home Guard by Churchill.

Though the TV programme *Dad's Army* may have implied that most Home Guard volunteers were elderly, in reality, figures show that only 40 per cent of men had previous military experience, primarily during the First World War. Probably the oldest man to have served was Thomas Walton, aged 84. He had served in the Sudan during the 1890s. An increasing number of members were young men who received basic training before enlisting in the services.

Their work was rarely glamorous. Units manned road blocks and fixed defences around vital positions such as bridges and viaducts and looked out for German paratrooper or seaborne landings. Often, they were called to help in the aftermath of air raids, by guarding houses where live bombs were suspected of being present, and patrolling shops to prevent looting. Later in the war, members manned anti-aircraft guns and coastal artillery, thus releasing regular troops for other duties.

In the early stages of the Home Guard, weapons were hard to come by. Volunteers instead made do with old hunting guns, trophy weapons from other conflicts or even shotguns, which were well sought after. As an alternative, Home Guard volunteers went about their duties sporting knives tied to broom handles or agricultural equipment like scythes to demonstrate their position. In Richmond, one platoon patrolled with sticks loaded with lead shot made by employees of the Poppy Factory, which was based locally.

Eventually, old and disused rifles were issued to the Home Guard, purchased from the Canadian and American governments. Even at the height of the invasion scare, many units were severely lacking in both equipment and training, some never having fired a practise shot. On 3 July 1940, the War Diary of 19th Battalion Kent Home Guard is noted: 'Permission received to fire 3 rounds per rifle.' During the winter of 1940–41 in Richmond, 'C' Company guarded Kew and Chiswick bridges 'more or less unarmed and unequipped, not a steel helmet between them, during terrific air raids, to do their duty, as only they knew how to, and wondering at the swish of every bomb how their families were faring'.[11]

Home Guard volunteers generally appointed their own officers, a result of the swift creation and mobilisation of their units that meant leaders required organisation and experience. These men had often already been officers in the First World War. In rarer cases, some units set up elections, but often they were led by senior managers. This was because most Home Guard platoons and sections were based in factories and other workplaces. For a short period, the Home Guard in Richmond was led by the director of Kew Gardens.

Despite the common perception that the Home Guard was an all-male reserve, women were integral to the running of the service. They frequently worked in units, providing refreshments and completing the necessary administrative procedures. As a result, in 1943 the Women's Auxiliary was formally established, known as the 'Wassies'. The unit in Richmond comprised 120 members who provided first aid, clerical help, signalling, transport and, most appreciated by the men, a canteen 'and what's more they washed up after we had eaten'.[12]

Following D-Day and the success of the Allied armies in France it became increasingly clear that the role of the Home Guard was over. They were stood down on 1 November 1944 with a final parade down Whitehall in London a month later.

AUXILIARY UNITS (AUXUNITS)

Among the Home Guard were special and very secretive Auxiliary Units, who were to become the nucleus of a British resistance movement had the Germans invaded. Members of the War Office and the British Secret Intelligence Service were not convinced by the policy of appeasement chosen by the Allied powers, believing the risk of Nazi invasion remained. Together, they prepared pre-emptive 'Last Ditch' survival plans in direct defiance of Whitehall. These plans included secret resistance networks, known as GHQ Auxiliary Units. This was the only body in Europe that was expecting an enemy assault.

The 'Auxunits' were essentially civilian 'stay-behinds', often local farmers and landowners who knew the area well. A particular feature of this group was the small and discreet patrols (around half a dozen men) that remained hidden in underground bases. Those involved were hastily selected after the Dunkirk evacuation, before being trained and equipped with firearms, explosives and booby traps. Once entrenched underground, the mission was to emerge at night, after the enemy had passed over, and cause as much havoc as possible, for as long as they were able. Other members, men and women alike, would remain above ground to observe the enemy and report intelligence back to the Defence Force via radio networks. Even today, very little is known about them and the volunteers who ran them, partly because many units remained available in case of a Russian invasion during the Cold War.

Finding out more

With the exception of records for County Durham, service records are with the Ministry of Defence and will be transferred to TNA over the next few years. The Durham Home Guard enrolment forms can already be loaded from TNA's website (series WO 409). They are also searchable on Findmypast. The records, however, are not terribly informative. They consist of the forms that individuals filled in when they joined up and include name and place and date of birth as well as the battalion they joined.

TNA has some war diaries in series WO 166. It is also worth looking at the unit histories in series WO 199. Neither collection is complete, however.

Local and regimental archives may well also have material, such as muster lists, diaries and collections of press cuttings. This material is unlikely to be online, although Ancestry has records related to the Home Guard in Lancashire. Its collection includes casualty records, battalion nominal registers (with addresses) and discharge and transfer registers. There is also a little about activities in Berkshire.

There may well be stories in local **newspapers**, often about social events, training and appointments within the Home Guard. Details of fatalities were recorded by the Commonwealth War Graves Commission.

Further reading

- www.home-guard.org.uk – an excellent website devoted to the Home Guard.
- www.auxunit.org.uk – devoted to the Home Guard Auxiliary Units.
- www.staybehinds.com – another excellent site on the Auxiliary Units. Includes short biographies of some members.
- www.parhamairfieldmuseum.co.uk/british-resistance-organisation – a very good summary of the work of the Auxiliary Units.

Donald Brown, *Somerset v Hitler: Secret Operations in the Mendips 1939–1945* (Countryside Press, 1999)
Norman Longmate, *The Real Dad's Army: The History of The Home Guard* (Amberley, 2016)
S.P. Mackenzie, *The Home Guard: A Military and Political History* (Oxford, 1995)
John Warricker, *Churchill's Underground Army* (Frontline Books, 2013)

Museum

Museum of the British Resistance Organisation
Parham Airfield
Great Glenham
IP13 9AF

There is a display at Coleshill House, a National Trust property in Wiltshire, which was the training centre for the Auxiliary Units.

Use these records for

- Researching men (and women) who served in the Home Guard.
- They can provide an insight into life on the home front.

Pitfalls

- The records are very patchy.
- There is very little about the Auxiliary Units or the Women's Auxiliaries.

WOMEN'S LAND ARMY (WLA)

Originally established during the First World War before being disbanded in 1919, the Women's Land Army was re-mobilised in 1939 to help the war effort. These 'land girls', as they became known, were critical to increasing food production. At the height of its influence, the Women's Land Army was comprised of more than 80,000 women working on the farms and in the fields, in a variety of ways. This included tasks such poultry farming, rodent catching and hay bailing. These women hailed from range of different lifestyles, whether from town, city or village all were integral to the success of the service. The government initially asked for volunteers, but later moved to conscripting women.

Josie Kurton, who had grown up in a Jewish family in the East End, joined the Women's Land Army In her reminiscences published on the Hastingleigh One Place Study website, she wrote:

> Apart from patriotic reasons there was a dream of living in the country one day. As a child we sometimes went to Epping Forest in Essex for walks and picnics. My grandmother inspired me with a longing for the country. I loved fields and woods and also tales of her beautiful homeland of forests and lakes of Lithuania.

She was stationed in the remote Kentish village of Hastingleigh, where she 'felt that the countryside was my home and I belonged to it'.[13]

Not all volunteers were well treated. In her contribution to the BBC People's History project, Grace Wallace, who was sent to rural West Wales, found that:

> Some of the farmers thought we were there just to do all the dirty jobs that no one else would do. I remember going to one place with another girl. The Lady of the Manor took us to a field about one-and-a-half acres. It was covered with weeds and thistles almost as tall as ourselves. We were told to clear it. We had no gloves to wear so you can imagine what our hands were like at the end of the day. Even our faces were scratched. She used to sit in her car at the far end of the field to watch us. If it rained and we went to shelter under a tree she would come round and make us go back ... One day we decided we had had enough. The lady came to the hostel and asked us to go back, and we were supplied with a pair of gloves each, and cups of tea. It took a long time for the farmers to realise we were quite capable of doing a man's job when we had to.[14]

The Land Army was disbanded in 1950. Unfortunately, the service records themselves do not survive. However, there are 90,000 **index cards** revealing the employment details of the land girls in England and Wales. They are available on Ancestry. The cards include names, addresses and birth dates of the women, their civilian occupations, when they resigned and the circumstances for their resignation. They do not appear to be complete.

Similar records for the Scottish Women's Land Army are with the National Records of Scotland. These include some records for the Women's Timber Corps.

Use these records for

- Finding basic information about members of the Women's Land Army.

Pitfalls

- The information on the cards is very sparse, but is still useful as the service records have been destroyed.
- Not all the cards appear to survive.

Finding out more

There is an interesting Women's Land Army website with plenty about its work and the women who served in it. TNA has a useful blog entry on the work of the Land Army and the index cards. Finally, an article 'What was the Women's Land Army?' can be found on the IWM's website.

Useful address

National Records of Scotland: www.nrscotland.gov.uk
General Register House
2 Princes Street
Edinburgh
EH1 3YY

NATIONAL FARM SURVEY

On the outbreak of war, Britain faced an urgent need to grow more crops. Land that was once assumed to be unsuitable was put under the plough. Between 1941 and 1943 some 300,000 farms and other agricultural holdings of 5 acres or more were surveyed for the National Farm Survey, a 'permanent and comprehensive record of the conditions on the farms of England and Wales' which was to form the basis of post-war agricultural planning. Farmers were required to complete the survey, and many were interviewed as well. Completed forms are in series MAF 32 (with maps in MAF 73). The landowner and tenant farmers are given as well as the name of the property. They are arranged by county and then parish. These records are not yet online, but should be available by 2028.

Further reading

There is TNA Research Guide on the National Farm Survey.

Geraldine Beech and Rose Mitchell, *Maps for Family and Local History* (The National Archives, 2004)

Brian Short, Charles Watkins, William Foot and Phil Kinsman, *The National Farm Survey 1941–43* (CABI, 1999)

PUBLIC SERVANTS

CIVIL SERVANTS

There was a massive increase in the Civil Service during the Second World War with the creation of new ministries such as those for Food, War Transport, and Aircraft Production, never mind quasi-military bodies such as the Political Warfare and Special Operations executives. Total war forced other departments to take on additional roles, from directing agricultural planting to blockading the Axis powers.

Unfortunately, it is almost impossible to find very much about individual civil servants. No personal records survive. But there are some sources, particularly if the person you are researching was a senior official. Even so, you might only find out which department within a ministry they worked in and possibly their job title. Occasionally, a date or appointment might be given together with letters after their names showing any honours they had received.

Senior civil servants (as well as senior army, air force and navy officers) may have entries in *Who's Who*.

Civil servants are listed in the *Imperial Calendar* (now the *Civil Service List*). In addition, people employed by the Foreign Office or the Colonial Office are listed in the *Foreign Office List* and the *Colonial Office List*. The lists often include short biographies, listing postings and other details. Unfortunately, it is difficult to track these books down, although big reference libraries may have sets and copies are on the open shelves in the reference room at TNA. Few, if any, volumes appear to be online for the period of the war.

The Army, Navy and Air lists also list senior civilian employees at the War Office, Admiralty and Air Ministry respectively.

The appointment and promotion of civil servants, particularly if they worked in an organisation that worked with the military, such as the dockyards, are sometimes recorded in the *London Gazette*.

LOCAL GOVERNMENT

Local government too played an important role in the war, particularly with air raid precautions, providing allotments, education and libraries and in the repair of damaged properties.

The employment of staff, promotions (and dismissals) as well as pay rises are covered in council minutes. Councils operated through a system of committees for education, parks, civil defence and other services, which

'WVS members making gauze bandages, 1942', a charcoal drawing by Erund Hudson. (Wellcome Library Ref 660086i)

reported to the full council. The committee minutes and attached papers will record appointments etc. They should also be very well indexed, although, in my experience, indexing sometimes lapsed during wartime.

The records should be with the county record office or local studies libraries.

VOLUNTARY WORK

Almost forgotten is the voluntary work that people – particularly women – carried out, knitting garments for the troops or those in hospital, collecting items for recycling and selling flags for war charities. Few, if any, records survive, but their activities feature in many newspaper articles. Occasionally, there may be collections of ephemera or minutes of local organisations at local archives.

If you have an aunt or grandmother who joined the Women's [Royal] Voluntary Service it is worth contacting the Royal Voluntary Service archives to see whether it has anything. For members of the wartime Women's Institute there may be material in its archives.

THE CHANNEL ISLANDS

On 30 June 1940, Guernsey, Jersey and the smaller islands that make up the Channel Islands were occupied by the Nazis. The British had decided that the islands were impossible to defend. In the days before the Germans arrived, many islanders, particularly children, were evacuated to England.

For just under five years, the islands were under Nazi occupation. Initially, German control was relatively benign, but this changed as the war turned against them. The islands eventually became the most heavily fortified areas of Hitler's 'Atlantic Wall' – a line of massive defence works that stretched from the Baltic to the Spanish frontier. The local fortifications include some of the best-surviving examples of their kind in Western Europe and many are of a design that is unique to the Channel Islands. The islanders came close to starvation in the months leading to liberation on 9 May 1945, which is still celebrated as a public holiday.

Thousands of local men, and a few women, were deported to Europe either to a concentration camp, if they were in the resistance, or to work in factories. In turn, tens of thousands of forced labourers were imported to build the fortifications, barracks and military hospitals. In particular, they worked on several small labour camps that were built on Alderney.

Because of the size of the islands, there was little effective resistance against the occupiers. Most residents were more interested in survival rather than striking a probably pointless blow for freedom.

RESEARCH

TNA has, of course, some material. Of particular interest are the interrogations of Channel Islanders who managed to escape to Britain, including several East European slave labourers. which are in series WO 208. One such person was Machansek Duquemin, who is described in the catalogue as being a 'loafer', he escaped with a friend in a fishing boat while employed ferrying supplies to Alderney. The reports contain eyewitness accounts of life on Guernsey and Jersey.[15]

GUERNSEY, ALDERNEY AND SARK

Most records are held by Guernsey Archives in St Peter Port. A little material is held by the Priaulx Library, which is, in effect, the island's local studies library. The Guernsey branch of the Channel Islands Occupation Society also has a useful website.

JERSEY

Here, Jersey Heritage is the place to start. Quite a lot of material has been digitised and can be downloaded, for a fee. Start your research by looking for an Occupation Registration Card. Each card contains personal details including name, address, date of birth, and many have a photograph. Children under the age of 14 are recorded on the back of a parent's card. They can be downloaded from the site above. An index, giving brief details, is also available on both Ancestry and Findmypast.

Between 1943 and 1945 many families who had been evacuated to the mainland completed applications to return to Jersey at the end of the war. Jersey Heritage has an incomplete set of applications.

Further reading

Madeleine Bunting, *The Model Occupation: The Channel Islands under German Rule, 1940–1945* (HarperCollins, 1995)

Barry Turner, *Outpost of Occupation: The Nazi Occupation of the Channel Islands, 1940–1945* (Aurum, 2011)

The Frank Falla Archive is a brilliant resource for anybody interested in the German occupation, particularly the deportation of islanders to Europe to the death camps or the munitions factories. There are lists of individual deportees, as well as articles about the individual camps that the men were sent to. Falla himself was a journalist on Guernsey and was deported to Germany for publishing an underground newspaper.

Museums

Both Guernsey and Jersey have a variety of visitor attractions and museums devoted to the German occupation.

BRITISH CITIZENS OVERSEAS

Tens of thousands of British citizens were living in Europe at the outbreak of war. Some managed to return home, but most stayed. Either they were too old to move, had married local people or felt, wrongly, that the war would not affect them.

The most famous British resident was the writer P.G. Wodehouse, who found himself on the wrong side of history when Nazi Germany invaded France. Wodehouse was living in Le Touquet, a prosperous French coastal town, with his wife Ethel, their dogs, and Coco the parrot. According to Wodehouse:

> All that happened, as far as I was concerned, was that I was strolling on the lawn with my wife one morning, when she lowered her voice and said, 'Don't look now, but there comes the German army.' And there they were, a fine body of men, rather prettily dressed in green, carrying machine guns.[16]

In July 1940, the German occupiers announced that all British men in occupied France under the age of 60 were to be interned immediately. As a result, Wodehouse spent nearly a year in internment camps, before making five fairly innocuous broadcasts on German radio trying to reassure his American readers that he was in good spirits. His reputation never recovered from this act of co-operation, however naive. In the words of George Orwell, one of the few outspoken defenders of Wodehouse after the war: 'His main idea … was to keep in touch with his public and – the comedian's ruling passion – to get a laugh.'[17]

Wodehouse spent the rest of the war in Berlin and then returned to France, where he was interrogated by MI5 after Paris was liberated. Because of his fame and his wealth, Wodehouse largely escaped the worst aspects of being an enemy alien in occupied Europe.

Several hundred unfortunate British citizens died in concentration camps. Mary Young was a Scottish nurse who moved to Paris before the First World War and made her life there. In late 1943, she was arrested by the Gestapo, who accused her of aiding escaped prisoners of war and allowing SOE agents to send messages from her attic, although it is unclear whether this was actually the case. Miss Young was sent to the concentration camp at Ravensbrück, where she died a few weeks before it was liberated by the Russians. When the news eventually reached Scotland, she was proclaimed as being the country's own Nurse Cavell.[18]

Details of British civilian deaths in concentration camps and in air raids can be found in the records of the Commonwealth War Graves Commission.

The best place to find information on British citizens overseas is in the records of the Foreign Office. The records themselves are not online but detailed indexes to the FO General Correspondence are in series FO 409 at Kew and can be consulted on TNA's website. However, as there is no keyword search, using the indexes can be cumbersome. As well as descriptions of the great events of the day, there are entries for many individuals who contacted the Office for some reason or other together with a brief description of the reason, perhaps an enquiry about a passport, pension or the award of a decoration. Unfortunately, the correspondence has almost always been destroyed, but occasionally something does survive. The records are described in a TNA Research Guide: 'Foreign Office and-Foreign-and-Commonwealth Office Correspondence 1920 onward'.

Much about the relief and support of British civilians, particularly in Europe, with many lists of individuals, are in series FO 916. The series contains rather less about civilian internees in the Far East. Occasionally, material about civilian internees in enemy hands can be found among the records of British prisoners of war (see Chapter 3).

Further reading

Katherine Lack, *Frontstalag142: The Internment Diary of an English lady* (The History Press, 2010)

8

THE WIDER WAR

THE BRITISH COMMONWEALTH

With the exception of the Irish Free State, the dominions of Australia, Canada, New Zealand and South Africa all declared war on Germany in September 1939. Together with India and the British colonies, they played a very full part in the war effort.

By 1945, it was clear that the British Empire could no longer survive. The surrender of the supposedly impregnable island of Singapore to the Japanese in 1942 had demonstrated dramatically that Britain was no longer a world power. Australia and New Zealand, in particular, became closely allied with the United States. As the result of agreements made during the war, India, Pakistan and Burma (Myanmar) became independent in 1947, followed by most other British colonies in the two decades that followed.

When serving in the European and Mediterranean theatres of war, Commonwealth forces were often under British command and subsumed for operational purposes into British forces. For example, there were a number of Canadian, Australian and New Zealand squadrons in the RAF. So if you are tracing a Commonwealth serviceman you may need to consult the records described elsewhere in this book. And, of course, many British-born immigrants served in local forces.

There was also the semi-autonomous Indian Empire (now India, Pakistan and Bangladesh), which was run by the British under a viceroy. The Raj was made up of British-controlled India and a number of nominally independent native states, although here the dominant figure was always the British resident. During the war, the sub-continent was often in turmoil as politicians such as Nehru, Gandhi and Jinnah pressed for independence. Eventually, this was promised in return for support for the war effort. The British Army maintained a number of garrisons in the sub-continent. In addition, there was a separate Indian army, air force and navy under the control of the viceroy and commanded by British officers with an increasing number of Indian junior officers.

COMMON SOURCES

With few exceptions, records are very similar to those you might encounter researching the British services. These are described in Chapter 3.

Promotions of officers of Commonwealth and Imperial forces are noted in the *London Gazette*. Promotions etc. also appeared in government gazettes published by individual dominions and colonies. TNA has an almost complete set of volumes.

MEDALS AND AWARDS

Campaign and gallantry medals were almost identical to those awarded in Britain, although the dominions also issued a separate campaign medal to their veterans. The award of gallantry medals to Commonwealth and Imperial forces are also noted in the *London Gazette*.

CASUALTIES

The deaths of all dominion and colonial forces are recorded by the Commonwealth War Graves Commission.

There are various memorials to forces from the Commonwealth who served in Britain during the war in or near Green Park in London. Of particular note are the Memorial Gates, which pay powerful tribute to the 5 million people from India, Africa and the Caribbean who served in two world wars.

OPERATIONAL RECORDS

Commonwealth forces were largely embedded within British command structures, so there may be records at TNA or, for the Indian services, at the British Library.

A selection of Commonwealth Orders of Battle (often referred to as Orbats) is on the British & Commonwealth Orders of Battle website. Orders of Battle are listings of military units in a given division or brigade and are useful if you want to research particular units that ancestors served in.

Further reading

Stephen Bourne, *Mother Country: Britain's Black Community on the Home Front, 1939–45* (The History Press, 2010)

Ashley Jackson, *The British Empire and the Second World War* (Hambledon, 2006)
Jonathan Fennell, *Fighting the People's War: The British and Commonwealth Armies and the Second World War* (Cambridge University Press, 2019)

AUSTRALIA

The Japanese attack on Pearl Harbor and, more particularly, the fall of Singapore, removed Australia from the protective wing of the United Kingdom and turned it towards the United States. The British could not protect the country, and for the first time in its history Australia faced a real threat from another nation. In reality there were only minor attacks on its soil – a midget submarine in Sydney Harbour and air raids on Darwin. Over the next three years, Australian forces fought to clear the Japanese from New Guinea, special forces launched raids on Singapore and Borneo, and Australian civilians welcomed tens of thousands of American service personnel who were based in the country.

That is not to say that the needs of the Mother Country were neglected. Until 1942, Australian soldiers fought bravely in Crete and North Africa, and tens of thousands of Aussies joined the Air Offensive over Europe or crewed merchant ships. Ships from the Royal Australian Navy operated as part the Royal Navy until the Pacific War, when those ships took part in US Navy offensives or defended Australian waters against enemy attacks. By the end of the war it was the fourth largest navy in the world.

Nearly 1 million men and women served in the nation's armed services (navy, army and air force) or the Merchant Navy, of whom about half served overseas.

About 10,000 Australian servicemen became prisoners of war in Europe. Another 22,000 were prisoners in the Asia-Pacific theatres. Here almost 8,000 died in captivity under horrendous slave labour conditions.

THE RECORDS

The National Archives of Australia has service records for the Australian Army, Royal Australian Navy (RAN) and Royal Australian Air Force (RAAF). They are very similar to their British equivalents. Like those in the UK, they are being digitised at present. There is a well-designed and informative introduction to the records in the Explore Collection pages of the archives' website.

The best place to start, however, is with the nominal rolls for Australian service personnel. Indexes to the rolls are available on the Department of Veteran Affairs website. They will tell you an individual's service number and unit, date of death if it occurred while on military service, and give various personal details, including the next of kin.

The Australian equivalent to the Imperial War Museum is the Australian War Memorial (AWM) in Canberra, which has a superb collection of research material online. It maintains an online roll of honour indicating the unit, date and place of death of the fallen. The information is based on the Roll of Honour displayed at the museum itself. There is also a much smaller Commemorative Roll for civilians who were killed during the war in Australia itself.

The key resource on the website are the unit war diaries and the equivalents for the RAAF and RAN.

CANADA

Canada's greatest effort to the Allied victory may have been the supply of munitions and military material for Britain. Like that of her great neighbour to the South, production boomed during the war. Many RAF pilots came to Canada as part of the Empire Flying Training Scheme and enemy prisoners of war together with enemy aliens were interned in camps.

Over a million Canadians served in the nation's armed forces, of whom 42,000 were killed and another 55,000 wounded. Canadian troops played important roles in many key battles of the war, particularly the ill-fated 1942 Dieppe Raid and the Normandy landings. Canada provided asylum for the Dutch monarchy, and Canadian troops were largely responsible for the liberation of the Netherlands in April and May 1945.

Canadian industries saw a significant increase in business during the war, as they supplied miliary materiel not only for themselves but for Britain, China and the Soviet Union. As a result, the Canadian economy boomed. [1]

THE RECORDS

Canadian records are largely with Library and Archives Canada in Ottawa.

Service records for Canadian servicemen of the Second World War who were discharged after the war's end are still closed to public access. You will need to submit an Access to Information and Privacy (ATIP) request to Library and Archives Canada (LAC). It is possible to do this online.

Canadian troops land on Juno Beach during the Normandy landings, June 1944. The taking of the beach was primarily a Canadian operation. (National Archives of Canada/Wikimedia Commons)

For service personnel who are deceased you may need to supply a death certificate or other evidence of their decease.

However, if the individual you are interested in was one of the 44,000 men and women who died while in the services, or during 1946 or 1947 of injuries related to service after their discharge, then the records can be downloaded free of charge. Unlike their British equivalents, they include detailed medical records.

Medals and replacement medals can be obtained from the Honours and Awards Section, Veterans Affairs Canada, Honours & Awards Section, Ottawa, Ontario, K1A 0P4. Email: awards-citations@veterans.gc.ca

Lists and citations for Canadians in the RCAF and RAF who were awarded gallantry medals, arranged in alphabetical order, can be found on the RCAF Association website. The website also has a lot about the RCAF in wartime.

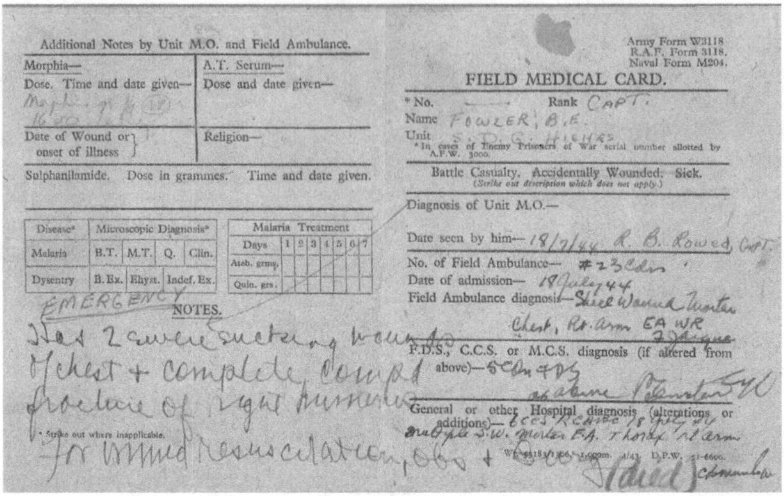
Additional Notes by Unit M.O. and Field Ambulance.

Morphia— Dose. Time and date given—	A.T. Serum— Dose and date given—
Date of Wound or onset of illness	Religion—

Sulphanilamide. Dose in grammes. Time and date given.

Disease*	Microscopic Diagnosis*			
Malaria	B.T.	M.T.	Q.	Clin.
Dysentry	B. Ex.	Bhyst.	Indef. Ex.	

Malaria Treatment							
Days	1	2	3	4	5	6	7
Atab. grms.							
Quin. grs.							

EMERGENCY
NOTES.
Has 2 severe sucking wounds of chest + complete compd fracture of right humerus
For immed resuscitation

* Strike out where inapplicable.

Army Form W3118
R.A.F. Form 3118.
Naval Form M204.
FIELD MEDICAL CARD.
* No. Rank CAPT.
Name FOWLER, B.E.
Unit S.D.G. HIGHRS
* In cases of Enemy Prisoners of War serial number allotted by A.F.W. 3000.
Battle Casualty. Accidentally Wounded. Sick.
(Strike out description which does not apply.)
Diagnosis of Unit M.O.—
Date seen by him— 18/7/44 R. B. Rowed, Capt.
No. of Field Ambulance— #23 Cdn.
Date of admission— 18 July 44
Field Ambulance diagnosis— Shell Wound Mortar Chest, Rt. Arm EA WR
F.D.S., C.C.S. or M.C.S. diagnosis (if altered from above)—
General or other Hospital diagnosis (alterations or additions)—
Died

Medical card, taken from the service record for Captain Byron Fowler, Stormont, Dundas and Glengarry Highlanders, who died of wounds on 18 July 1944 from mortar fire. (Library and Archives Canada/Veteran Affairs Canada)

The Canadian Virtual War Memorial contains details of the last resting places of 116,000 Canadian and Newfoundland servicemen from all wars of the twentieth century. As well as including the details found on the Commonwealth War Graves Commission website, there is additional information about places where an individual is commemorated in Canada, and photographs of the grave and sometimes the individual themselves.

War diaries, log books and operation record books for Canadian army and air force units and ships are with Library and Archives Canada. Many are also available on the Canadiana Héritage website. They are normally digitised microfilms, so the quality does vary somewhat. In addition, indexing is pretty minimal.

Miscellaneous records

Many resources relating to Canada's contribution to the Second World War can be found on the website of the Department of Veteran Affairs.

Small collections of Canadian material are available on both Ancestry and Findmypast. British subscribers will need to have the worldwide subscription package to access it.

Further reading

The Canadian military historian Tim Cook has written a number of well-regarded books about the Canadian experience in the Second World War.

Much about the Canadian Army in the war can be found on the excellent Canadian Soldiers website.

Guides to researching Canadian military personnel in the Second World War can be found in Military History Research Centre, part of the Canadian War Museum website.

INDIA

India made a large but often overlooked contribution to Allied victory. By August 1945, the Indian Army had become the largest volunteer army in history, with 2.5 million men in the colours. The Indian Army fought in Italy and North Africa, although by 1942 it was largely fighting the Japanese in Burma. Some 87,000 Indian service personnel lost their lives. Eighteen members of the Indian Army were awarded the Victoria Cross or the George Cross. At the end of the war, Winston Churchill paid tribute to 'the unsurpassed bravery of Indian soldiers and officers.'

The majority of the officers in the British Indian Army were British men who had joined the army, trained at the Royal Military College, Sandhurst and were then sent out to India.

There was also an increasing number of Viceroy's commissioned officers (VCOs), experienced Indian soldiers who were granted a commission by the Viceroy of India. They served as platoon commanders (jemadars) and second in command of companies (subadars). Each battalion or regiment had one subadar-major, who was the most senior Indian officer in the unit and a key person for the British commanding officer to work with.

In the early 1920s, Indian soldiers started to attend Sandhurst and on commission they became King's commissioned officers (KCOs) with the same status as their British colleagues. The war inevitably hastened a process of 'Indianisation' with a large increase in native officers. Even so, at the end of the war, the highest rank held by an Indian was that of brigadier.

Sources in the UK

Many records for the Indian Army are with the British Library (BL) in London as they inherited the records of the India and Burma offices in Whitehall after Indian, Pakistani and Burmese independence in 1947. An excellent guide to the Records is Ian A. Baxter, *Baxter's Guide: Biographical Sources in the India Office Records* (3rd edition, Families in British India Society, 2004).

The National Army Museum may also be able to help, as it has major collections relating to the Indian Army before 1947. For the Garhwal Rifles, for example, there are uniforms, details of reunion dinners, regimental histories, oral histories, personal diaries and, of course, many photographs. Some material, mainly photographs and paintings, is online. Otherwise you may need to visit the Templar Centre at the museum to consult original material.

Service records

Personal files of British officers and warrant officers in the Indian Army (including women's units such as the Women's Auxiliary Army Corps) are in series L/MIL/14 and Royal Indian Navy and Royal Indian Naval Volunteer Reserve in L/MIL/16 at the British Library. Other papers and correspondence can be found in series L/MIL/7. Officers, both British and Indian, are also listed in the *India Army Lists* and the equivalents for other services. The BL has a complete set and incomplete runs may be found elsewhere. Promotions of officers are also given in the *London Gazette*.

For service records of Indian officers and other ranks, contact the Adjutant General's Office, Indian Headquarters of the Ministry of Defence (Army), Room No. 280, South Block, New Delhi 110011. Email: agbrancharmyhq@gmail.com. The personal files are organised by the service record numbers, so it is necessary to have one to find an individual.

After independence in August 1947, most regiments of the old Indian Army were absorbed into either the new Indian or Pakistan armies and many are still in existence. Some have regimental museums and archives, so it may be worth contacting the appropriate unit to see whether they have any material.

Casualty returns for officers can be found at the British Library in items L/MIL/14/128–143.

TNA has war diaries for many Indian units. Those for units in the Middle East are in WO 169, Italy WO 170, and Burma WO 172 (see Chapter 4 for more details).

The National Army Museum and, to a lesser extent, the Imperial War Museum have copies of official histories together with other material, including collections of private papers and interviews with veterans.

Further reading

Diya Gupta, *India in the Second World War* (Oxford University Press, 2023)
Yasmin Khan, *The Raj at War: A People's History of India's Second World War* (Oxford University Press, 2015)

The Families in British India Society has a very good website with lots of useful information for researching the British in India.

The British Military History website offers a good introduction to the Indian Army.

The Burma Campaign is an excellent website devoted to the campaign in Burma, and the Burmese forces who fought in it. The Burma Star Memorial website includes details of individual members of the Burma Star Association as well as the Association's newsletter *Decko*.

Useful addresses

British Library
96 Euston Road
London
NW1 2DB
www.bl.uk

NEWFOUNDLAND

Now part of Canada (which it joined in 1949), Newfoundland in 1939 was technically a dominion. However, as a result of the Great Depression it had become bankrupt in 1933 and reverted to British control. During the war, men were recruited and trained for two regiments in the Royal Artillery. The largest single contingent of Newfoundlanders to go overseas, however, was the Newfoundland Forestry Unit. Of a total population of 321,819 in 1945 (including Labrador) more than

12,000 were involved, through service in the Newfoundland Militia, the Forestry Unit and the seamen in the Merchant Navy. The Royal Newfoundland Regiment was a home defence militia.

Newfoundland's geographical position as the eastern-most point in North America meant that it became an important staging point for aircraft crossing the Atlantic and to allow anti-submarine patrols to extend into the ocean to protect the convoys from U-boat attack.

Service records for Newfoundlanders in the Royal Artillery are with the Ministry of Defence/TNA.

No records of the Forestry Unit are known to survive.

Further reading

An account of the province's role in the war is provided by the Canadian War Museum in its Despatches blog.

Also of interest are the Heritage Newfoundland and Labrador webpages about the Second World War.

NEW ZEALAND

Of all the British dominions, New Zealand remained closest to the United Kingdom. Early in the war it was agreed that the country's security depended on British success around 11,500 miles away in Europe. Only here could the enemy be defeated and New Zealand's contribution, necessarily relatively small, could best help achieve such an outcome. The New Zealand Expeditionary force fought gallantly in Crete and across North Africa and Italy. New Zealanders were encouraged to join the RAF and Royal Navy rather than their national air forces and navies, as was the case in the other dominions.

In total, 194,000 men and 10,000 women served in the armed forces, of whom 11,928 lost their lives. New Zealand's ratio of killed per million of population (at 6,684) was the highest in the Commonwealth. The British ratio was 5,123 and the Australian 3,232.

THE RECORDS

Service records for New Zealand personnel are still held by the New Zealand Defence Force's Personnel Archives. There is no access to service records for personnel still alive. To get access to records of deceased servicemen you will need to prove their death. More information can be found on the New Zealand Government's Military History, Records and Medals webpages.

Archives New Zealand has nominal rolls for troops who went overseas. Rolls usually include name, number, rank, occupation, unit, conjugal status, place of enlistment, last New Zealand address, and name and address of next of kin. Some are organised by brigade or similar level unit. They are not online.

The Personnel Archives will also help with enquiries about medals. Archives New Zealand also has files about the award of gallantry medals.

Casualty records

An 'Online cenotaph' giving details of New Zealanders who lost their lives during the war is maintained by the Auckland War Memorial.

At the end of the war, details of some fifty official histories recording New Zealand's war effort, including battalion level studies, were prepared. They are online at the Official History of New Zealand in the Second World War website.

Official records of the three services including war diaries and the like are held by Archives New Zealand, in Wellington.

Unofficial records relating to the New Zealand Army during the war, including unit records, newspapers and personnel papers, are with the Army Museum, in Waiouru, www.armymuseum.co.nz. The Air Force Museum in Christchurch maintains a specialist research collection covering the history of the RNZAF and military aviation in general.

Further reading

Ian McGibbon, *New Zealand and the Second World War: The People, The Battles and The Legacy* (Hodder Moa Beckett, 2004)

The excellent New Zealand History website has much about the country's experience during the war.

A guide to the key holdings of Archives New Zealand relating to the war is on its website.

RHODESIA

In 1939, Zimbabwe (then known as Southern Rhodesia) was a self-governing colony largely run by the European minority. It had considerable autonomy in domestic matters, although foreign and military affairs still continued to be controlled by London. The colony's most important contribution to the war effort was probably the Empire Air Training Scheme (EATS), which trained British and Allied airmen at local flying schools.

Over 25,000 Rhodesians served in the armed forces, a third of whom served overseas. Many of those who served became members of British or South African units in order to try to prevent high losses. However, a Rhodesian unit, the Rhodesian African Rifles – comprised of Black troops and white officers – served in Burma from late 1944.

Tens of thousands of local men were conscripted from rural communities to work, initially to build aerodromes and later labouring on white-owned farms.

If individual service personnel served in the British or South African forces, service and related records should be with the appropriate archives. It is not known where records of the Rhodesian African Rifles are, but the National Archives of Zimbabwe may be able to help. Its email is: archives@isp.gov.zw.

War diaries for the Rifles are with TNA.

SOUTH AFRICA

South Africa's role in the Second World War was limited, largely for political reasons. The white population, which ran the country, was split between the Afrikaners, who were suspicious of British intentions and many of whom were sympathetic to the Nazis, and the English speakers, who strongly supported the war. British and Allied troops breaking their journey at Cape Town or Durban on their way to the Middle East were always assured of a warm welcome in South African homes.

Only Europeans were recruited for front-line service, although the majority Black population could join various support units working behind the lines. About 334,000 men, largely white, volunteered for full-time service in the Union Defence Force (UDF). The Force fought in East Africa, in the Western Desert and finally in Italy.

THE RECORDS

Most official records are held by the Department of Defence Archives. In particular, they have personnel records for all former members of the wartime Union Defence Force. Researchers should contact the Department of Defence Archives, Private Bag X289, Pretoria 0001, South Africa. Email: sandfdoc@mweb.co.za or archive@dod.mil.za. At the time of writing, the archives does not appear to have a website. It might be sensible to employ a local researcher with experience of the system to undertake the work for you.

Copies of operations record books for the South African Air Force are in series AIR 54 at TNA. They can be downloaded from TNA's website.

Further information

The South African Military History Society is a brilliant resource for researching the country's involvement in the Second World War, as there is free access to the Society's journal, which has many articles about the war.

The Ditsong National Museum of Military History, located in the Johannesburg suburbs, is South Africa's national history museum. There are various displays relating to the Union's involvement in the Second World War.

SA Air Force, is an excellent website devoted to the current and past of the South African Air Force. Usefully, it contains a list of potential researchers who can help you deal with the Department of Defence Archives.

THE COLONIES AND PROTECTORATES

As well as the dominions there were many colonies and protectorates. Most were poor and generally contributed little to the war effort, except perhaps occupying a strategic position or supplying raw materials for factories in Britain. Some supplied volunteers to come to the UK to work on the land or in factories, including the British Honduras Forestry Unit. In addition, individuals, particularly from the West Indian islands, made their way to Britain in order to enlist in the forces.

Men also volunteered to serve in local regiments. Some 100,000 men from Nigeria and the Gold Coast (Ghana) fought in Italian East Africa and then played a major role in the Burma Campaign. During the Japanese invasions of Malaya and Hong Kong, local volunteer forces put up some gallant resistance. In Hong Kong, out of the mobilised strength of 2,200 in the local Volunteer Defence Corps, 289 were listed either as missing or killed, and many others became prisoners of war. The services of the corps were later recognised by the award of nineteen gallantry awards and a further eighteen Mentions in Despatches for gallantry and good service. The corps' regimental association maintains an interesting website.

A number of colonies raised pioneer battalions to help supply front-line units or build and maintain facilities. The Cyprus Regiment, for example, included infantry, mechanical transport and mule pack transport corps. Another such unit was the African Auxiliary Pioneer Corps, later the African Pioneer Corps, which recruited men from Lesotho (Basutoland), Botswana (Bechuanaland), and Eswatini (Swaziland) in Southern Africa. The corps provided crucial logistical support to the Allied war effort during the North African, Dodecanese and Italian campaigns. Its duties were gradually expanded to include anti-aircraft artillery operation and other combat duties. Beside the appropriate campaign stars and service medals, they were awarded two MBEs, seven MMs, eight BEMs, sixty-one Mentions in Despatches and twenty-three Commendations for Gallantry. Some 36,000 men volunteered for service, 1,216 of whom died during the war; nearly 700 were drowned in one incident on 1 May 1943 when the British troopship SS *Erinpura* was torpedoed and sunk.

Service records for members of colonial regiments that were directly under the control of the War Office are considered as being part of the British Army: the Cyprus Regiment; the Palestine Regiment (which was subsumed into the Jewish Brigade in 1944); the King's African Rifles; and the Royal West African Frontier Force. They are with the Ministry of Defence and will be transferred to TNA in due course.

Most colonies formed small units, generally with volunteers, in the title to defend the colony. Where this is the case, the records should be with the local archives or possibly still with the military.

Further reading

West Indies Calling is an interesting short film, made in 1944, about the West Indians in Britain at www.youtube.com/watch?v=ViGwxJloI70. A film about the participation of Trinidad and Tobago in the war is at www.youtube.com/watch?v=8XC_Gyfff8Y

IRELAND

The twenty-six counties of southern Ireland – then known as the Irish Free State or Éire – remained neutral during what it called 'The Emergency', but it could not entirely escape the war. There were several German air raids on Dublin, for example, and food was always in short supply. Aircrew of the belligerent countries who crashed on Irish soil were interned, although those from the Allies were eventually repatriated. Inevitably, bearing in mind Ireland's geographical location, there was planning between British and Irish military in case of a German invasion. More importantly, nearly 50,000 men volunteered for the British services, including over 4,000 deserters from the Irish Army, and another 250,000 men and women found work in British factories, hospitals and offices.

Northern Ireland, as part of the United Kingdom, played a full part in the war, except that there was no conscription. There was a major raid on Belfast in April 1941, which caused much damage. American troops were stationed there from 1942.

THE RECORDS

The Military Archives in Dublin has service records for men in the Irish forces. Other material can be found at the National Archives of Ireland which is also in Dublin.

Northern Ireland had considerable autonomy during the Second World War and most records relating to internal affairs are with the Public Record Office of Northern Ireland (PRONI) in Belfast. Military records, however, are largely with TNA at Kew.

Further reading

Brian Barton, *Northern Ireland in the Second World War* (Ulster Historical Foundation, 1995)

Tony Gray, *The Lost Years: The Emergency in Ireland 1939–1945* (Warner, 1997)

Ian Maxwell, *Tracing Irish Ancestors* (Pen & Sword, 2009)

Ian Maxwell, *Tracing your Northern Irish Ancestors* (Pen & Sword, 2010)

The WW2 in NI website includes a useful section on museums in the Province that have displays about the war.

THE UNITED STATES OF AMERICA

Nearly 3 million American men and women were stationed in the United Kingdom (including Northern Ireland) during the Second World War. The first personnel arrived even before America entered the war in December 1941.

On the outbreak of war in 1939, the United States was strictly neutral but increasingly leant towards the Western allies. Lend-lease, for example, allowed the supply of war goods to the belligerents at no cost to the recipients. As Conrad Black, one of biographers of Franklin D. Roosevelt noted: 'If there was no practical alternative, there was certainly no moral one either. Britain and the Commonwealth were carrying the battle for all civilization, and the overwhelming majority of Americans wished to help them.'[2] As Roosevelt himself put it: 'There can be no reasoning with incendiary bombs.'[3] At least initially, the equipment supplied was of little use to the war effort, but for the British it was a sign of American commitment to the Allied cause.

Probably of more long-term value was the decision made by Winston Churchill in September 1940 to share all British scientific secrets with the United States, which was a major factor in the development of the Atomic Bomb, radar and a host of other technologies. By mid-1943, the Americans were the dominant partner in the Western alliance as a result of the huge production of munitions of all kinds and the spread of US armed forces across the world.

After the United States entered the war in December 1941, the number of Americans in bases and airfields across the United Kingdom increased rapidly as service personnel arrived in preparation for the invasion of France. Only after D-Day did the numbers fall away. As well as GIs training for the great day, there were dozens of airfields for American fighter and bomber squadrons, naval facilities in the ports, and a variety of other establishments. Almost every town and village appears to have had an American base of some kind.

The site where TNA in Kew is now, for example, housed a unit of mapmakers. The first cartographers arrived in September 1942. 'They were welcomed, first by a band of the Irish Guards in kilts at Richmond station, then by the Coldstream Guards with a meal in Ruskin Avenue and finally by a Luftwaffe air raid just after they had gone to bed.'[4]

Despite grumbles about Americans flaunting their wealth, relations were generally cordial. Relatively few Americans had been overseas before and their hosts, brought up on a diet of Hollywood movies, were curious to know more about the world they had seen in the films.[5] There was much puzzlement over the colour bar imposed by the American military authorities; the troops were widely welcomed by their British hosts.

Inevitably, there were romances. It is estimated that 70,000 British girls married American soldiers and another 40,000 married Canadian men.[6] One of the first Americans to find an English bride was Lieutenant Stephen Paull, who married Hilda May Smith of Twickenham after a whirlwind romance on 24 January 1942. A physics teacher from Michigan, he had enlisted in the US Signal Corps and had arrived in England during the previous November to receive training at the Radar Research Establishment in Richmond.[7]

The United States Army Air Force (USAAF) was formally established in June 1941. Technically it was part of the army but in practice was an independent service. It quickly became the world's most powerful air force.American air units, under the command of VIII Bomber Command, later the Eighth Air Force, began to arrive in Britain in the spring of 1942. By mid-1943 the USAAF was playing a key part in the strategic bombing offensive on Germany. The Americans concentrated on day raids, leaving night raids to the RAF, flying largely from airfields across eastern England.

SERVICE RECORDS

As with British service records, it is helpful to have a full name, date and place of birth, as well as service. In addition, it is useful to have an address, particularly the state where the individual lived at the time they enlisted.

Service records for militia, volunteer, or regular forces document that an individual served in the military and can provide your ancestor's unit or organisation. The National Personnel Records Center (NPRC) in St Louis has personnel files for men and women who served in the army, army air force, navy, marine corps and the coast guard. In July 1973, a fire destroyed about 85 per cent of the army and army air force individual personnel files, but staff are often able to locate basic information relevant to a person's service from other records in their care. Navy, marine corps and coast guard records were unaffected by the fire. You can contact the centre at www.archives.gov/veterans/military-service-records. There's a simple form to complete and a copying fee. However, at the time of writing there was a considerable backlog, and it may be some months before you receive the record.

DRAFT, CONSCRIPTION, OR SELECTIVE SERVICE RECORDS

Since 1863, the federal government has registered millions of men who may have been eligible for military service. Enrolment and Draft information includes name, residence, age, occupation, marital status, birthplace, physical description, and other information. They tend to be arranged by state. About half of army enlistment records are listed on the National Archives and Records Administration's (NARA) Access to Archival Databases service. It does not include officers. You can either search all the databases, which will provide the Social Security number if you were asked for this when ordering a service record from the NPRC, or you can just search this specific database. The information provided is pretty basic, but it does list a man's state, which allows researchers to see what is available at state level.

Many draft records are available online on FamilySearch or through the commercial services Ancestry/Fold3 or Findmypast. If you have an 'all areas' subscription, rather than just access to British resources, then you should be able to use all American material.

CASUALTY RECORDS

The American Battle Monuments Commission (ABMC) is comparable to the Commonwealth War Graves Commission. The information about individuals on its website is very similar to that found on the CWGC's, although there is no mention of the deceased's family. Unlike in Britain, the families of service personnel who die overseas can ask to have the bodies of deceased members repatriated.

The only American war cemetery in the United Kingdom is at Madingley, just outside Cambridge. The site was donated by the University of Cambridge. It lies on a slope with the west and south sides framed by woodland. The cemetery contains the remains of 3,811 war dead, and another 5,127 names are recorded on the Walls of the Missing. Rosettes mark the names of those whose bodies have since been recovered and identified. Most died during the Battle of the Atlantic or in the strategic air bombardment of north-west Europe. A visitor centre includes interpretive exhibits that incorporate personal stories, photographs, films, and interactive displays.

In Washington DC, the impressive World War II Memorial honours the 16 million people who served in the American armed forces, over 400,000 of whom died, and all who supported the war effort from afar.

The Memorial's website maintains a Registry of Remembrances, listing Americans who contributed to the war effort. Any American citizen who was involved in the war effort, whether a veteran or someone contributing to the home front, is eligible for inclusion on the Registry.

OPERATIONAL (UNIT) RECORDS

Use these records for

- Researching men and women who served in the US armed forces during the Second World War.

A DNA test may help identify a father or grandfather if you suspect that a GI was more just good friends with a family member. If you need assistance chasing down an American serviceman who you believe might be your father or grandfather, the GI Trace Service may be able to help in researching American troops who were based in your town or village.

Pitfalls

- Beware of false friends! Although the terminology used may look similar to that used in the British (and Commonwealth) armed services it can mean different things.
- The arrangement and storage of the archives is very different to that we may be familiar with in the UK, in part because, even during the war, American armed forces were so much larger than their British equivalents. If you are planning a large research project then it might be a good idea to employ a professional researcher or, at least, find books and websites that can help. A selection is given below.
- Only 15 per cent of army and army air force personnel files for the period of the Second World War survive. The rest were destroyed by fire in 1973.

Further reading

Duncan Barratt and Nuala Calvi, *GI Brides: The Wartime Girls Who Crossed the Atlantic for Love* (HarperCollins, 2013)
Juliet Gardiner, *'Over Here': the GIs in Wartime Britain* (Collins, 1992)
Jonathan Gawne, *Finding Your Father's War* (3rd edition, Casemate, 2020)
Debra Johnson Knox, *World War II Military Records: A Family Historian's Guide* (Mie Publishing, 2003)

Aerial view of the National World War II Memorial in Washington DC. (Carol M. Highsmith/Wikimedia Commons)

Norman Longmate, *The GIs: The Americans in Britain 1942–1945* (Hutchinson, 1975)
US War Department, *Instructions for American Servicemen in Britain, 1942* (republished Bodleian Library, 2005)

Useful addresses

National Personnel Records Center (Military Personnel Records), 1 Archives Drive, St Louis, MO 63138: www.archives.gov/veterans

National Archives at College Park, 8601 Adelphi Road, College Park, MD 207406: www.archives.gov

National WWII Museum, 945 Magazine St, New Orleans, LA 7013: www.nationalww2museum.org

US Army

US Army Center of Military History, 950 Soldiers Drive, Carlisle, PA 17013: https://history.army.mil/index.html

National Museum of the US Army, 1775 Liberty Drive, Fort Belvoir, VA 22060: https://www.thenmusa.org

US Air Force

Air Force Historical Research Agency, 600 Chennault Circle, Maxwell AFB, AL 36112: www.afhra.af.mi

National Museum of the US Air Force, 1100 Spaatz Street, Wright-Patterson AFB, OH 45433: www.nationalmuseum.af.mil

US Navy

US Navy Archives: www.history.navy.mil/research/archives/resources-for-researchers.html
National Museum of the US Navy, Washington Navy Yard, Washington DC

US Marine Corps

USMC History Division: www.usmcu.edu/Research/History-Division

Further reading

The best simple introduction to researching American military personnel is published by the National Archives and Records Administration (NARA) at www.archives.gov/files/research/military/ww2/ww2-participation.pdf

Another very useful starting place is FamilySearch's genealogy wiki. There is a basic guide to American Military Genealogy at www.familysearch.org/en/wiki/United_States_Military_Records

The Military Records Class Handout is particularly useful at www.familysearch.org/en/wiki/U.S._Military_Records_Class_Handout

There is another webpage about the Second World War with many links to online resources at www.familysearch.org/en/wiki/World_War_II_United_States_Military_Records,_1941_to_1945

A more comprehensive guide, *Research A Veteran: How to locate someone who fought in World War II*, is available free of charge from the National WWII Museum.

Museums

The American Air Museum at the Imperial War Museum Duxford is a brilliant exploration of the American air presence in Britain. More homely is Halesworth Airfield Museum, which is dedicated to the memory of several USAAF fighter and bomber units that were based there between 1942 and 1945.

THE EUROPEAN ALLIES

Thousands of troops from across Europe escaped the Nazis to Britain.

In the small Worcestershire town of Malvern, at various times during the war, for example, Free French troops boarded at Malvern College, the town's public school. Staff of the exiled Belgian Army occupied the Abbey Hotel. Elsewhere at times, French Canadian troops and Polish Naval officers worked at the telecommunications research establishment, which arrived in early 1942. Later in the war, thousands of wounded American soldiers were treated in military hospitals locally. In 1945, two of these hospitals were handed over to train 10,000 Dutch servicemen before they transferred to the Far East. In addition, numerous Italian and German prisoners of war stayed in camps locally. Before the war Malvern had been a resort town and a long way from any possible invasion site, so it was natural for the War Office to commandeer local hotels and schools for soldiers. Even so, except in the industrial areas where there was no suitable accommodation, troops from a dozen countries and more were scattered across the United Kingdom.

They played an important role in winning the war, whether it be Norwegian Commandos destroying the German heavy water plants in Norway and thereby wrecking the Nazi atomic bomb programme, Polish squadrons coming to the aid of the RAF during the Battle of Britain or the French resistance harassing German forces across France. Individual

Europeans, such as the Danish VC winner Anders Lassen, and the Czech soldiers Jozef Gabčik and Jan Kubiš, who assassinated Reinhard Heydrich in 1942, showed great bravery in the cause of the Allies. Most left for home after VE-Day, but with the changing political situation in Eastern Europe many Poles and Czechs found themselves unable to go back to their native countries.

RESEARCH

Many archives, particularly in Eastern Europe, are not geared up to dealing with researchers, although with the rapid growth of genealogy worldwide matters are considerably better than they used to be. Almost every archive now has a website – many with pages in English – but it can still be difficult to find anything about the records and how to access them. It certainly helps if you correspond in the language of the country your ancestors came from, although increasingly archivists understand English (even if they are not always willing to reply in it). There are several increasingly accurate translation websites, such as Google Translate or Deepl, to assist in writing emails and letters or in translating webpages.

Using European archives can seem baffling, as the records are different to the ones you may be used to. The Family Search Research Wiki has pages of advice for every country in the world, often including guidance in using military archives.

Another useful resource is Cyndi's List with links to over 250,000 genealogical websites arranged by country and subject. It is a bit hit and miss what you will find, however.

The European Holocaust Research Infrastructure website has information about most European archives, including descriptions of their military holdings.

If you are tracing a prisoner of war or civilian internee then the first place to try may be the International Committee of the Red Cross Archive in Geneva, which maintains records for prisoners of war and refugees helped by the Red Cross during the war. Unfortunately, it has a strict quota of the numbers of inquiries that it can deal with.

If you are researching somebody who arrived in Britain during or after the war as a Displaced Person (as refugees were described), then the Arolsen Archives may be able to help. Almost all the records have been digitised and can be searched by name. It is easy to use and largely in English, although the material itself is likely to be in German or another language.

A fascinating source for people who escaped from occupied Europe and crossed the Channel to Britain during the war are the interrogations reports. Each individual was interrogated by MI9 at the Royal Patriotic School in Wandsworth to ensure they weren't spies and to discover what they knew about the Nazi war machine and the conditions from where they came. The reports are in series WO 208 at TNA. They aren't online, but they have been indexed by name in TNA's Discovery Catalogue (although the names of people under 100 years old have been redacted). Many were fishermen, for whom getting to England was easy, but others took many months to arrive in the UK, bringing descriptions and plans of the factories and harbours where they had worked.

Another interesting source is the helpers' awards. After the war, awards were made to resistance members and others who had helped the Allied cause, mainly in Western Europe. Most recipients were given the King's Medal for Courage in the Cause of Freedom, although in some cases awards were made of the MBE or OBE. The recommendations are in series WO 208 and have been fully indexed in TNA's online catalogue. 'Indexing WO 208: Helpers of Allied prisoners of war' is a useful blog posting about the records on TNA's website.

The forces of the European allies, but not the Free French, were normally under operational command of the appropriate British service. As a result, you should be able to find operational records for individual units as you might for British units.

Further reading

Alan Brown, *Airmen in Exile: The Allied Air Forces in WWII* (Sutton, 2000)

BELGIUM

By 1944, the Free Belgian forces in the United Kingdom numbered some 4,500 men. Belgian soldiers formed the 1st Belgian Infantry Brigade (which also included an artillery battery of soldiers from Luxembourg) more often known as the Brigade Piron after its commanding officer, Jean-Baptiste Piron. The brigade took part in the Normandy invasion as well as in battles in France and the Netherlands. The 5th Special Air Service (which was part of the elite SAS) was the first Allied unit to enter Belgium in September 1944, and was comprised solely of Belgians.

Four hundred Belgian pilots served in the RAF. Two all-Belgian fighter units, Nos. 349 and 350 Squadrons, were formed. Two corvettes and a group of minesweepers were also operated by the Belgians during the Battle of the Atlantic.

Service records are with the Belgian Armed Forces documentation centre in Evere: Quarters Queen Elisabeth, rue d'Evere1, B-1140 Evere; email: info.ca@mil.be. They are slowly being transferred to the General State Archives in Brussels.

The General State Archives also has some 120,000 files for men and women who served in the Belgian resistance.

The Royal Military Museum in Brussels also keeps private archives relating to Belgian military history. The museum is splendidly old-fashioned and is well worth visiting.

Further reading

www.be4046.eu is a website devoted to the Belgian Free Forces.

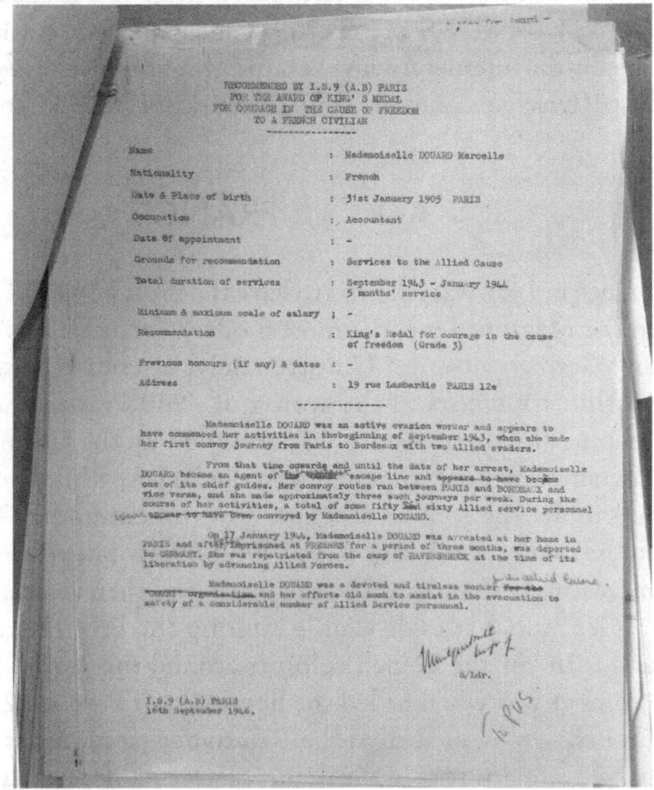

RECOMMENDED BY I.S.9 (A.B) PARIS
FOR THE AWARD OF KING'S MEDAL
FOR COURAGE IN THE CAUSE OF FREEDOM
TO A FRENCH CIVILIAN

Name	: Mademoiselle DOUARD Marcelle
Nationality	: French
Date & Place of birth	: 31st January 1905 PARIS
Occupation	: Accountant
Date of appointment	: -
Grounds for recommendation	: Services to the Allied Cause
Total duration of services	: September 1943 - January 1944 5 months' service
Minimum & maximum scale of salary	: -
Recommendation	: King's Medal for courage in the cause of freedom (Grade 3)
Previous honours (if any) & dates	: -
Address	: 19 rue Lamballe PARIS 12e

Mademoiselle DOUARD was an active evasion worker and appears to have commenced her activities in thebeginning of September 1943, when she made her first convoy journey from Paris to Bordeaux with two Allied evaders.

From that time onwards and until the date of her arrest, Mademoiselle DOUARD became an agent of the "COMET" escape line and appears to have become one of its chief guides. Her convoy routes ran between PARIS and BORDEAUX and vice versa, and she made approximately three such journeys per week. During the course of her activities, a total of some fifty and sixty Allied service personnel appear to have been convoyed by Mademoiselle DOUARD.

On 17 January 1944, Mademoiselle DOUARD was arrested at her home in PARIS and after imprisoned at FRESNES for a period of three months, was deported to GERMANY. She was repatriated from the camp of RAVENSBRUCK at the time of its liberation by advancing Allied Forces.

Mademoiselle DOUARD was a devoted and tireless worker for the "COMET" organisation and her efforts did much to assist in the evacuation to safety of a considerable number of Allied Service personnel.

S/Ldr.

I.S.9 (A.B) PARIS
16th September 1946.

Recommendation for a King's Commendation for helping the Allied cause. Mademoiselle Marcelle Douard was a guide on the Comet escape line until her arrest by the Germans. (TNA WO 208/5459)

CZECHOSLOVAKIA

Czechoslovakia was occupied by Germany after the Munich Agreement of October 1939. The pre-war army was disbanded in 1939 and many Czech and Slovak servicemen and volunteers found their way to Britain. A Czech Independent Armoured Brigade became part of the Canadian Army. There were four Czech squadrons in the RAF – 310 to 313 Squadrons.

Brief descriptions of the personnel holdings of Czech and Slovak military archives are on the My Czech Roots website. Service records for some Czech aircrew and groundcrew can be obtained from the UK Ministry of Defence/TNA in the same way as for British personnel in the RAF.

Further reading

An introduction to the Czech forces in exile is at www.militaryhistory-online.com/WWII/CzechExilesOfWWII

The Czech Independent Armoured Brigade besieged the French port of Dunkirk between September 1944 and May 1945. An account of the siege is kept by the Internet Archive at https://web.archive.org/web/20110714154719/http://www.nasenoviny.com/DunkirkEN1944_45.html

FRANCE

France in 1939 was believed to have the most powerful army in Europe and, in the Maginot Line, the most modern fortifications capable of repelling any German advance. Unfortunately, of course neither much mattered. Within six weeks in the spring of 1940 France was comprehensively beaten. Northern France was occupied by the Germans, and Alsace and Lorraine were incorporated into the Reich, while the rest of the country was under the control of a new government under General Petain, based in the small spa town of Vichy. Nominally independent, inevitably it was increasingly dominated by the Nazis and their needs.

General Charles de Gaulle built up the Free French forces in London and many of the French colonies around the world. De Gaulle's greatest moment was when he led the liberation of Paris on 25 August 1944. Free French forces, as well as the Resistance (sometimes called the Maquis), played a major part in the defeat of Germany across France.

SERVICE RECORDS

The French Ministry of Defence has various archives. Full details are given on its website, www.servicehistorique.sga.defense.gouv.fr. It is in French, although there are some English language webpages.

The most important archive centre is at Vincennes near Paris: Centre Historique des Archives (SHD), Château de Vincennes, Avenue de Paris, 94306 Vincennes Cedex, which has most of the operational records. In addition, it holds records of Resistance (Maquis) members.

Service records, however, are in Pau, at the Centre des archives du personnel militaire (CAAPC) Place de Verdun, Caserne Bernadotte, 64023 Pau Cedex. Also at Pau are records of foreign military personnel who served in the French armed forces, particularly from the French colonies and protectorates.

Details of French prisoners of war, deportees, forced and voluntary labourers, and volunteers for the Compulsory Work Service Brigades in Germany are with the Service historique de la Défense, Division des archives des victimes des conflits contemporains, Rue Neuve du Bourg l'Abbé, BP 552, 14307 Caen Cedex, France.

Access to military records for non-family members is restricted for 120 years from the soldier's birth. However, operational files and some pension papers are now largely open.

CASUALTY RECORDS

Graves and memorials for French servicemen who lost their lives during the war are maintained by the Office des Anciens Combattants et Victimes de Guerre, 139 Rue de Bercy, F-75012 Paris.

OPERATIONAL RECORDS

Most operational records are available at the military archives in Vincennes.

The French Army Museum has extensive galleries devoted to the Second World War and France's part in it at Musée de l'Armée, Hôtel national des Invalides, 129 Rue de Grenelle, F-75700 Paris 07 SP.

Further reading

Julian Jackson, *France: The Dark Years 1940–1944* (Oxford University Press, 2011)

France Libre was a very useful website about the Free French forces across the world. It is now archived on the Wayback Machine: https://web.archive.org/web/20090417002650/http://www.france-libre.net/unites_combats/Unites_combats.htm

Another useful site, created by Simon Kitson, this time about Vichy France, is also on the Internet Archive, https://web.archive.org/web/20140911225053/http://artsweb.bham.ac.uk/vichy

THE NETHERLANDS

On 10 May 1940, neutral Netherlands was invaded by Nazi Germany. The country was increasingly badly treated by the occupiers, particularly during the long winter of 1944–45, before it was liberated by British and Canadian forces. In Asia, the Dutch East Indies (now Indonesia) was occupied by the Japanese.

Service records for men and women who served in the Dutch armed forces up to May 1940 are with the National Archives in The Hague. The Archives has major collections of material relating to the Second World War, although service records for the period of the war are with the Dutch Ministry of Defence.

The Archives also has records of the Dutch War Graves Commission, which maintains a number of war cemeteries across Europe (including a plot at Paddington Cemetery, Mill Hill, in north London).

NORWAY

Norway was occupied by the Germans in April 1940 and not liberated by the British until May 1945. There was considerable resistance against the occupiers, of which the best-known action was the destruction of the German heavy water production in a series of raids by Norwegian members of SOE.

Operational records of Norwegian forces are kept by the Riksarkivet (National Archives), Postboks 4013, Ullevål Stadion, N-0806 Oslo.

Norwegian aircrew flew in 333 and 334 Squadrons RAF, whose operation record books are in series AIR 27 and online. Most of the ships in the Norwegian navy found their way to Britain, where they served with the Royal Navy. The 'Shetland Bus' transported supplies and men across to the resistance in Norway, utilizing a number of the many Norwegian fishing boats that had escaped to do so. They were crewed by volunteers, mostly fishermen and seafarers, who made many hazardous trips across the North Sea, especially in wintertime.

Museum

There is an excellent display about the Shetland Bus organisation at the Scalloway Museum.

Further reading

Damien Lewis, *Hunting Hitler's Nukes: The Secret Race to Stop the Nazi Bomb* (Quercus, 2015)

POLAND

Poland was carved up by Nazi Germany and Soviet Russia in 1939. Over the next few months large numbers of Polish service personnel crossed Europe to France, before eventually reaching Britain. Most remarkably, nearly 100,000 Polish servicemen and their families who had ended up in Russia made their way from Turkmenistan to Palestine via Iran during the spring and summer of 1942. Anders Army, as these men were nicknamed, formed the basis of the Polish II Corps which fought in Italy notably during the Battle of Monte Cassino. The most famous member was an actual brown bear with the name Wojtek.

Polish pilots played a major part in the Battle of Britain 303 (Polish) Squadron shot down more enemy aircraft than any other squadron, while Sergeant Josef Frantisek was the top ace of battle with 17 kills to his name.

At the end of the war, Poland fell under Soviet control. Members of the Polish forces in the west were regarded as traitors. As a result, most service men and their families settled in Britain or emigrated overseas.

Service records for Poles who served in British forces during the war are with the Ministry of Defence and will be transferred to TNA in due course.

The Polish Institute and Sikorski Museum in London holds an extensive archive of some 10,000 military items arranged on display in rooms primarily dedicated to the armed forces, many of which served in the Second World War.

Records of Poles who served in Polish forces are held by the Centralne Archiwum Wojskowe, ul. Poligonowa 2, 00–910 Warszawa. You will need to write to them in Polish.

Further reading

The Polonica website in Scotland is devoted to the wartime and post-war experiences of Poles there, although unfortunately it appears to be a work in progress.

SOVIET UNION (RUSSIA)

In the two decades after the end of the Cold War the first accurate histories of the war on the Eastern Front appeared in the west. They were written by authors such as Anthony Beevor, who had access to previously closed archives. Service records for officers and men, together with other information about the Russian forces, are held by the Central Archive of the Russian Ministry of Defence, ul. Kirova 74, 142100, g. Podolsk, Moscow Region, Russian Federation. At the time of writing, it is difficult to know how receptive they are to enquiries from the West.

RESEARCHING THE ENEMY

GERMANY

It is perfectly possible that Germany could have won the Second World War. In 1939, the German economy was the largest in Europe. In particular, their scientific research was more advanced than its enemies. For the most part, the German people remained loyal to the regime until almost the final collapse.

The Nazis came within an inch of defeating Britain in the summer of 1940, and had Operation Barbarossa been launched against Russia in May rather than June 1941 as had originally been planned, it is hard to see how the Soviets would have survived. But by May 1945 the Germans had been comprehensively defeated: their cities in ruins, the economy in tatters. It is not for nothing that the period is called *Jahre Null* – Year Zero – in Germany.

Defeat was certain once Russia – with its immense reserve of manpower – and the United States – the world's most powerful economy – entered the war. However, it did not help that the Nazi leadership made

The last resting place of a Polish officer unable to return home after the war in Richmond Cemetery. (Author)

increasingly erratic decisions, notably the decision to fight on at Stalingrad long after it was clear that the battle had been lost. The economy was badly managed, with little mass production of a small range of weapons that the Allies adopted. And then there was the Holocaust.

German losses were immense, particularly on the Eastern Front. Even today, the bodies of ten thousand German soldiers are uncovered each year across Eastern Europe. Many hundreds of thousands of civilians were either killed or had their lives ruined by the destruction of cities across the Reich.

Service records

German service records can be found in one of three different archive repositories, so it is important to know which service a man served with. Austria joined Germany as a result of the *Anschluss* in March 1938, so records for Austrians (and for the nationals of the parts of other countries absorbed into the Reich, such as the Sudetenland and Alsace) are also to be found in the archives described below.

Records of the Luftwaffe, including service personnel, were largely destroyed during an air raid in March 1945. A few other series of records suffered similar a similar fate during the last few months of the war. Surviving records are mainly with one of the branches of the Bundesarchiv (the German Federal Archives) in Berlin. It has an excellent website with many pages in English. However, it can be hard to understand how actually to get access to the records. Again, the European Holocaust Research Infrastructure website can help.

Most German military service records for the Second World War are held by the Deutsche Dienststelle (WASt)), Eichborndamm 179, D-13403 Berlin. There is a useful website in German and English.

The archives include the Central Registry, with over 19 million record cards about Wehrmacht personnel and members of other military/paramilitary organisations; over 2 million personal files on German naval personnel; over 15 million files on German and Austrian prisoners of war, mainly captured by the Western allies; 3 million registrations of death; and much about honours and awards.

Access is allowed to records for personnel who were killed in action or have been dead for ten years. Records for men who were presumed missing in action are available ninety years after their birth date. There is a fee of approximately €20: the actual amount depends on how much photocopying is required.

Records of members of the Nazi Party and related bodies (including the SS and SA) were kept by the American-run Berlin Document Center, before they were passed to the Bundesarchiv in 1994. These records are now available at the Bundesarchiv, Abteilung Deutsches Reich, in Berlin.

Casualty records

The German equivalent of the CWGC is the Volksbund Deutsche Kriegsgräberfürsorge.

The website (in German) describes the work of the Volksbund, and contains details of German cemeteries around the world. There is also a searchable database to the war dead, although information is posted to you, rather than directly available online.

Records of Luftwaffe losses in or around the UK were kept in the Luftwaffe Quartermaster General's daily returns, microfilm copies of which are held at the Imperial War Museum, London. All Luftwaffe losses over the UK are summarised in Nigel Parker's *Luftwaffe Crash Archive*

(12 vols, Naval & Military Press, 2022). Researched over twenty years, the book offers a definitive guide to every enemy aircraft that came down over Britain. A database of Luftwaffe casualties is available on the Aircrew Remembered website.

Operational records

Operational records of the German Army and Waffen-SS are with the Bundesarchiv military archive in Freiburg-in-Breisgau, Unfortunately, Luftwaffe records were largely destroyed in the last weeks of the war. An increasing proportion of records have been digitised, including records of the Afrika Korps.

From 1940, much German signal traffic was intercepted by codebreakers at Bletchley Park. The raw Ultra Decrypts (as their transcripts were called) are available at TNA in series DEFE 3, although it is better to use the edited material found in the two-dozen series within GCHQ letter code HW. These files also contain decrypts of Italian, German and even Soviet messages. They make very interesting reading and cover a vast range of topics from the shortage of tyres to Himmler's secret negotiations with the British and Americans in April 1945.

Further reading

FamilySearch's Research Wiki has many pages on how to use German records of all kinds, including those relating to the armed forces.

Nicholas Stargardt, *The German War: A Nation Under Arms 1939–45* (Bodley Head, 2015)

ITALY

Italy joined the war on the German side in June 1940 and agreed an armistice with the Allies in September 1943. Italian troops fought largely in North Africa, with the Italian fleet a powerful presence in the Mediterranean.

Service records for Italian forces are held by the Direzione Generale del Personale Militare, 5 Reparto – 15a Divisione, Piazzale della Marina 2, I-00196 ROMA. Some guidance is available on FamilySearch's Research Wiki pages on how best to research Italian ancestors.

JAPAN

It is arguable that the Second World War began in 1937 with the Japanese attack on China. In December 1941, Japanese forces launched a pre-emptive attack on Western forces in the Pacific, notably at Pearl Harbor, and subsequently occupied much of South-East Asia. The Japanese were slowly pushed back from their conquests by the British in Burma and the Americans in the Pacific. However, the war came to a speedy conclusion in August 1945 after two atomic bombs were dropped on Hiroshima and Nagasaki.

Many records were destroyed during bombing raids on Tokyo in the last few months of the war. Only records for the Imperial Japanese Navy appear to survive. The *Kaigan Shōhei rirekesho* are records of naval officers and ratings, 1872–1945, including names, dates of birth and death and length of service. These records are with the Ministry of Health and Welfare's Relief Bureau in Tokyo. Records are available only to the families of the deceased.

Junkokusha Meibo is a roll of honour for the dead, which is kept at the Yasukuni Shrine in Tokyo, which commemorates all of Japan's war dead. Details about how to access the roll is available at on FamilySearch's Research Wiki pages on Japan.

The National Institute for Defense Studies in Tokyo has numerous records for both the army and navy, including war diaries and naval action reports. Decrypts of intercepted Japanese signals are at TNA in series DEFE 3 and under the HW letter code.

ENEMY PRISONERS OF WAR IN ALLIED HANDS

Hundreds of thousands of enemy soldiers ended up in Allied hands. German prisoners who were captured by the Soviets, in particular, endured many years of hardship. The final men were only released by the Russians a decade after the war's end in 1955.[8] Fortunately, men serving in the Axis forces captured by the Western allies were generally better treated.

There are very few records relating to individual German and Italian prisoners of war in British archives, as the paperwork was transferred to the German and Italian authorities in 1949. There may be some records about individual camps at local archives and in newspapers.[9]

The Eden Camp Second World War Museum in North Yorkshire was originally a PoW camp for Italian prisoners and was largely built by them. Its official title was P.W. Work Camp 83. At its peak, in addition to Eden Camp's forty-five huts, tented accommodation was added to increase the camp's capacity, which enabled it to house around 1,200 prisoners at any one time. The Italian prisoners gave way to Germans during the summer of 1944. Like the Italians before them, the Germans mainly worked locally in agriculture. The camp finally closed in 1948 three years after the war had ended.[10]

Repatriated Landscape is a very good website that shows former Second World War PoW sites within the British landscape as they appear today.

German records are with the WASt division of the Bundesarchiv found in Berlin.

WAR CRIMES

In the months after the collapse of Nazi Germany, the Allies tried to locate and arrest known or suspected war criminals with the intention of trying them for war crimes. The most important war criminals were tried by the International Military Tribunal in Nuremberg. Each of the occupying powers also sought war criminals in their zone with varying degrees of success. A few war criminals, most famously Adolf Eichmann and Josef Mengele, made their way out of Europe mainly to South America, with the help of sympathetic Catholic priests on a variety of escape routes.[11]

By late 1946, the hunt was beginning to flag. The demobilisation of Allied forces meant reductions in the men who were assigned to the work of finding and trying war criminals. There were other, more

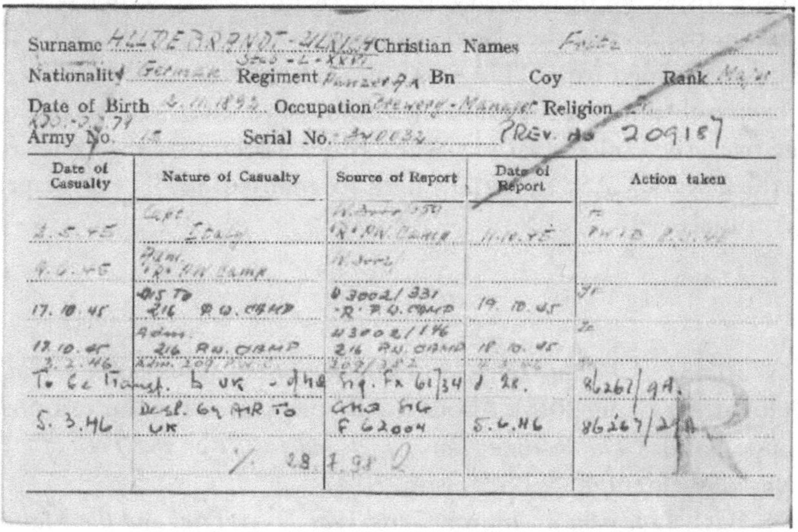
Surname ... Christian Names ...
Nationality ... Regiment ... Bn ... Coy ... Rank ...
Date of Birth ... Occupation ... Religion ...
Army No. ... Serial No. ...

Date of Casualty	Nature of Casualty	Source of Report	Date of Report	Action taken

Prisoner of war card for Franz Hildebrandt, who was in camps in Britain between 1946 and 1948. (Bundesarchiv)

important developments; the emerging Cold War with Russia and the need to rebuild a democratic Germany were increasingly important priorities. As a result, many Nazis had successful careers in post-war Germany and the German governments – both West and East – had little interest in raking over their past. Most convicted war criminals were eventually released, leaving only Rudolf Hess to live the rest of his long life in Berlin's Spandau Prison, until his death by suicide in August 1987 aged 93.

TNA at Kew has papers related to the war crimes that took place either in the British Zone or by Germans normally resident there. There is also information about the trial of Japanese war criminals. This material largely comprises transcripts of trials that were conducted by the British, together with voluminous volumes of evidence. However, there is very little about individual members of the War Crimes Teams or the people who ran the courts. More about the records can be found in a TNA Research Guide: 'War Crimes 1939–1945'.

An interesting account of the Nuremberg trials can be found on the American National WWII Museum website.

Of particular interest are the Consolidated Wanted Lists prepared by the Central Registry of War Criminals and Security Aspects (CROWCASS), which was established by the British and Americans to trace former enemy nationals suspected of committing war crimes or atrocities. These lists contain over 50,000 names of known war criminals and those suspected of brutality, torture or murder, together with their position in the SS or other Nazi organisation. Lists in piece WO 229/1 can be downloaded from TNA's website. Lists current at the end of 1947 have been published by the Naval & Military Press. Others can be downloaded from the United Nations War Crimes Commission website. Apart from the CROWCASS material, there are many other lists of suspected war criminals.

Further reading

A.T. Williams, *A Passing Fury: Searching for Justice at the end of World War II* (Jonathan Cape, 2016). About the British search for war criminals.

Phillippe Sands, *The Ratline: Love, Lies and Justice on the Trail of a Nazi Fugitive* (Weidenfeld & Nicholson, 2020)

Gary J. Bass, *Judgment at Tokyo: World War II on Trial and the Making of Modern Asia* (Picador, 2024)

THE HOLOCAUST

The Holocaust, that is the murder of 6 million Jews and hundreds of thousands of Roma and Sinti people, LGBTQ+ people and opponents of the Nazi regime, is perhaps the greatest war crime in modern history.

In reality, there were two separate holocausts. Not every victim died in a concentration camp, like Auschwitz; millions of men, women and children were murdered in cold blood in villages and towns across Russia and Eastern Europe by special *Einzatzgruppen*, or in labour camps, such as the one at Treblinka.

There is a mass of information available about the victims, as well as the survivors. Detailed records were kept by the Nazis.

However, as the United States Holocaust Memorial Museum points out: 'There is no single list of victims and survivors of Nazi persecution. Instead, researching an individual's story during the Holocaust is a process of following trails and piecing together bits of information.'

For researchers, it is much more difficult to find out about those who were murdered by the death squads across Eastern Europe, because no records were kept or have long since disappeared. Many of my wife's family were killed when the Germans massacred the Jewish residents of Svislach, a town now on the Belarus-Polish border, in November 1942. So far as I can tell, there is no list of the dead. It is doubtful whether the Nazi murderers thought it was worth compiling. Only her cousin Rakhmel Livschitz is known to have survived. He spent the remainder of the war with Russian partisans. We know he survived as he emigrated to Uruguay at the end of the war.

However, if your relative was German, or Austrian, or to a lesser extent came from elsewhere in Western Europe, then they will be described in the records at some stage, which are largely available for free online.

The International Tracing Service is the place to start. This is the complete set of the material held by the Arolsen Archives (see below). Experienced staff at the **Wiener Holocaust Library** will do a search through the records and provide a detailed report. The library was established in 1933 to record the growth of antisemitism in Germany. It has one of the world's leading and most extensive archives on the Holocaust, the Nazi era and genocide.

Yad Vashem – Hebrew for 'A Memorial and a Name' – is Israel's official memorial to the victims of the Holocaust. It was established in 1953 to record the names of the victims and research the Holocaust.

A major part of its work has been to collect details of about 4.8 million victims (out of a likely 6 million names) in the Central Database of Shoah Victims' Names. *Shoah* is the Hebrew word for catastrophe and it is sometimes used as an alternative to the Holocaust. The database is easy to use and contains links to lists of victims held by Yad Vashem, as well as some other records. There is a form, for example, recording Rakhmel Livschitz's service with the Russian partisans. The database and much else besides is on its website. The most important set of records here – and the most frustrating – are the **Pages of Testimony** submitted by survivors, relations and friends. These one-page forms contain the names, biographical details and, when available, photographs, of individuals and provide symbolic 'tombstones' for people who might otherwise be forgotten. It is still possible to submit forms. The problem is that there is no verification of the information provided, so inevitably there are errors and duplication.

The **Arolsen Archives** is the international centre on Nazi persecution, based in the German town of Bad Arolsen. It holds the world's most comprehensive archive on victims and survivors of National Socialism. It has records for nearly 18 million individuals from a wide range of sources. The records can now largely be searched online by name or place. The names are not just for Holocaust victims, they also include many refugees. There are many lists providing details of men and women who sought to emigrate to America.

There is potentially a lot of useful information here, but it can be difficult to interpret. What turns up is seemingly random. For my grandfather Ismar there is what appears to be a death certificate, in Czech, giving the date of his death at Theresienstadt. For my grandmother Ida there is a letter dated July 1945 to the International Red Cross from my mother asking for information about her fate.

There are also some useful German sources relating to Jews who lived in Germany, notably the *Gedenkbuch* (Memorial Book) for the 'Victims of the Persecution of Jews under the National Socialist Tyranny in Germany 1933–1945', which is maintained by the Bundesarchiv on its website. It provides details of the fate of nearly 180,000 German (and a few Polish) Jews and where they lived. For both my grandparents it gives birth dates and places and dates of death.

In May 1939, a census was taken across Germany and Austria to identify Jewish households. It provides basic information about the names and ages of people in each household on census night. The records are now available through My Heritage. The subscription website has a number of useful resources on the Holocaust, although it primarily offers DNA testing.

RED CROSS ENQUIRY/MESSAGE
ROTES, KREUZ ANFRAGE/NACHRICHT

BC/UKSB/ONA

Stamp of issuing Red Cross
FOREIGN RELATIONS DEPARTMENT
BRITISH RED CROSS & ORDER OF ST. JOHN,
WIMBORNE HOUSE, ARLINGTON STREET,
LONDON, S.W.1.

ENQUIRER
ANFRAGER

Name/Zuname Schoenwald
First Names/Vornamen Ge-da Ilse
Date of Birth/Geburtsdatum 10.6.1921. Place of Birth/Geburtsort Oels, Sil.
Nationality/Nationalitaet – stateless
Address/Adresse St. Andrew's Hospital, Devon Road, Bow, London E.3.
Original Home Address (in the case of a Displaced Person).
Heimatsadresse im Falle von Auswanderung

Relationship of Enquirer to Addressee/Verwandschaftsgrad Daughter
The enquirer desires news of the Addressee and asks that the following message should be transmitted to him.
Der Anfrager wuenscht Nachrichten vom Empfaenger und ersucht die folgende Botschaft zu uebermitteln.

Date/Datum 30.1.1946.

ADDRESSEE
EMPFAENGER

Name/Zuname Schoenwald nee Cohn
First Names/Vornamen Ida
Date of Birth/Geburtsdatum 86537739 ?.1885. Place of Birth/Geburtsort Muenste-be-g
Nationality/Nationalitaet stateless – Jewish
Ledig Verheiratet Widow (er) Witwe (er) Geschieden (Delete all irrelevant matter). (Unerwuenschtes durch zu streichen).
Profession/Beruf
Last known address/Letzte Adresse B-eslau, Hoefchenst-asse 99. Ge-many. 1941.

The Addressee's reply to be written overleaf (not more than 25 words).
Antwort umseitig (Hochstzahl 25 Worte).

< 3 >

S & D Ltd

The letter my mother sent to the Red Cross seeking information about her family. (Arolsen Archives)

BRITISH RECORDS

Despite official reluctance and suspicion, many German Jews ended up in Britain. The most famous group were the children who left as part of the Kindertransport programme in late 1938 and early 1939. There is no complete register of the refugees, although some lists, taken from official files, can be found on Findmypast.

A number of diplomats at British consulates across Germany and other countries helped Jews escape the Nazis, often at great personal cost. One of the best known was Frank Foley, who was the passport officer at the consulate in Berlin. He helped perhaps 10,000 to escape almost certain death. Unfortunately, no lists for those he assisted survive. It is entirely possible that Foley provided the papers that enabled my mother to leave, but we will never know.

In the mid-1960s claims for compensation from the West German government could be submitted. Surviving files are at TNA in series FO 950.

They are not online. However, detailed descriptions, including names, can be found in TNA's Discovery Catalogue

You can ask Jewish World Relief to provide details about individuals. Normally you'll just receive a copy of the index card on which details were recorded. My mother's card confirmed the exact date she arrived in England.

OTHER SOURCES

JewishGen serves as the global home for Jewish genealogy. Its Holocaust Database comprises a collection of databases containing information about Holocaust victims and survivors. It contains more than 3.79 million records, from more than 400 component datasets.

The **United States Holocaust Memorial Museum** in Washington DC provides a detailed guide to many aspects of the Shoah and has collected many records, some of which are online. It is possible to run a name search of its resources.

The **Jewish Genealogical Society of Great Britain** also has many resources and offers members a chance to discuss research problems with experts.

Further reading

There are many books on the Holocaust, detailing how it occurred, providing eyewitness accounts of the horrors, and describing the fate of writers' families. Many describe the research journeys, although of course they may well be different to your journey. A general introduction is James Bulgin, *The Holocaust* (IWM Books, 2021), which is based on the items displayed at IWM's Holocaust Galleries.

TNA has Research Guides to 'Internment of Enemy Aliens', 'Nazi Persecution and the Holocaust', and 'War Crimes'.

Damien Lewis, *SAS Ghost Patrol: The Ultra-Secret Unit That Posed As Nazi Stormtroopers* (Quercus, 2017)

Museums

The Imperial War Museum's Holocaust Galleries is a brilliant and heartbreaking account of the atrocities perpetrated by the Nazis.

The Wiener Holocaust Library has a small gallery, usually with an exhibition relating to some aspect of the Holocaust.

If you visit Germany and other Western European countries, look out for the *Stolpersteine* (stumble stones), small brass plaques set into the pavement recording the fate of Jews and other victims of the Nazis who lived in the street between the wars.

REFUGEES

During the 1930s and 1940s, Britain welcomed tens of thousands of refugees from Europe, who brought with them much to enrich British society – from the architectural critic Nikolas Pevsner and the journalist Hella Pick, as well as the thousands who worked in the mines or on the land during and after the war.

The British authorities and trade unions were reluctant to admit too many refugees for fear of antagonising the host population and, frankly, because of antisemitism. The first wave, which came after the rise of the Nazis, were intellectuals and others who feared persecution or worse. The pace of arrivals increased in 1938 and 1939 with the arrival of 10,000 children under the Kindertransport scheme and thousands of other young people in other ways (including my mother). In 1940 and 1941, tens of thousands more arrived as the result of the Nazi occupation of much of Europe. And finally, many settled here in the immediate aftermath of the war as Britain was a safe haven or stepping stone on the way to new lives in America or Australia.

An example of Stolpersteine in Wiesbaden. The two men, presumably brothers, had been in care homes for many years before being murdered as part of the Nazi eugenics programme. (Author)

Most care for the new arrivals was provided by charities, particularly those run by Quakers and the Jews. As a result, it can be difficult to find very much about individuals.

OFFICIAL SOURCES

1939 Register

All refugees who were in England and Wales in September 1939 should appear in the 1939 Register. The register will give you the individual's name, date of birth, occupation and who else was in the household. However, details of children may be redacted to protect personal details.

Internment cards

Refugees from countries with which the UK was at war could be interned. They were mainly German and Italians. In May 1940, it was decided to intern German and Italian men. 'Collar the lot' was Churchill's instruction. In the end, only men of working age were interned, mainly on the Isle of Man. It was both cruel and pointless as the overwhelming majority of internees were vehemently anti-Nazi.

Tribunals were set up at the beginning of the Second World War to determine whether an enemy alien should be interned, exempt from internment with restrictions, or exempt from internment without restrictions. Those who were not interned were recorded as 'at liberty'. Cards were prepared for each individual, which recorded their full name, their address and occupation in the UK, date and place of birth and former occupation in Germany. If an individual was actually interned, the card will give the date of internment and the date of his release. The originals are in series HO 326 at TNA. But more usefully they are also on Findmypast. Findmypast also has rolls of men in the camps on the Isle of Man. They date from 1943.

Service records

A number of enemy aliens subsequently joined the British armed services. Some joined special forces, while others became translators in war crimes investigations, but most were in the Pioneer Corps, which was a non-fighting unit in which men did essential but unskilled work, such as guarding bases and erecting and maintaining buildings.[12] Their service records can be obtained from TNA/MOD in the normal way.

FEMALE ENEMY ALIEN—EXEMPTION FROM INTERNMENT—REFUGEE

(1) Surname (*block capitals*) SCHOENWALD
Forenames Gerda Ilse
Alias
(2) Date and place of birth 10.6.1921 Oslo
(3) Nationality German
(4) Police Regn. Cert. No. 656718 Home Office reference if known
Special Procedure Card Number if known
(5) Address Nurses' Quarters, Mansion House, Waldenhurst
(6) Normal occupation Probationer Nurse
(7) Present Occupation do
(8) Name and address of employer Royal Victoria Hospital as above
(9) Decision of Tribunal Exempt Date 25/11/39
(10) Whether exempted from Article 6 (*a*) and 9 (*a*) (Yes or No) Yes
(11) Whether desires to be repatriated (Yes or No) No

"KENT MESSENGER," MAIDSTONE (OVER)

The Aliens Registration Card for Gerda Ilse Schoenwald. (Findmypast/TNA)

Further reading

Martin Sugarman, *Fighting Back: British Jewry's Military Contribution in the Second World War* (Valentine Mitchell, 2017)

NATURALISATION

Although at the end of the war some refugees returned home to try to rebuild their lives and others emigrated to Israel, many stayed and became British citizens. Those granted citizenship were issued with a certificate, copies of which are in series HO 334. There may be also a case file for an individual applicant, although not all survive. The file will contain correspondence with local police forces and the security services to ensure that the applicant had no criminal record, together with statements from referees about the applicant's suitability to become a British citizen. These are in series HO 405. Technically they are closed to public access for 100 years after the application was made. However, if a file has yet to be opened, researchers can submit a Freedom of Information request. This should be a formality.

Further reading

Information can be found in a TNA Research Guide: 'Naturalisation, Registration and British-Citizenship'.

CZECHS AND SLOVAKS

Papers of the Czechoslovak Refugee Trust, established by the British government in 1939 to help Czech and Slovak refugees in the United Kingdom, and of its voluntary predecessor the British Committee for Refugees from Czechoslovakia, are in series HO 294.

POLES

Records of the Polish Resettlement Corps, which helped ex-servicemen and women adjust to new lives in Britain in the immediate post-war years, are at TNA in series WO 315. There are, however, few references to individuals and many records are in Polish.

What does not survive or was never kept in the first place

- There are no passenger lists for liners, ferries etc. arriving in the United Kingdom from Europe or the Mediterranean.
- Most files relating to individual aliens have been destroyed.

UNOFFICIAL SOURCES

Newspapers

Throughout much of 1938 and for most of 1939, the *Manchester Guardian* and *The Times*, as well as other newspapers, contained small advertisements from Jews from Germany and Austria who sought safety in jobs as domestic servants. It was hoped that their new employers would sponsor their immigration to Britain. On 30 August 1938, for example, the Situations Wanted column in the *Manchester Guardian* contained adverts such as:

- Chauffeur (with licence), footman, 43 years old. Seeks post. Cultivated Viennese Jew. Josef Kernegg, 9 Marc Aurelstrasse, Vienna 9.
- Childless married couple of good family, likeable appearance, well educated, good English and French. Seeks position as caretakers, receptionists, cook and gentleman-butler, go anywhere Baach, 20 Lowengasse, Vienna 5.[13]

Apart from such tragic advertisements, newspapers may contain:

- News stories about individuals. My mother is mentioned twice, once performing in a play at St Andrews Hospital in the East End in January 1943, and the other for receiving a certificate for distinction in passing an exam in nursing in July 1945.
- Official notices about applications for naturalisation.

The *Jewish Chronicle* is full of stories about refugees in Britain. It is available online via My Heritage. This is a commercial website, but it does offer a free trial. Alternatively, you can do a basic search for free at https://archive.thejc.com. If there is anything in which you are interested there is a small charge for accessing the paper itself.

Further reading

Julian Borger, *I Seek a Kind Person: My Father, Seven Children and the Adverts that Helped Them Escape the Holocaust* (John Murray, 2024)

The UK Holocaust Map includes sites all across the UK help to tell the story of the Holocaust and British responses to Nazism.

CHARITIES

Much help to new arrivals was provided by charities. Key among them was (and remains) the **Association of Jewish Refugees** – the national charity supporting Holocaust refugees and survivors living in Great Britain.

Also of interest is the **World Jewish Relief**, which was established as the Central British Fund for German Jewry in 1933 to help refugees from Nazi Europe. It succeeded in bringing around 65,000 Jewish refugees to safety. It has records for many of the people it helped in the 1930s, including children who arrived here as part of the Kindertransport.

Museums and Libraries

There may well be information at specialist libraries and museums, the largest of which is the **Wiener Holocaust Library**, founded by Dr Alfred

Wiener in 1934 to alert the world to the threat posed by the Third Reich. It has a huge range of material not just about the Holocaust, but also refugees in Britain.

For the Polish communities there are two London-based institutions: the **Polish Institute and Sikorski Museum** in London holds an extensive archive and an extensive library relating to Poland and Polish people abroad is kept by the Polish Social and Cultural Association.

APPENDICES

APPENDIX I

THE KOREAN WAR (1950–53)

After the Second World War, the peninsula of Korea, which had been a Japanese colony, was split along the 38th Parallel. North of the line was allocated to the Soviet Union and the south to the United States. There were considerable tensions between the two occupying powers and the regimes they had established.

On 25 June 1950, North Korea launched a major attack on the South. The United Nations Security Council denounced North Korea's actions and authorised the formation of the United Nations Command and the dispatch of forces to Korea to repel it. Twenty-one UN members eventually contributed to the UN force, including the United Kingdom and many Commonwealth countries. The Americans, however, provided around 90 per cent of the military personnel supplied by the United Nations.

After the first two months of war, the South Korean army (ROKA) and the American forces were on the point of defeat, retreating to a small area behind a defensive line known as the Pusan Perimeter. In September 1950, a risky amphibious counteroffensive was launched at Incheon, cutting off North Korean (KPA) troops and their supply lines in South Korea. UN forces then invaded North Korea in October 1950 and moved rapidly towards the border with China – but on 19 October 1950, Chinese forces – the People's Volunteer Army (PVA) – crossed into Korea.

The UN retreated from North Korea following the PVA's First Phase Offensive and the Second Phase Offensive. China, along with its North Korean and Soviet allies, pressed its offensive, invading the South and capturing Seoul by early January 1951. A UN force recaptured Seoul and the communists were pushed back to positions around the 38th Parallel. After this, the front stabilised, and the last two years were a war of attrition. The fighting ended on 27 July 1953 when the Korean Armistice Agreement was signed. The agreement created the Korean Demilitarized Zone (DMZ) to separate North and South Korea, and allowed the return of prisoners. However, no peace treaty has ever been signed, and the two Koreas are technically still at war, engaged in a frozen conflict.

The UK was the third largest contributor of forces to the UN, although some way behind South Korea and the US. UK forces were part of the British Commonwealth Forces Korea, later 1st Commonwealth Division, which also included soldiers from Canada, Australia and other Commonwealth nations. British infantry battalions rotated through the theatre of operations. They often included National Servicemen, such as the actor Michael Caine, who remembered his time there:

> I was just a National Service. I couldn't wait to get out. I was dragged off to Korea screaming. It was like the First World War. It was trench warfare with patrols at night into the paddy fields. Well, that was terrifying, because you know, there you are from the Elephant and Castle trying to sort out Koreans in a paddy field, I wonder whose got the advantage here?[1]

The most famous action was conducted by the 1st Battalion, Gloucestershire Regiment, who, against considerable odds, defended a position against Chinese forces on the Imjin River in April 1951. General James Van Fleet, commander of the US Eighth Army, described the stand as 'the most outstanding example of unit bravery in modern war'.

The Royal Navy usually had at least one aircraft carrier on station during the war. The Royal Australian Navy provided the carrier HMAS *Sydney*. The RN, RAN, RNZN, and the Royal Canadian Navy also provided other warships.

On 9 August 1952 a propeller-driven Sea Fury, piloted by Lieutenant Peter Carmichael of 802 Squadron, Fleet Air Arm, based on HMS *Ocean*, shot down a MiG-15 jet fighter, becoming one of only a handful of pilots of propeller planes to have shot down a jet.

British casualties were 1,078 killed, 2,674 wounded, 179 missing and 976 prisoners of war.

The Korean War has largely been forgotten in Britain. If you are interested in understanding why this is the case, it is well worth reading Francis Pike's article at: www.spectator.co.uk/article/why-do-we-forget-britains-role-in-the-korean-war.

THE RECORDS

The records are very similar to those of the Second World War. Service records may be ordered from the Ministry of Defence/TNA in the normal way. Recommendations for gallantry awards to army personnel are in series WO 373 and can be downloaded from TNA's website. Recommendations to naval personnel can be found in files in ADM 1. They are not arranged by name.

However, there are no Commonwealth War Graves Commission listings for British and Commonwealth war dead. Instead, Findmypast has brief details of the 4,502 service personnel who were killed or injured between 1950 and 1953. Most of the war dead are buried in the UN Memorial Cemetery at Busan. More details about individuals can be found at www.unmck.or.kr. The British national memorial to the men who lost their lives in the war was dedicated in December 2014. It is on the Victoria Embankment in London.

TNA also has several lists of prisoners of war and there are files in series WO 208 about their treatment by the Chinese and attempts to brainwash them. The references are given in its Research Guide to the Korean War.

War diaries for British units in Korea are in series WO 281, with other historical records and reports in WO 308. United Nations Command operational reports are in DEFE 12. Records of naval participation are in ADM 1 and ADM 116, logs of Royal Naval ships are in ADM 53, record books of Fleet Air Arm Squadrons in ADM 227. Unit diaries of 41 Commando Royal Marines are in ADM 202.

Many photographs of the conflict are available on the Imperial War Museum website. www.iwm.org.uk/collections. The IWM, the National Army Museum and some regimental museums have small displays devoted to the war.

A memorial to the Korean War on the village memorial at Croxley near Watford. (Author)

Further reading

TNA's holdings are summarised in a Research Guide: 'British Army Operations-After-1945'.

Useful short histories of the war can be found on the Imperial War Museum and Royal British Legion websites.

Michael Cullinane and Iain Johnston-White, *A Forgotten British War: The accounts of Korean War Veterans* (Palgrave Macmillan, 2023)
Max Hastings, *The Korean War* (Michael Joseph, 1987)
S.P. Mackenzie, *British Prisoners of the Korean War* (Oxford University Press, 2012)
Andrew Salmon, *To the Last Round: The Epic British Stand on the Imjin River, Korea 1951* (Aurum, 2009)

APPENDIX 2

ARMY SERVICE RECORDS

Completing this form might help you understand what the service record is telling you.

Personal Details

Full name: ______________________________

Service number: ____________

Date of birth: ____________

Place of birth: ____________

Occupation: ____________

Citizenship: ____________

Home address: ____________

____

____

____

Next of kin (name, relationship, address): ______________

____

____

Marriage (Spouse, date, place): ______________

____

____

KEY SERVICE DATES

Date of attestation: ______________________

Date of call up: ______________________

Date released to Army Reserve (Class Z): ____________________________

Date of end of engagement (final discharge): _______________________

Regiment(s) served with

Name (and battalion or sub-unit): _____________________

Date when taken on strength (TOS): ____________________

Date when struck off strength (SOS): _____________________

Any notes:

Promotions (and demotions)

Rank: ____

Date: ____

Any notes:

Military history sheet – service home and abroad

Country Served: ____

From (date): _______________________

To (date): _______________________

Medals awarded (where given)

Name of award: ______________________________

Date of award: __________________

Any notes:

Service and casualty form

Use this section to record additional information, such as training courses attended, time spent in hospital (and hospital when given), when exactly left UK (with troop-ship if given)

Date of event:__________________

Unit: ________________________

Event type:

APPENDIX 3

ABBREVIATIONS

There were thousands of abbreviations in common use during the Second World War. After nearly ninety years it may not always be easy to work out what they meant.

However, the following websites might help:

- For all the services: www.researchingww2.co.uk/ww2-abbreviations-acronyms
- For the RAF: ww2memories.wordpress.com/tag/abbreviations
- For the Royal Navy: www.naval-history.net/xDKCas1005-Abbreviations.htm
- For Australian services: www.awm.gov.au/learn/glossary
- For Canadian services: http://cmhs.ca

Or you could post a query in the WW2 talk forum: ww2talk.com/index.php

Here are some of the abbreviations commonly used in the records or mentioned in this book:

A/	Acting
AFS	Auxiliary Fire Service
AM	Air Ministry
AOC	Air Officer Commanding
ARP	Air Raid Precautions
ATS	Auxiliary Territorial Service
BBC	British Broadcasting Corporation
Bn	Battalion (sometimes Btn)
CD	Civil Defence
CDO	Commando
CDR	Commander
CPO	Chief Petty Officer

CWGC	Commonwealth War Graves Commission (technically during the war it was known as the IWGC Imperial War Graves Commission)
Coy	Company (part of an infantry battalion)
Cpl	Corporal
DFC	Distinguished Flying Cross
DFM	Distinguished Flying Medal
DSO	Distinguished Service Order
E/A	Enemy aircraft
ENSA	Entertainments National Service Association
FAA	Fleet Air Arm
F/	Flight (as in F/Lt for Flight Lieutenant)
GC	George Cross
GHQ	General Headquarters
GI	American soldier
GM	George Medal
Gp	Group
HAA	Heavy Anti-aircraft Artillery
HCU	Heavy Conversion Unit (RAF)
HG	Home Guard
IWM	Imperial War Museum
LAA	Light Anti-aircraft Artillery
L/	Lance (L/CPL – Lance Corporal)
L of C	Lines of Communication
LG	*London Gazette*
LT	Lieutenant
MBE	Member of the Order of the British Empire
MC	Military Cross
MM	Military Medal
MiD	Mention in Despatches
MOD	Ministry of Defence
MN	Merchant Navy
NAM	National Army Museum
OBE	Officer of the Order of the British Empire
OC	Officer in Charge
OTU	Officer Training Unit
Pte	Private (never Pvt, which is the American usage)
P/O	Pilot Officer (RAF) Petty Officer (RN)

PTC	Primary Training Centre
PWE	Political Warfare Executive
RAF	Royal Air Force
RAAF	Royal Australian Air Force
RCAF	Royal Canadian Air Force
RM	Royal Marines
RN	Royal Navy
RAN	Royal Australian Navy
RCN	Royal Canadian Navy
RNR	Royal Naval Reserve
RNVR	Royal Naval Reserve
Sgt	Sergeant
S/L	Squadron Leader
SOE	Special Operations Executive
SOS	Struck off Strength (service records)
Sqn	Squadron
T/	Temporary
TNA	The National Archives
TOS	Taken on Strength (service records)
VC	Victoria Cross
VCO	Viceroy Commissioned Officer
WO	Warrant Officer (also War Office)

APPENDIX 4

BATTLEFIELD TOURS

In recent years a whole industry has sprung into being catering for the increasing numbers of people who want to see where their forebears fought in both world wars.

There are several companies, large and small, who offer tours. A selection of the larger ones is given below, but Google will suggest other firms. As part of the package, they provide accommodation, meals and guides and are normally flexible enough to allow clients to visit particular war cemeteries or other sites of interest, provided they are close to the itinerary.

Most guided tours relating to the Second World War are for the battlefields of Western Europe – particularly the D-Day beaches, Arnhem, and Auschwitz and the concentration camps of Poland. There are less frequent tours to Italy and South-East Asia. Unfortunately, rather sadly, certain areas, such as Burma and much of the Middle East and the Western Desert, are now almost off limits to the tourist altogether.

It is a good idea to choose companies who use members of the Guild of Battlefield Guides because you will be guaranteed a high level of knowledge and the ability to express it. A list of members can be found on the Guild's website: www.gbg-international.com. Some guides will provide a personalised tour, although this is likely to be expensive.

It is perfectly possible to do your own self-guided tour of Western Europe. The roads are good. There are plentiful hotels and restaurants and the welcome is likely to be warm. This is ideal if you want to follow in the footsteps of a particular ancestor or would like to explore a particular battlefield in detail.

Selected tour companies

- Holts: www.holts.co.uk/destinations
- Leger Battlefield Tours: www.legerbattlefields.co.uk/ww2-tours
- Cultural Experience: www.theculturalexperience.com/historical-periods/guided-world-war-2-tours
- Matt Limb Battlefield Tours offers a more personal experience to clients: https//mlbft.co.uk

Guide books

There are a number of guides to particular battlefields and campaigns, although far fewer than there are to the Western Front of the First World War. Always try to buy the most up to date edition. The biggest publisher is Pen and Sword. The Naval & Military Press also sells a variety of guides.

ENDNOTES

Routine Orders

1 www.bankofengland.co.uk/monetary-policy/inflation/inflation-calculator. Due to inflation and other reasons, the pound lost a third of value during the war.
2 http://barclayperkins.blogspot.com/2018/12/draught-beer-prices-1939-1948.html
3 www.britishmilitaryhistory.co.uk/docs-services-royal-army-pay-corps
4 www.key.aero/forum/historic-aviation/114990-raf-pay-in-wwii

1. Introduction

1 Quoted from https://winstonchurchill.org/resources/speeches/1940-the-finest-hour/war-of-the-unknown-warriors/
2 Quoted in Lara Feigel, 'The Thirties: an intimate history by Juliet Gardiner', *The Guardian*, 7 February 2010, www.theguardian.com/books/2010/feb/07/thirties-intimate-history-juliet-gardiner
3 www.frankfallaarchive.org/people/frank-falla/
4 The only major exception is the 1931 Census, which was destroyed in an accidental fire in December 1942. See www.ons.gov.uk/visualisations/storyofthecensus/#
5 Ned Sheridan, 'Terence Alan (Spike) Milligan', *Oxford Dictionary of National Biography* (2006).
6 The best of the seven volumes is probably the first *Adolf Hitler: My Part in His Downfall* (Penguin,1971).
7 Technically there were three. Clement Attlee was prime minister for the last six weeks of the war with Japan (which formally surrendered on 2 September 1945) and then navigated Britain through the choppy post-war world.
8 Even now there is a thrill when one comes across a minute scribbled by Churchill (he had terrible handwriting) or even one initialled just WSC in red ink indicating that the prime minister had read the document.
9 In the First World War some 5 million men served in the army out of an estimated 6 million men in uniform. Figures taken from a House of Lords written question 'Allied Casualties in Second World War', found at HL.Deb 03 2961, Vol. 234 pp. 316–7 WA online at https://api.parliament.uk/historic-hansard/written-answers/1961/aug/03/allied-casualties-in-second-world-war#column_317wa
10 More about Army Groups can be found at https://en.wikipedia.org/wiki/Army_group#Western_Allies
11 George Forty, *British Army Handbook 1939–1945* (Sutton, 1998), pp. 36–45.
12 Forty, *British Army Handbook*, pp. 52–4. Roman numerals are normally used for corps, so 12 Corps should be written XII Corps.

13 Forty, *British Army Handbook*, pp. 328–35. Numbering of divisions seem to have been random, and many were assigned quite high numbers.
14 Forty, *British Army Handbook*, pp. 146–56. The example is based on entries in TNA Discovery Catalogue of war diaries. There may have been smaller units, but those war diaries do not survive.
15 www.nam.ac.uk/explore/worcestershire-regiment
16 Masterbomber Craig has a very good description of a Lancaster aircrew and the tasks they performed at https://masterbombercraig.wordpress.com/avro-lancaster-bomber/lancaster-crews/air-crew-personnel/
17 www.bcar.org.uk/elsham-history.php
18 Wikipedia has a complete lists of Royal Navy shore establishments at https://en.wikipedia.org/wiki/List_of_Royal_Navy_shore_establishments
19 For more about Motor Torpedo Boats visit the Spitfires of the Sea website, https://spitfiresofthesea.com
20 Angus Calder, *The People's War: Britain 1939–1945* (Panther, 1971), p. 311.
21 They were universally known as 'the grey mice' from the colour of their uniforms.
22 Jeremy Crang, *The British Army and the People's War 1939–1945* (Manchester University Press, 2000), pp. 9–10.
23 Crang, p. 14.
24 'Worker's Week-end' is a fascinating wartime film about the construction of a Wellington bomber in just 30 hours, showing the women who undertook the work, see https://www.youtube.com/watch?v=YPx-NqHH5fc
25 His story can be found at www.bbc.co.uk/history/ww2peopleswar/stories/30/a4252330.shtml. Eventually Mr Mitchell went to prison rather than spend more time in the mines.
26 Mr Dowden's experiences are at www.bbc.co.uk/history/ww2peopleswar/stories/78/a3391878.shtml
27 Crang, p. 23.
28 Crang, p. 29.
29 *Sunday Express*, 13 April 1941.
30 Quoted in Crang, p. 33.
31 George Macdonald Fraser, *The General Danced at Dawn* (Barrie & Jenkins, 1970), p. 2.
32 Much of the information in this section can be found on the webpage 'Conscription and the Second World War' at https://spartacus-educational.com/2WWconscription.htm
33 *Manchester Guardian*, 10 March 1941.
34 Forty, *British Army Handbook*, p. 318.
35 Joyce Storey, *Joyce's War* (Bristol Writers Workshop, 1992), p. 84.
36 Frederick Pile, *Ack-Ack: Britain's defence against air attack during the Second World War* (Harrap, 1949), p. 169.

2. Starting Your Research

1 You can perhaps understand why from accounts of the conditions when the British arrived on 15–16 April 1945, see https://en.wikipedia.org/wiki/Bergen-Belsen_concentration_camp#Liberation, https://encyclopedia.ushmm.org/content/en/article/the-11th-armoured-division-great-britain and Ben Shephard, *After Daybreak: The Liberation of Belsen, 1945* (Pimlico, 2006).
2 The plan was code-named Operation Foxley. See Mark Seaman, *Operation Foxley: The British Plan to Kill Hitler* (Public Record Office, 1998).
3 Footage can be found at www.youtube.com/watch?v=N-k3SH6eLcs

4 IWM JER Parsons papers Documents 18760.
5 An interesting article on identity cards and their use is at www.statewatch.org/news/2003/july/statewatch-news-online-identity-cards-in-the-uk-a-lesson-from-history/
6 Quoted in Brian Bond & Michael Taylor, *The Battle of France and Flanders 1940: Sixty Years On* (Pen & Sword, 2001), p. 14.
7 Forty, *British Army Handbook*, p. 177. As a tank officer during the war, he was speaking from experience.
8 https://en.wikipedia.org/wiki/Uniforms_of_the_British_Army
9 As well as wasting a great deal of time, as social media is so addictive.
10 Such as TTFN – Ta Ta for Now. Characters and catchphrases included the charlady Mrs Mopp ('Can I do you now, sir?'), and the lugubrious Mona Lott ('It's being so cheerful that keeps me going.'). However, to modern ears, the show is woefully unfunny.
11 The TV service was taken off air halfway through a Disney cartoon. Fittingly, programmes restarted at the exact moment the programme had stopped.
12 Despite what you might have seen on *Who Do You Think You Are* and similar programmes, archives rarely ask readers to wear cotton gloves.
13 www.gov.ie/en/press-release/678fc-digitisation-of-the-1926-census/
14 Thanks to Chris Paton describing the current situation in Northern Ireland.
15 Scotland's People suggest he left an infant daughter, Caroline Mary.
16 It has not been possible to find more about this officer, although he seems to have survived the war.
17 *Surrey Comet*, 17 May 1941, p. 4.
18 *Oxford Dictionary of National Biography*, entry for Sir Dirk Bogarde by David Parkinson. VJ-Day was 15 August 1945 (2 September 1945 in the USA).

3. Common Sources

1 22 March 1944. The speech is given in full in Hansard (HC Deb, 22 March 1944, c872).
2 The criteria is given in full at https://victoriacrosstrust.org.
3 *London Gazette*, 14 October 1941, Supplement 35306, p. 5935.
4 *London Gazette*, 26 September 1945, Supplement 37283, p. 4779.
5 The full Royal Warrant about the award of the George Cross can be found in the *London Gazette*, 31 January 1941, Supplement 35060, p. 622.
6 P.E. Abbott and J.M.A. Tamplin, *British Gallantry Awards* (Nimrod Dix) pp. 124–9.
7 A biography can be found at https://en.wikipedia.org/wiki/Jock_Pearson
8 WO 373/80/269. The award was gazetted in the *London Gazette*, 26 June 1945, p. 3374. No citation is given.
9 *London Gazette*, 14 July 1942, p. 3151. The air raid was probably the one that took place on 1 June 1942, one of the series of Baedeker Raids on historic cities.
10 Abbott and Tamplin, pp. 110–1, 220–7.
11 TNA WO 373/36/271. *London Gazette*, Supplement 36994, 20 March 1945, p. 1545.
12 Abbott and Tamplin, pp. 95–8, 104.
13 Abbott and Tamplin, pp. 8–10.
14 Abbott and Tamplin, pp. 110–1.
15 *Kentish Express*, 10 October 1947.
16 https://en.wikipedia.org/wiki/Bernard_Montgomery#Casualty_conservation_policy
17 For more about the disaster see www.historic-uk.com/HistoryUK/HistoryofBritain/Sinking-Of-RMS-Lancastria and www.bbc.com/news/uk-scotland-33092351

18 Max Hastings, *Bomber Command* (Pan, 1979) p. 334.
19 As the name suggests, aircrew were the men who flew the planes – the pilots, navigators, radio operators, air gunners and flight engineers. Everybody else were groundcrew.
20 Figures given by Rob Davies on his Nor the Years Condemn website: https://web.archive.org/web/20080615144021/http://www.elsham.pwp.blueyonder.co.uk/raf_bc/'
21 Figures taken from Commonwealth War Graves Commission, *Annual Report 2015–16* (CWGC, 2016), p. 35
22 *Annual Report 2015–16*, p. 35.
23 There's an interesting webpage on what happened at Grangues on D-Day at www.normandythenandnow.com/the-disappearing-war-criminal-of-chateau-de-grangues
24 Numbers given at www.tracesofwar.com/sights/19829/War-Memorial-Basingstoke.htm
25 Details of the Basingstoke memorial, for example, are at www.iwm.org.uk/memorials/item/memorial/2203 and www.warmemorialsonline.org.uk/memorial/120366
26 There's a time capsule at the Bomber Command memorial containing messages of love and remembrance from those connected with Second World War bomber missions. The case of the capsule is salvaged from a Lancaster aircraft, which crashed with the loss of all crew.
27 See www.royalparks.org.uk/parks/green-park/things-to-see-and-do
28 www.cwgc.org/visit-us/find-cemeteries-memorials/cemetery-details/2012400/brookwood-1939-1945-memorial/
29 Figures based on Allied Casualties in Second World War HL Debate, 03 August 1961, Vol. 234 pp. 216–7, WA online at https://api.parliament.uk/historic-hansard/written-answers/1961/aug/03/allied-casualties-in-second-world-war#column_317wa
30 The experiences of one such prisoner, Private Arthur Dodd, RASC, is told in Colin Rushton, *Spectator in Hell: A British Soldier's Story of Imprisonment in Auschwitz* (Summerdale, 2001)
31 Figures based on report by Captain D. Nelson, *Straits Settlement Volunteers August 1945*, summarised by Neil MacPherson at www.mansell.com/pow_resources/camplists/death_rr/movements_1.html
32 WO 416/14/131; WO 416/98/260, WO 416/236/1
33 This work and much more was co-ordinated by MI9, see https://en.wikipedia.org/wiki/MI9
34 https://en.wikipedia.org/wiki/British_Army_Aid_Group

4. The British Army

1 TNA WO 416/315/157-158
2 *Porthcawl Guardian*, 25 November 1949, p. 2. See also *Leamington Spa Courier*, 30 January 1953, p. 9.
3 War diaries are still kept today.
4 'Instructions for compiling and disposing of the war diary', printed inside cover sheets used to contain monthly war diaries.
5 War diary for 5th Battalion, Hampshire Regiment, 3 March 1942 (TNA WO 166/8716).
6 The Entertainments National Service Association (ENSA) provided entertainment for British armed forces personnel across the world. Although their programmes were immensely popular, it was commonly said that the initials stood for Every Night Something Awful. Few records appear to survive.

7 War diary for 2/4th Battalion, Hampshire Regiment, 6–12 May 1944 (TNA WO 170/2399). After heavy fighting, which resulted in many enemy prisoners of war being taken, the battalion were relieved on the 16th. The following day was devoted to 'baths and admin'.
8 TNA WO 171/4773.
9 Winston S. Churchill, *The Second World War: Their Finest Hour* (Boston: Houghton Mifflin Company, 1949), pp. 246–7.
10 Taylor Downing, *Night Raid: The True Story of the First Victorious British Para Raid of WWII* (Hachette, 2013), p. 194.
11 Hugh Trevor-Roper, *The Philby Affair* (William Kimber, 1968), pp. 73–4.
12 The daily summaries, with Churchill's comments, are in TNA series HW 1.
13 TNA WO 373/7/425. See also https://www.paradata.org.uk/people/anthony-greville-bell

5. The Royal Air Force

1 Abbott and Tamplin, pp. 95–8, 104
2 *London Gazette* (no. 3614), 27 August 1943, p. 3824.
3 Statistics taken from https://en.wikipedia.org/wiki/RAF_Bomber_Command#Casualties
4 TNA AIR 27/2076/13 entry for 13 July 1942. F/O Edgar Mostyn Innes-Jones was a 30-year-old New Zealander. It is likely that he was shot down by a German Focke-Wulf that had taken off to intercept the intruders. He is commemorated on the memorial to the missing of the RAF at Runnymede.
5 TNA AIR 27/2076/13 entry for 16 July 1942.
6 TNA AIR 27/1089/46, entry for 2 November 1944.
7 TNA AIR 27/2134/21-22 entries for 6 June 1944.
8 For more about the recovery and management of aircraft wrecks see https://historic-england.org.uk/images-books/publications/military-aircraft-crash-sites/milaircsites
9 *Aeroplane*, 30 March 1940, p. 2.

6. The Royal Navy

1 Quoted in an MoD e-publication *A History of our Reserves* (2013) https://assets.publishing.service.gov.uk/media/5a7c054140f0b63f7572ad85/a-history-our-Reserves-Epub-v2.pdf
2 For more about the list see the National Maritime Museum Research Guide E2 at www.rmg.co.uk/collections/research-guides/research-guide-e2-world-war-two-guide-dunkirk-list
3 For a complete list see www.royalnavyresearcharchive.org.uk/SQUADRONS/Index.htm
4 John Keegan, *The Second World War* (Penguin, 1989), p. 94.

7. The Home Front

1 Borough of Twickenham Local History Society Newsletter 146 (December 2007). Letters were also reprinted in issues 148–56. http://botlhs.co.uk/portfolio-tags/newsletters/
2 Quoted at https://spartacus-educational.com/2WWhughesS.htm
3 *Manchester Guardian*, 17 February 1945, p. 3

4 The wartime diaries of the politician and social butterfly 'Chips' Channon, for example, rarely mention rationing or any restrictions in the menus offered at the London restaurants at which he and his circle ate regularly.
5 *The Westminster*, spring 1945, p. 15.
6 *The Westminster*, spring 1943, p. 116.
7 Supplement to the *London Gazette*, 4 February 1941, p. 740. There is also some paperwork at TNA T 336/14/21.
8 *Middlesex Chronicle*, 15 February 1941, p. 7.
9 Simon Fowler, *Richmond at War* (Richmond Local History Society, 2015), p. 34.
10 A.E. Redfern, *Reminiscences of the 63rd Surrey (Richmond) Battalion Home Guard*, (Richmond, 1946), p. 7. TNA WO 199/3371.
11 Redfern, p. 44.
12 Redfern, p. 48.
13 www.hastingleigh.com/hast-ww2-landarmy.html
14 www.striking-women.org/module/women-and-work/world-war-ii-1939-1945
15 TNA WO 208/3729, WO 208/5499
16 Transcripts of all five broadcasts can be found at www.oocities.org/indeedsir/radiomenu.htm. See also https://southwestreview.com/a-grave-moral-mistake-the-tragedy-of-p-g-wodehouses-berlin-broadcasts/ and the Wikipedia entry for Wodehouse.
17 George Orwell, 'In Defence of PG Wodehouse', *Windmill* (July 1946), see https://orwell.ru/library/reviews/plum/english/e_plum
18 See her entry in the *Oxford Dictionary of National Biography*.

8. The Wider War

1 A more detailed introduction to Canada and the Second World War can be found at www.canadiansoldiers.com/history/wars/secondworldwar.htm
2 Conrad Black, *Franklin Delano Roosevelt: Champion of Freedom* (New York, 2003)
3 *The New York Times*, 30 December 1940.
4 David Blomfield and Chris May, *Kew at War: 1939–1945* (Richmond Local History Society, 2016), p. 26. There's a plaque in the grounds of the Archives.
5 If you are interested, watch the short film *Welcome to Britain* (1943), which was shown to American troops before their arrival in the UK to help them adjust to life here: www.youtube.com/watch?v=SyYSBBE1DFw
6 An excellent website devoted to Canadian War Brides is at www.canadianwarbrides.com
7 Oddly, apart from a single mention of his marriage, there is nothing about the romance in his wartime diary, which is now at the Imperial War Museum. Like so many such relationships, it seems to have ended in divorce.
8 Phillip Kerr's novel *Field Grey* (Quercus, 2010) is a moving account of the experiences of the German prisoners. See also a poignant 1955 newsreel: 'The prisoners came back', www.youtube.com/watch?v=8QsjbdWY1a0.
9 Fun fact: TNA at Kew is on the site of Camp 144, which housed Italian prisoners. There is a plaque in the grounds.
10 https://edencamp.co.uk/about-us/
11 For an introduction see https://en.wikipedia.org/wiki/Ratlines_(World_War_II)#
12 There is a family story that a cousin of my mother was dismissed from the Pioneer Corps for being unable to march properly! It has been impossible to verify it.
13 *Manchester Guardian*, 30 August 1938, p. 2. There is no evidence that either Herr Kernegg or the Baachs were successful in finding employment in the UK.

Appendix 1. The Korean War (1950–53)

1 Interviewed by The History Chap at www.youtube.com/watch?v=iB0ptJoND-E

Miklós Radnóti Quote, p. 4

1 https://hungarytoday.hu/84-years-since-the-outbreak-of-the-history-shaping-world-war-ii/

X and Y Lists Box p. 117

1 See www.commandoveterans.org/x_lists

2 Based on ww2talk.com/index.php?threads/info-on-y-list-please.61446/

INDEX

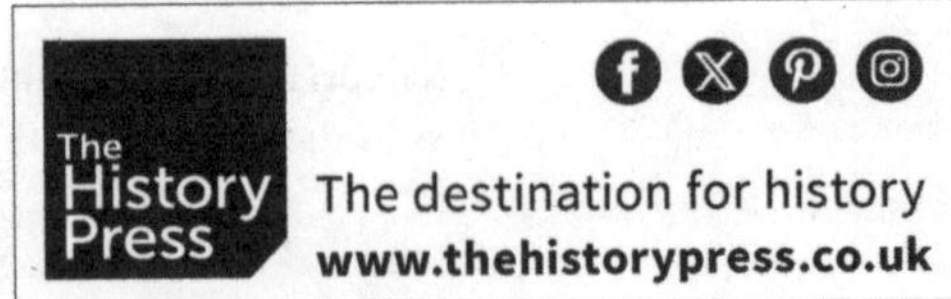
The History Press
The destination for history
www.thehistorypress.co.uk